Privilege and Prerogative

Privilege and Prerogative

New York's Provincial Elite, 1710–1776

Mary Lou Lustig

Madison • Teaneck
Fairleigh Dickinson University Press
London and Toronto: Associated University Presses

Associated University Presses
440 Forsgate Drive
Cranbury, NJ 08512

Associated University Presses
25 Sicilian Avenue
London WC1A 2QH, England

Associated University Presses
P.O.Box 338, Port Credit
Mississauga, Ontario
Canada L5G 4L8

The paper used in this publication meets the requirements of the American National Standard for Permanence of Paper for Printed Library Materials Z39.48–1984.

Library of Congress Cataloging-in-Publication Data

Lustig, Mary Lou
    Privilege and prerogative : New York's provincial elite, 1710-1776 / Mary Lou Lustig.
      p.   cm.
    Includes bibliographical references (p.) and index.
    ISBN 0-8386-3554-7 (alk. paper)
    1. New York (State)—Politics and government—To 1775.   2. Elite (Social sciences)—New York (State)—History—18th century. I. Title.
F122.L97   1995
974.7'102'08621—dc20
                                          93-51010
                                             CIP

PRINTED IN THE UNITED STATES OF AMERICA

To my parents

An oligarchy . . . certainly gives the many their share of
dangers, but when it comes to the good things of life not
only claims the largest share, but goes off with the whole lot.

—Thucydides, The Peloponnesian War, Book 6, 39

Contents

Preface

The elite families of colonial New York wielded an influence that far exceeded their relatively small number. It was to the colony's elite that royal governors turned for advice and assistance. New York's royal governors enjoyed considerable power, but the most consistent source of influence rested with the elite. Knowledgeable about provincial affairs, the elite provided continuity for imperial administration. In fact, imperial government would have been impossible without their cooperation.

The elite were the large landowners, wealthy merchants, and their families who constituted only a small fraction of New York's population, certainly no more than ten percent. This group, which dominated the colony's economic, social, and political life, formulated and popularized the rhetoric that led New York to join the struggle for independence. It was also the elite, who, however unwittingly, roused the urban lower classes from political apathy to activism. When the lower classes initiated the move to separation, the elite used their knowledge of politics and human nature to seize from the lower classes the direction of the revolutionary movement. After the Revolution, the elite of New York and other states formulated a lasting constitution based on principles they advocated when opposing British rule.

Robert C. Ritchie, in *The Duke's Province*, has called the years from 1664 to 1691 in the colonies the "period when political institutions and practices were formulated; . . . when the basic structure of the English empire was created; and when the colonists reshaped the social structures of the Old World to fit the imperatives of life in the new. These developments created strains that came to the fore in rebellion, riot, resistance to authority, personal anxiety, and religious doubt. . . . Between 1664 and 1691 there emerged an elite group that was to dominate life in New York for over a century."[1]

While New York's eighteenth-century history has been explored by many historians, few have treated the entire period to the Revolution and fewer still have dealt with the emergence of local elites. This lack has been commented upon by other historians, most notably Patricia U. Bonomi. In *A Factious People*, Bonomi observes that "one subject that certainly needs some fresh examination is that of the New York 'aristocracy.'"[2]

This book will follow the development of the elite from 1710 to 1776. The first date, which marks the beginning of Robert Hunter's administration, was chosen because it was during Hunter's governorship that the elite in New York's assembly made their first successful and dramatic assault on the royal prerogative. The latter date, of course, was when royal rule was finally and completely rejected. Within this time frame, I will trace the development of the themes outlined by Ritchie and the concerns voiced by Bonomi. The concentration will be on the emergence of dominant elite factions during the eighteenth century, as the elite saw their position threatened by one assault from the British ministry and another from the lower classes.

Since the struggle between privilege and prerogative centered on the royal governors, I have divided the work by administrations after the introductory chapter. I have grouped those administrations where it was convenient to do so or when they spoke to a specific problem or issue. The friction created by the continued clashes between privilege and prerogative brought independence from Great Britain, but that had not been the original intent or goal of New York's elite. In fact, the elite were pleased to be part of a system that permitted them to prosper and then protected their wealth and status. As in England, oligarchic rule was the practice in New York and had been since the seventeenth century. Members of the wealthiest and most influential families dominated New York politics generation after generation. They were kept in power in New York, as in England, by infrequent elections that tended to shut the door to outsiders. Factionalism rose within the ranks of the elite about who among them would wield influence. Governors unwittingly contributed to this factionalism when they allied with an elite group, forming a governor's—or court—party, thereby creating an opposition, or country, party, whose members gravitated to the assembly. Although such one-sided alliances were necessary for the governor, they had a divisive effect in the colony.

New York was notorious for lacking political stability because of the persistent discord in the province. Discord was produced in part by New York's assembly. The intent of the New York assembly was to increase its sphere of influence to further its own local, provincial interests while reducing the metropolitan interests represented by the governor. The executive's efforts to resist such encroachments contributed to the unrest in the province. Unrest was further exacerbated by other factors, such as the struggle within the legislature between the assembly and the council, between the legislature and the executive, the nature of imperial administration, and New York's peculiar history.

Some of that peculiarity lies in New York's uniqueness among England's North American colonies. The province exhibited a religious and ethnic diversity unknown in New England or the Chesapeake. This same diversity made New York a prototype of modern American society. Originally settled by the Dutch, New York after its 1664 conquest, retained a sizeable Dutch-speaking population, particularly in Albany. That city, the center of the lucrative fur trade, also served as the conference site for diplomatic meetings between the British and the influential Five (later Six) Nations of the Iroquois, whose allegiance was essential to British interests. New York's strategic location adjacent to French Canada made it particularly important to Great Britain.

New York was also unique in that it had a manorial system, unlike most other colonies. This system, which put large parcels of land into the hands of a relatively few, created a small, but powerful, land-based elite and a permanent rural underclass of disgruntled tenant farmers. The dominance of elite families, whose power and status were buttressed through intermarriage, was ensured because manors were usually passed intact to eldest sons, who consistently added to the family's landholdings. Younger sons, often given acreage apart from the manor, were frequently established as merchants or trained as attorneys. They thus continued to protect and expand their families's considerable business interests.

Unrest spread to the ranks of the elite as aristocrats struggled to gain entry into the court faction or to be effective opposition leaders. Membership in both factions was constantly changing. While New York's elite shifted from one faction to the other, dependent on the governor's favor, they were fairly constant in their attachment to Whig or Tory principles. By mid-eighteenth century, New York's two leading families, the DeLanceys and the Livingstons, gave their names to political factions, with the former embodying Tory and the latter Whig philosophy. Strong leaders rose at that time: James DeLancey and William Livingston assumed the leadership of their respective factions. DeLancey remained active until his 1760 death; Livingston until his 1772 retirement to New Jersey. The DeLanceys, a wealthy merchant family, favored mercantile interests, while the Livingstons, with extensive landholdings, favored the interests of manor lords.

These political factions formed the nucleus of the political parties that would develop during the early national period.

The long political dominance of the DeLanceys and Livingstons has led some historians, such as Roger Champagne, to assert that family antagonism between the DeLanceys and Livingstons was the most significant factor in shaping New York politics.[3] This work will show that the DeLancey-Livingston friction was only the tip of a much deeper and more fundamental disagreement between the contending ideologies represented by Whigs and Tories.

Friction was also a product of the desire for upward social mobility. New York offered many opportunities for economic and social advancement. Virtually all of New York's wealthy manor lords and merchants were self-made men who started life in the colony with few resources. White members of the lower class were certain that, given good fortune and the right set of circumstances, they, too, could gain wealth and status. Economic opportunity existed for whites throughout most of the colonial era. In the 1760s, as the population grew rapidly and England and its colonies faced an economic depression, opportunities for advancement dwindled, heightening discontent among the lower orders.

Little economic opportunity existed for black freemen and virtually none for black slaves or Native Americans. Slave uprisings threatened the lives and property of the elite. Hence, they were even more ruthlessly suppressed than tenant uprisings. The elite, contrary to reason and British policy, worked against their own long-term interests in their dealings with Native Americans, including the Iroquois. British survival in North America depended in large measure on the continued friendship of the Iroquois, who were situated between the English settlements in New York and the French in Canada. Despite this, manor lords and Albany merchants continually cheated the Iroquois in land sales and the fur trade. The result was that by mid-eigtheenth century, the Iroquois were reluctant to assist New Yorkers in Great Britain's continuing war against France. During the Revolution, four of the six Iroquois tribes, with keen memories of past oppressions at the hands of Americans, allied with the British against the former colonists.

Short-sightedness, such as that exhibited by colonists toward the Iroquois, was also apparent in colonial administration. The crown gave royal governors excessive power and rigid instructions that, if followed to the letter, made it virtually impossible to govern. The crown also gave assemblies exclusive control of raising money for all government expenses, including the governor's salary. By simply declining to raise a revenue, the New York assembly was able to wrest significant concessions from a succession of royal governors, thus weakening respect for the executive and the monarch he represented.

Opposition elite, both landowners and merchants, continually strove to expand their power at the expense of the royal prerogative as personified in the governor. The logical base for doing so was the assembly, whose membership was composed almost exclusively of the elite. The assembly filled the traditional role of the lower house in England by attempting to limit the power of the executive. Assemblymen were vigilant against attempts by the governor and the ruling ministry in England to reduce their privileges and liberties. Such vigilance was particularly appropriate in New York since residents shared an inherited memory and fear of absolutism. New York bore the name of its proprietor, a Stuart tyrant, James, duke of York, who was later James II. The duke's rule sensitized New Yorkers to the threat of absolute power. Their fears were further heightened by English opposition writers of the seventeenth and eighteenth centuries. New York's elite responded quickly to what they interpreted as the potential oppression of Parliament. After 1763, it seemed to the elite that the British Parliament was acting as arbitrarily as had the Stuart kings. Parliament altered charters, passed discriminatory economic legislation, ignored basic rights to trial by jury through the use of vice-admiralty and other prerogative courts, stifled freedom of expression, used the courts to punish dissenting writers, and imposed taxes without consent.

Colonial protest was at first centered in the assemblies, which had grown more effective during the course of the eighteenth century. This has rightly led many historians, such as Jack P. Greene, to view this period as significant. While Greene's *The Quest for Power* deals primarily with the southern colonies, he extends his view to all colonies in his preface where he states that "it was the lower houses that took the lead in defending American rights and liberties when they were challenged by Crown and Parliament after 1763...."[4] In line with this, Greene sees a commensurate decline in executive power. He does not note that much of the executive's power was theoretical even in the early century and much power was retained even into the 1760s. More significant than the theoretical power conveyed in the governor's instructions and commissions were the force of personality and the determination of the governor. A strong executive, like Robert Hunter, made concessions, but received favors in return. Weak executives, like George Clinton, also made concessions, but received nothing in return.

In the assembly, New York's elite objected to Parliament's measures because of a deep-seated conviction that accepting them would reduce their personal liberties and property. Such conviction was sincere, as

Greene implies, but not the only reason for resistance to British measures. Self–interest figured largely in the elite's decision to oppose the British ministry. The old colonial system brought the elite wealth, power, and influence. The New York elite did not want the ministry to change that system, but rather to preserve it as it had been from 1691 to 1763. New Yorkers meant it when they said that they desired a return to conditions as they had been prior to the end of the French and Indian War. They wanted "a Restoration of those Rights which we enjoyed by General Consent before the Close of the last War; we desire no more than a Continuation of that ancient Government."[5]

If timing is everything, then the British ministry's decision to change the system after 1763 was a miscalculation. Acting on the complaints and suggestions of numerous royal officials, the ministry was determined to tighten colonial administration. These officials had complained to the Board of Trade and the ministry of continued attempts by the assembly to wrest power from the executive. The Board of Trade repeatedly urged the ministry to curb the power of provincial assemblies, and, beginning in 1763, the ministry did just that. In a series of actions, the British government worked to restore the power of the executive while reducing severely that of the assembly. By 1774, the program appeared so threatening to New York's elite that many realized that continued allegiance to Britain would be overly costly to their interests. Many elite conservatives who previously rejected the idea of separation now usurped leadership of the movement from lower class radicals to lead them in opposition to Great Britain. Hence the protests of the elite against parliamentary measures, while undoubtedly based on principle, were also predicated by a self-serving desire to preserve the status quo.

The status quo was also threatened by New York's lower and middling sort, a view eloquently stated by Carl Lotus Becker. Virtually all modern historians who write about prerevolutionary New York, acknowledge the debt they owe to Becker's seminal work, *The History of Political Parties in the Province of New York, 1760–1776.* This work is no exception. The most influential portion of Becker's work was his first chapter, meant as an introduction or background to New York's prerevolutionary politics. His conclusions were summed up in the now classic statement that the most important issue concerning New York's party history during the period of his inquiry was "the question of home rule; the second was the question, if we may so put it, of who should rule at home."[6] Many of the conclusions advanced by Becker have been challenged by new generations of historians. It is now evident, for instance, that the electorate in colonial New York was much broader than Becker could have known. It is my contention that the prerevolutionary chaos in New York sprang from a number of contending forces and was thus more complex than Becker indicated.[7]

Some of those forces arose from a power struggle between social classes. The elite recognized the importance of the lower and middling sort and believed they had a role in politics, but it was a distinctly subordinate one. Through the press, both court and country oligarchs politicized the masses to gain their support for elite platforms. Voters were still constrained in this era of oral balloting by the presence of the candidate, who was often their manor lord or the local magistrate. In fact, those manors that had the privilege of electing representatives were pocket boroughs, electing the manor lord or whomever he proposed. But some degree of free choice existed in other areas so that, in 1733, Lewis Morris and his anti–William Cosby faction could exert enough influence on voters that they rejected the governor's candidate. New York City voters were also fairly independent, and the four delegates elected from there were consistently the most influential, hence those seats the most contested, in the house. It was well worth the candidate's time to court the electorate, although their response was never as predictable or mechanical as the elite might have wished.

The rise of the lower classes to political activism was an unforeseen side effect of elite opposition to Great Britain. The politicization of the lower class was made possible by the growing availability of the printing press in the eighteenth century. Newspapers, broadsides, pamphlets, and the like were widely circulated in the province among the literate members of the lower orders. In bars, taverns, inns, and churches and on streetcorners, the literate passed on information to their illiterate compatriots. The lower and middling sort responded to elite press propaganda, although not always in the fashion the elite desired.

Despite indoctrination by the elite, the lower and middling sort remained a collective loose cannon, absorbing the political philosophy fed to them by the elite, but giving it their own interpretation. Elite opposition propaganda stressed that all authority for government came from the people. The lower and middling sort after 1765 defined the phrase "the people" much more broadly than did the elite. They demanded a secret ballot, rather than the customary oral voting in the presence of candidates. They began to stage their own demonstrations and to voice open criticism of the elite, particularly those in the assembly. In time, the elite realized that, through the press, a popular force was raised that proved increasingly difficult to control.

The participation of the lower classes affected the outcome of many of the issues that pitted prerogative and privilege. The influence of these classes was exerted on numerous occasions between 1710 and 1776: at the polls in the election of assembly candidates, by pressure on representatives in the house, and through street demonstrations, which always carried the potential of violence. Popular pressure in whatever form ensured that representatives would consider local interests before imperial concerns. The influence of the lower and middling sort was also seen in the failure of the crown's prosecution of seditious libel charges against Samuel Mulford and John Peter Zenger and was evident in the futile attempts of Governors Cosby, Monckton, and Dunmore to collect money from their lieutenant governors. It was prominent in the dispute over King's College when Anglicans failed to secure full funding support. The influence of the lower and middling sort was also felt in the tenure of judges controversy and the *Forsey v. Cunningham* appeal and reached its height in the protests against the Stamp, Townshend, Quartering, Tea, and Intolerable acts.

The lower classes often expressed their concerns about such political issues by taking to the streets. The reasons for popular protests were diverse and included economic hardships and frustrated ambitions. The white poor in New York were by no means reconciled to their impoverished lot. New York was essentially a frontier society that offered greater economic opportunity for members of the lower classes than did Europe. Opportunity raised aspirations, but for those who did not succeed, disappointment brought discontent, thus increasing unrest. Democratic elements were at work in sparking the revolution but democracy did not enjoy any immediate or long-term success, despite the contention of Edward Countryman, who sees "a democratic revolution with a deep, though complicated, social content."[8]

Discontent was often expressed through street demonstrations. Rioting was not unique to New York or to the North American colonies. Riots occurred frequently in eighteenth-century England, most notably against the excise tax, to protest the presence in England of German mercenaries and to express outrage at the ministry's conduct of the Seven Years' War.

Early in the colonial period, New York riots were occasionally spontaneous, but often were conducted at the direction of the opposition elite, who wanted to get the message to the ministry that the governor could not control the province.[9] Signs of incompetence might well lead to the governor's recall. With the 1765 Stamp Act riots, the New York City crowds, rejecting the leadership of the elite, began to think and act for themselves. In 1765 and thereafter, the mobs chose their elite victims with care, usually those who had the bad taste to flaunt their wealth.

New York was also shaken by rural riots. Tenant farmers, landless in a society that linked land ownership with status and privilege, periodically protested their exploited condition. This added to the persistent turmoil in the province. The elite, who prior to 1765 encouraged urban riots, were horrified by tenant uprisings for the simple reason that tenant riots were directed at them, not the imperial government.

Some historians, such as Sung Bok Kim in *Landlords and Tenants in Colonial New York*, see a similarity of interests between rural upper and lower classes, or manor lords and tenants.[10] There was in fact little similarity of interest. Instead the relationship was exploitive on the part of landlords and marked by extreme bitterness and anger on the part of tenants. Tension also existed in urban areas between elites and working men, producing class antagonisms throughout the colony.

Kim's work provides part of the basis for Greene's argument in *Pursuits of Happiness* that New York society grew more coherent as the colonial period progressed.[11] Greene states that tenant rioters had no levelling intentions because their aim was not to destroy but to join the existing social order. The latter contention is true. Tenants wanted to own their own land. It was their efforts to accomplish this that brought bloody reprisals on the part of manor lords. Frustrated tenants frequently threatened to murder manor lords, who had to protect themselves from their "contented" tenants with local militia and regular army troops. Far from growing more coherent as the colonial period progressed, class tensions in society heightened and by the revolution New York was a splintered society in both rural and urban areas.

While rural riots were disturbing to the elite, they did not impel New York toward independence. Tenant rioting added to the discord in the colony, but the impetus for revolution in New York came largely from urban mobs. More than rhetoric and more than an ideological platform were needed to inspire New Yorkers to revolution. Also necessary was a large segment of society willing and able to effect change. New York's elite did not want change. Instead, they wanted a return to conditions as they had been prior to 1763; the lower classes did not. Revolution did not occur in England's West Indian islands because the lower class black population was enslaved and helpless while the elite preferred to live in England. The middle and lower white classes had been largely driven off the islands with the introduction of sugar cultivation, so there was no group in a position to rebel. Such a group, grown increasingly sophisticated, existed in New York.

All these factors worked together to produce a revolution. This revolution occurred in New York because the free white urban lower classes spurred the movement to independence. It came because of long-standing hostility among New Yorkers toward English rule and because of a climate of unrest in the colonies as different elite factions struggled for power.

The basis of the struggle was partly a quest for provincial power and partly a commitment to ideals. Both family and politics were of the utmost importance and both were strongly linked with religious beliefs which provided the basis for political ideologies categorized as Whig and Tory.[12] The commitment of these families to differing political ideologies produced divisions in New York that were further worsened by contention between executive and legislature, court and country, metropolitan and provincial interests, landowners and merchants, manor lords and tenant farmers, urban and rural interests, black slaves and white owners, Albanians and Manhattanites, and Indians and frontier settlers. The discord in New York was also a result of class conflict between the haves and have-nots. All worked to create a climate of dissension and turmoil in which defiance of authority became a commonplace and revolution became the plausible alternative.

Acknowledgments

This project would not have been possible without the assistance of many people and institutions. I would particularly like to express my thanks to the librarians and archivists of the following institutions: British Library; Public Record Office, London; Scottish Public Record Office, Edinburgh; Elmer Holmes Bobst Library, New York University; Charles C. Wise, Jr., Library, West Virginia University; New-York Historical Society; New York Public Library; Franklin Delano Roosevelt Library, Hyde Park; New Jersey State Library; Newark Public Library; Massachusets Historical Society; Yale University Library; State Library at Albany.

I would like to thank the Folger Institute for a grant–in-aid that made possible research in the fine collection of the Folger Shakespeare Library.

Research for this project was also made possible in part by a grant from the West Virginia University Senate. My thanks to the members of the committee and to Dean Gerald Lang of the College of Arts and Sciences for approving a leave of absence which enabled me to turn my full attention to this study. I would like to thank two successive chairmen of the history department, Robert Maxon and Ronald Lewis, for their continued support and encouragement..

I am indebted to the members of the Columbia University Seminar of Early American History for their perceptive comments on an earlier version of part of this work. I would particularly like to thank Graham R. Hodges, who read the entire manuscript with great care. His efforts are much appreciated as are those of Patricia U. Bonomi, Milton M. Klein, Carl E. Prince, and David William Voorhees, who read and made helpful suggestions and pertinent observations on earlier drafts of portions of this study. Stephen Saunders Webb read most of the manuscript in one form or another and it benefits from his insight. I am grateful for his time and attention.

Finally, my thanks to my family and friends for their continued support and interest.

Privilege and Prerogative

1
Privilege and Prerogative

The perpetual Struggle in Every Colony [is] between Privilege and Prerogative, and the Governor who is not so happy as to temporize (for it is impossible to reconcile difficulties on one side, or the other, and in either case his
recall is the only remedy that can restore quiet to the Colony).[1]

One of the chief functions of the House of Commons was to contain
the power of the executive. The elite in New York's assembly believed
they had the same duty. The assembly, weak and ineffectual in the
seventeenth century—in contrast to a strong executive—did not take
long to expand its power. By 1713, New York's assembly proclaimed
itself the protector of English liberties, with its self-imposed function
that of reducing the excessive power of the governor, just as Commons
did that of the monarch. This was a task that would be assumed by
all of New York's provincial assemblies, with varying degrees of success, until 1776.[2]

While the aim of Commons and the Whigs in England was to limit
executive power, few in England looked favorably on efforts of provincial oligarchs to defy executive authority. Colonies were subordinate
to the mother country, their interests of secondary, or perhaps tertiary,
importance to the well-being of the imperial power.

In the eighteenth century, Great Britain's internal government
made it one of the most liberal countries in Europe, guaranteeing
more individual freedom to its subjects than almost any other European country. Although Britain granted its colonies representative
internal government, colonial administration was arbitrary and autocratic. This imperial rule produced discontent in New York, which
was exacerbated as colonists realized they were imposed upon and
exploited by the home government.[3]

The pattern for imperial administration had been established in ancient history and in England's more recent experiences in Ireland and Scotland. The English, since 1169 during the reign of Henry II, had claimed sovereignty over Ireland. In 1494 during the reign of Henry VII, Poynings's Law was passed by the English Parliament to safeguard the rights of the crown and Anglo-Norman settlers in Ireland. Poynings's Law dictated that the Irish Parliament could not pass any law unless it had prior approval from the English Privy Council. Thus the power of the crown was far greater in Ireland than it was in England, Scotland, or the North American colonies. The English Parliament confirmed its right to legislate for Ireland by the 1719 Declaratory Act. Of the few protests, official or unofficial, made in Ireland against the act, the most notable came from Jonathan Swift. In a 1720 pamphlet, "A Proposal for the Universal Use of Irish Manufactures," Swift advocated nonconsumption of English goods by the Irish (a ploy later adopted by American patriots). Swift urged the Irish to buy Irish-made manufactures.[4]

To more firmly establish English rule in Ireland, colonization was promoted around 1550. What began as a trickle soon became a flood, with between seventy to one hundred thousand English and Scots migrating to Ireland from 1603 to 1643. Those Irish people who resisted English domination and culture were brutally suppressed. By the early eighteenth century, 90 to 95 percent of the land in Ireland was held by Anglo-Irish. The political and social supremacy of the Anglo-Irish was confirmed by the Test Act of 1704, which excluded from the franchise and from public office all who were not members of the Church of Ireland. To religious discrimination was added economic exploitation. Ireland was excluded from the Navigation Acts and subjected to trade restrictions so that its products, which undersold English-made goods because of cheap labor, would not compete with English manufactures. Those who suffered most from these measures were Roman Catholics, the vast majority of the population, and a numerically smaller group of Scots Presbyterians. Many of the latter, motivated by the Test Act and by a worsening economic situation in Ireland, migrated to England's North American colonies in the early eighteenth century, adding to the number of people in America who left their native land because they were discontented with England.[5]

Scotland was also considered a subordinate province by the English, but it was clearly neither a conquered province nor a colony. A union of the crowns in 1603 had joined the neighboring kingdoms when Scotland's James VI assumed the English throne as James I. A political union was considered in the seventeenth century but rejected by both countries. After the Restoration, Scots Presbyterians were persecuted by Charles II, with ministers driven from their parishes and covenanters killed. Scottish dissent was finally quieted after the Glorious Revolution when the Scottish church was established. In 1707, the failure of the Scottish-backed New World colonization scheme in Darien, a depressed economy, and the passage of the Alien Act by the English Parliament forced Scotland to agree to a political union with England.[6]

Both Ireland and Scotland provided the blueprint for England's colonial administration and settlement in America. Just as Ireland was colonized by the English, so was North America. Just as the Irish were dispossessed of their land, so were the American Indians. Just as those Irish who resisted acculturation or conversion to English Protestantism were reduced, so were belligerent American Indian tribes. The extreme lessons provided by Sir Humphrey Gilbert's lining of the walk to his tent with the heads of his Irish enemies or the slaughter of thousands of Scottish Covenanters who refused to accept episcopacy were not lost on Englishmen in America. English atrocities practiced against the Irish and the Scots were repeated against subordinate peoples in America, sometimes by the very same Englishmen.[7]

Imperial government in Ireland, Scotland, and the colonies shared many similarities. Metropolitan government in each operated with the willing assistance of local elites, loyal to the crown as long as their interests were being protected. Ireland and the American colonies both had a degraded labor force. In Ireland this labor force was composed primarily of Roman Catholics, stripped of land, the vote, and the ability to hold public office. In America the labor force was largely composed of black slaves and freemen and poor whites, without land, the vote, or the ability to hold public office. The Native American population, who once held all the land, were systematically deprived of it, just as were the Irish.

Significant differences also existed. Ireland and Scotland were close to England, while the colonies were three thousand miles away. Ireland and Scotland were settled countries, while America was a frontier environment. There was more upward mobility in America than in Ireland and Scotland and there were no landed aristocrats with inherited wealth and privilege. The wealthiest families in New York were founded by self-made men who rose only because of their wits. Unlike Ireland, the expectation in America among all white members of the lower classes was that they too could rise, given the right set of circumstances.[8]

While the English were determined to maintain as tight a control over their North American colonies as they did over Ireland and Scotland, the colonists were just as determined to resist that control and protect traditional English liberties. The New York assembly's determination to do exactly that began with its initial session on 17 October

1683, when fifteen laws were passed, including a Charter of Liberties and Privileges. The charter was sent to England for confirmation by the colony's proprietor, James, duke of York. The duke, a firm believer in autocratic government, permitted an assembly to be called in his colony with great reluctance. He was forced to do so by a combination of events in England and New York. The Roman Catholic duke, heir to the throne, was on the defensive in England as Whigs tried to influence Charles II to exclude his brother James and name a Protestant as successor. The furor raised by the Popish Plot and the Exclusion Crisis so weakened the duke that he could not resist Whig pressure to permit a representative assembly to meet in New York. The duke was also persuaded to call an assembly because he needed tax money for government expenditures in the province. The duke instructed his newly appointed governor, Thomas Dongan (1683–88) to call "a Genl Assembly of all the Freeholders, by the persons who they shall choose to reprsent ym." The duke made this concession in exchange for the assembly's passage of a permanent revenue act.[9]

The assembly, in session for three weeks, complied and passed such an act. It also passed a charter to guarantee "several ancient Customes, Priviledges and Immunityes which were confirmed and granted to them by Colln. Richard Nicholls the late Governor of this Province by authority under His Royall Highness." The charter sought to confirm traditional political rights and guaranteed freedom of religion in this ethnically and religiously mixed colony. Richard Nicolls had taken the province from the Dutch in 1664 for the English king, Charles II. Even before Nicolls landed in New Netherlands, the king had given the territory to his brother James. New York, renamed for its proprietor, was a conquered province, as was Jamaica. As such, the duke was free to impose on it any kind of government he pleased. His choice was a nonrepresentative government where the viceroy, James's governor, ruled the colony with the advice of an appointive council.[10]

The charter passed by the New York assembly in 1683 challenged such arbitrary rule. Received in London early in 1684, its consideration was delayed because conditions had changed in England since James had agreed to permit an assembly to meet in New York. By 1684, the Whigs had lost their influence, and Charles was conducting a purge of Whig officials. The king recalled the charters of numerous cities and towns, including that of London, so that new officials, loyal to him, could be appointed. One of the charters recalled in October 1684 was that of the defiant and contentious Massachusetts Bay Colony. The king's intent was to institute a centralized government, based on the French colonial model, for Massachusetts and other New England colonies. Charles died in February 1685, before he could

James II, 1684–85, by Sir Godfrey Kneller, National Portrait Gallery, London. Proprietor of New York, James favored an autocratic government and refused to permit a representative assembly in his province. New York's government may have been the model James hoped to implement as king in England.

implement the plan. James succeeded his brother as king, and New York became a royal colony.[11]

King James was determined to carry out his brother's plans for colonial consolidation and centralization. Since New York was next to New England, it seemed logical to the king that it should be incorporated into the New England government. The charter passed in 1683 by the New York assembly was considered by the king–in–council in March 1685. Specific objections were made to such phrases as "the Inhabitants of New York shall be governed by and according to the Laws of England." The ministry asserted that "This Priviledge is not granted to any of His Mts Plantations." The ministry also objected to the clause that provided the assembly would meet at least once every three years. The ministry felt this placed too great "an Obligation upon the government." Particular objection was made to the claim that the assembly "with the Governor and his Councill shall be the supream and only legislative power of the said Province." The ministry believed that would "abridge the Acts of Parliament that may be made concerning New York." After considering the charter, the king declared he did "not think fitt to confirm the same." Instead, James ordered that "New York . . . be assimilated to the Constitution that shall be agreed on for New England, to which it is adjoining."[12]

James was delayed in implementing the Dominion of New England by an internal rebellion mounted by his nephew, the duke of Monmouth. When the Dominion was finally organized, with Sir Edmund Andros as governor, it did not provide for a representative assembly. The Dominion government was overthrown in 1689 in the American phase of England's 1688 Glorious Revolution. In England, James was deposed by his daughter Mary and her husband William of Orange. The revolutionary settlement of 1689 brought a limited monarchy and the rise of parliamentary rule in England. The change in England was profound, but there was little or no affect on colonial administration, which continued to be arbitrary.[13]

This was evident in New York's government. The province was granted an official assembly in 1691, together with the standard government of any royal colony—with the executive wielding excessive power. The assembly almost immeditely began the process of reducing that power while enhancing its own. Representatives declared all acts passed by previous assemblies to be null and void, thereby invalidating the 1683 permanent revenue act. The assembly also passed a new version of the Charter of Liberties. This charter, like the one passed by the assembly in 1683, was also rejected by the crown. The rejection left New York as one of only two mainland British colonies without a written charter. Nevertheless New Yorkers believed that by tradition and custom they were entitled to all the rights of Englishmen. In fact, a later assembly claimed that all a written charter did was confirm "Rights and Privileges inherent in Us, in common with [all] . . . his Majesty's Free-born Natural Subjects."[14]

Disagreement over the balance of power between the executive and the legislature escalated factionalism and discontent in New York. Much discord sprang from the efforts of the assembly to reduce the royal prerogative through its control of the purse strings. Assemblies had the crown-assigned function of raising money to pay the governor's salary and government expenses. The crown consistently insisted that the New York assembly pass another permanent revenue bill to ensure government support and to remove governors from the assembly's control. The Board of Trade and Plantations, created in 1696 to handle colonial affairs, tried to restrict the power of assemblies by urging governors to obtain such revenues. The New York assembly consistently refused, determined to retain its financial control. The assembly was sensitized to the potential greed of royal officials by Governor Lord Cornbury (1702–08), who had misappropriated £1500 of public money slated for the colony's defense to build a "pleasure palace" for his amusement. Hence, succeeding assemblies were wary of putting money under the control of governors.[15]

Discord in New York was also spawned by the imperial system itself, created, it seemed, to foster discontent, factionalism, and turmoil. Much disharmony resulted from the fact that the royal governor was given extensive theoretical power—more power in the colony than the king had in eighteenth-century England. The governor could, for instance, dismiss judges and veto legislation, the first power having been lost by the monarch in 1689 and the second not exercised by the monarch in England after the reign of Queen Anne. The governor could also, at will, call for assembly elections, prorogue or dissolve the assembly, or keep it in existence. The monarch lacked similar power over the legislature in England.[16]

But while the governor was the representative of the monarch, he had "neither his Power, nor Regalia." Friendless on arrival in the colony, governors were bound by their rigid instructions. Their first task was to call the assembly into session and persuade that body to raise money for the governor's salary and other government expenses. The governor's task was made difficult because they had "very little personal influence" and were "dependent on the good-will of the assemblys for their susbsistence." The governor's reliance on the assembly for salary and revenue put them "under the necessity of either breaking the instructions or of starveing, at least of loosing the purpose for which they desire their Governments. It is easy to guess which of these two all of them have chosen." Imperial authority was reduced as governors gave up crown prerogatives in exchange for salaries and support of government.[17]

Despite the best efforts of the assembly, royal governors in eighteenth-century New York continued to wield considerable power. Although the governor's power was significant, within the colony, the most stable and enduring source of influence was a small coterie of men, drawn from the province's most affluent families. These oligarchs dominated the economic, social, and political life of New York with their influence passed down from generation to generation. Knowledgeable about provincial affairs and cognizant of events in the mother country, members of New York's miniscule elite sought alliances with each successive royal governor, just as in England elites sought the favor of the monarch and his or her chief minister. The governor in turn sought the advice of local experts to help him rule. These provincial leaders shared certain similarities. When allied with the governor, or when they themselves served as the chief executive, the oligarchs formed a court party, as their counterparts did in England. As a court faction, provincial oligarchs consistently supported imperial measures, whether those measures were the establishment of prerogative courts or the granting of a permanent revenue. Members of the court party, whether in England or New York, were expected to support administration policy and to neutralize opposition.

Just as consistently, these same men, when alienated from the governor, became commonwealthmen, embodying the principles of and serving the same functions as English country Whigs and country Tories. As the country party, provincial oligarchs opposed imperial measures—usually as members of the assembly. Representatives sought to obtain concessions from the governor and to weaken the royal prerogative by exerting the assembly's control over the pursestrings. The country party naturally gravitated to Parliament in England or the assembly in the provinces. In those bodies, they attempted to weaken the administration that had denied them close access to power. Country politicians in Parliament or assembly tried, in England to weaken the ministry so a new prime minister would be appointed or, in New York, to secure the recall of the governor [18]

Whether in England or New York, the country opposition, composed of both disgruntled Whigs and Tories, had similar political platforms. They deplored patronage, which they believed threatened the English constitution. They bitterly resented the crown's or the royal governor's influence over the legislature. They believed that such influence would bring the destruction of the British constitution since it interfered with the legislature's chief function as watchdog of the executive. Both country Whigs and country Tories were offended by government corruption and deplored uncontrolled government spending. The opposition also believed that standing armies represented a threat to traditional English liberties since they might well be used by a potential tyrant to gain power. The goal of the country party was to reduce the size of the army, eliminate patronage, and limit the government's influence over elections.[19]

While assembly members espoused republican principles to justify their defiance of imperial rule, the protection of these principles was not the primary reason elite New Yorkers became involved in politics. In fact, New York's elite had few principles that could not be swayed. Nor did the elite seek office to advance the best interests of the province. Their purpose in seeking office was largely self-serving, just as it was among the English elite. So too were their political alliances. As Philip Livingston candidly admitted in 1737, "we Change Sides as Serves our Interest best, not ye Countries." Oligarchs were eager to hold public office for the good they could do themselves, their families, and their class.[20]

Factionalism in New York was also heightened by the contention between religious and political groups that followed Leisler's 1689 Rebellion. The Leislerians were the followers and allies of Jacob Leisler, who in 1689 usurped control of New York's government from lieutenant governor Francis Nicholson. The Anti-Leislerians were those who opposed Leisler's regime and were persecuted by Leisler for their resistance. Anti-Leislerians took their revenge on the Leislerians when Leisler was deposed. The resultant turmoil led to decades of bitterness and strife in New York. The issues had as much to do with ideology as with political power. The terms Leislerians and Anti-Leislerians were merely the convenient labels that summed up the deep religious and ideological differences that separated the rivals. The Leislerians were essentially Whigs who favored an orthodox Calvinism with a presbyterian form of government in church and state that derived its authority from the people. Most Anti-Leislerians, close to English Tories, favored an episcopal form of church and state government with order imposed from above.[21]

The divisions between Leislerians and Anti-Leislerians lasted into the early eighteenth century, kept alive by alliances with succeeding governors. By the 1710s, the Leislerians, or Whigs, were in the ascendance through their alliance with Governor Robert Hunter. The Anti-Leislerians, or Tories, remained in existence as the opposition party, waiting for the appointment of a governor who would be sympathetic to their concerns. In England, the Whigs were primarily composed of the new mercantile-capitalist class while Tories were predominantly the older landowning class. The exact opposite was true in New York with the Leislerian-Whigs being primarily landowners while the Anti-Leislerian-Tories were largely merchants. The Livingston family eventually assumed the leadership of the Whig-landowning faction while the DeLancey family led the Tory-merchant group.[22]

Despite the obvious presence of political factions in New York, each with a distinctly different philosophic base, the existence of political parties was not acknowledged in the colony any more than it was in England. "Faction" was the word usually used by governors to characterize their opponents. The existence of factions or political parties was seen as evidence of a splintered and disjointed society. The common belief in England during the eighteenth century was that a nation could only survive and prosper if it was politically and religiously homogeneous. There could only be one state religion and one political party. There was as yet no concept of the loyal opposition. Any opposition to government was regarded as treason. In England, the political influence of Whigs and Tories alternated for the first few decades after the 1688 Glorious Revolution. This changed with the 1714 accession of George I to the throne. The Whigs were now firmly in power, while the Tories were seen merely as a troublesome faction. In New York, Whigs and Tories alternated as factions, or opposition groups, depending on which group was allied with the governor as the court party.[23]

The primary weapon used to undermine the governor was the press. Although the press was used by both court and country factions, it was most often the weapon of the less powerful against the more powerful. Through the press, both factions informed the middling and lower sort of political events, thus drawing them into the conflict and escalating discord within the colony. The intent of the elite, whether court or country, in informing the lower classes was to obtain voter support for their assembly candidates. The governor's court party could only maintain control of the assembly with a proadministration majority in that body. To accomplish this, it was necessary for a governor to get his candidates elected to assembly office. Governors had to gain the support of the bulk of the voting population. Voters would then elect the governor's men to the assembly, giving the governor a proadministration court majority in the house and nullifying the efforts of the country faction. This was accomplished most effectively through the press.[24]

By the same token, the opposition or country party needed to control the assembly so that they could wrest concessions from the governor. The need for support at the polls led both court and country to appeal to voters. The bulk of New York's voters were of the middling sort—small merchants, landowners with estates of more than £40, tenant farmers with lifelong leases, and freemen of New York City and Albany. The influence of voters was dramatic in New York and in other colonies, as noted by another royal governor Alexander Spotswood of Virginia. The governor voiced his frustration that "the meaner sort of People will ever carry the elections," while burgesses "for fear of not being chosen again, dare in Assembly do nothing that may be disrelished out of the House by the Common People."[25]

Court and country elite in New York also tried to reach the unfranchised, who constituted approximately one-third to one-half the adult male population. These were both urban and rural dwellers who comprised the lowest orders of New York society, with the exception of free blacks, slaves, and Indians. The unfranchised included carters, seamen, dockworkers, peddlars, tenant farmers on short-term leases, tavern owners, farm laborers, mechanics, porters, blacksmiths, and other lesser artisans and craftsmen. Elite polemicists realized this was an important segment of society. Even if they could not read, they were informed about public affairs because they frequented taverns and coffee houses where newspapers were read aloud. Even if they could not vote, they cared enough about public issues to indicate their approval or disapproval of events in the streets where they protested against unpopular measures or governors. Further it appears that many of the unfranchised did, in fact, vote, and their votes were counted. Hence, the middling and lower sorts of New York society, whether urban or rural, whether franchised or not, wielded considerable, if indirect, political influence in the province.[26]

Both court and country factions were aware of the influence exerted by the lower and middling sort in electing assembly candidates. The goal of both court and country was to accomplish and maintain a proadministration legislative majority. To achieve a court majority, the governor in New York or the ministry in London not only had to control elections through appeals to the electorate but also to reward loyal followers with offices. There were far fewer offices in New York than in England. Hence this program was most often successful in England, where the monarch and his chief minister had numerous offices at their disposal. By 1742, some 286 out of a total of 558 members of Parliament were placemen, beholden to the ministry for some government post or for the promise of a future government pension. When officials were rewarded with promotions, pensions, or peerages, the ministry made it clear that their parliamentary support was the price of these favors. The duke of Newcastle, for instance, informed Horace Walpole in 1755 that the king intended to elevate Walpole to the peerage. In return, Newcastle reminded Walpole that he was to support the king's policies, including "preventing, as far as is possible to be done, the War from extending itself to the Continent of Europe."[27]

The decline of colonial patronage during this same period was apparent in New York. In 1756, Governor Charles Hardy (1755–57) recommended to Newcastle his choice for comptroller of customs in New York. Hardy urged his nominee be accepted since "I need not point out how farr Recommendations of this kind from me, if accepted, may tend to promote the necessary Influence I ought to have, and if possible acquire, to enable me to carry on His Majesty's Service in this Country." In New York, royal governors lacked the extensive powers of patronage available to the king. Hence it was more difficult for governors, who were themselves placemen both representing and safeguarding the interests of the crown in the colony, to create and maintain a sizeable court party in the provincial assembly because they could not always satisfactorily reward allies.[28]

Even when provincial governors were able to establish a court party in the assembly, these parties did not always vote the way the administration wanted any more than did the court party in Parliament. Nevertheless, their presence was important to counter country politicians. In England and New York, the political compositions of both court and country factions were constantly changing. At any given time each might include Whigs or Tories, landowners or merchants, depending on which group was currently in favor.

The necessity for a governor to form alliances with one provincial faction or another led him "to be the Head of a Party, when he ought to have been the Head of the Government." While the king in England was above party and was the monarch of all Britons—Whigs and Tories, court and country—the governor did not enjoy similar stature in the colony. Forced by political necessity to form alliances, governors alienated other factions. All governors had to form alliances for all were ignorant of provincial affairs and needed the assistance and advice of local politicians. As Board of Trade secretary Alured Popple noted in 1734, "A Governor has at first a pretty difficult Lesson to learn, and if he falls into right Hands, he may certainly pave the Way for a peaceable, and an agreeable Way of making his Fortune."[29]

Governors did indeed make their fortunes in New York, one of the most lucrative of colonial governorships. This was particularly true prior to 1737 when it was combined with the governorship of New Jersey. Robert Hunter's (1710–19) income from salaries, fees, and perquisites brought the yearly total to well over £9,000. Despite the loss of the New Jersey governorship, New York was still a profitable post as shown by George Clinton (1743–53), who returned to England richer by some £80,000. That all governors came to New York to make money was obvious to provincials. A rare exception was William Bur net (1720 –28), who, according to William Smith, Jr., was free of this "disease common to all his predecessors and to some who succeeded him." Provincials were also aware that during the Walpolean era governors and other royal officials were chosen not on the basis of ability, but rather because of their political and social connections in the ministry or because they were owed a favor by the ministry.[30]

While the money was there to be made it could scarcely be enjoyed if dissension persisted. Governors had several potent weapons at their command with which to calm dissent and counter legislative assertiveness, foremost among them the Church of England. In England the Anglican Church, no longer troubled by dissenters, served as a buttress to government. Religious dissenters were quiet in England because their philosophy had become mainstream with the adoption of the 1689 revolutionary settlement. Religious unity, such as that achieved in England, was virtually impossible in New York, given the numerous religions and sects that existed in the province even before it was taken from the Dutch in 1664. Despite the multiplicity of sects, the Church of England was established in the four lower counties of New York, although religious dissenters repeatedly refused to acknowledge that fact.[31]

Governors also used the court system to gain control of the colony, a control assemblies consistently sought to weaken. New York's courts were patterned on the English models and created by New York's Judiciary Act of 1691. There was in every county an Inferior Court of Common Pleas, composed of three judges assisted by justices of the peace, all appointed by the governor and presumably loyal to him. The governor also appointed all sheriffs, clerks, and coroners. The supreme court, the highest common law court in the province, was modeled after the English courts of King's Bench, Common Pleas, and Exchequer. The supreme court met yearly in New York City, and the justices also went on circuit. The court's chief justice was usually recommended by the governor, and his appointment was approved by the king, as was that of the colony's attorney general. The governor appointed the subordinate justices in the supreme court. By virtue of his commission, the governor was empowered to erect a chancery court with equity jurisdiction and an admiralty court, both of which used civil law procedures. Both were prerogative courts that functioned without juries and, hence, were much resented by colonists. The governor could either sit in these courts himself as chief presiding magistrate, or appoint deputies. In addition, the governor and his council, acting together, constituted the provincial court of appeals, with the governor acting as chief appelate judge.[32]

The governor also appointed all councillors, who were confirmed by the monarch. The role of provincial councils was ill-defined.

Provincials believed the council was equivalent to the House of Lords. Britons at home did not agree since there was no hereditary aristocracy in the colonies. Despite this, Britons saw provincial councils as the more important of the two legislative bodies. The council alone had an inherent right to exist even in the governor's absence, with the senior councillor serving as acting governor. When the governor was present, the council was an advisory body to the governor, much as the Privy Council acted for the king.[33]

Although the council had an inherent right to exist, its precise function as a legislative body was disputed. British administrators claimed the council should be "a Second Estate separate and distinct from the Governor," part of whose function was "to propose, and amend Bills as a branch of the Legislature." Provincial assemblies asserted the council's function was "only to give their advice to the Governor as a Privy council, whether he should assent to or reject the Bills formed by the Assembly." The council should not, for instance, alter money bills passed by the assembly since Lords did not alter money bills passed by Commons. The council should "have nothing to do in the business of Legislation, but to advise the Governor." Royal officials believed such assertions "groundless," since the council shared "an equal Right with them [the assembly] in granting of Money."[34]

Colonial assemblies patterned their own functions on the British House of Commons. Provincials were aware that in England, after 1689, the power of Commons had increased while the power of Lords and the executive had declined. Hence provincials believed that the power of the provincial assemblies should grow while that of the council and governor should decrease. Britons did not agree with provincials that assemblies were equal to the House of Commons. To Britons, provincial assemblies existed only "upon the good pleasure of the King, as expressed in his Commission, and Instructions to his Governors." Further complicating imperial government was the difference in perception between how colonists saw themselves and their function within the system and how their role in the empire was viewed by Britons at home. New Yorkers believed "themselves as intituled to a greater measure of Liberty than is enjoy'd by the People of England." Britons agreed colonists were entitled to the rights of British subjects, but only to those rights of Britons living abroad.[35]

Such differences in perception spelled trouble for royal governors since it led to "the perpetual Struggle in every Colony between Privilege and Prerogative, and the Governor who is not so happy as to temporize (for it is impossible to reconcile difficulties on one side, or the other, and in either case his recall is the only remedy that can restore quiet to the Colony)." If the governor managed to retain his post, he was often forced "to gratify the People in demands highly injurious to the Prerogative; a fatal complaisance, and which had encouraged the Colonists to enlarge their Claims."[36]

American colonists resisted English rule, as had the Scots and the Irish. The latter two provinces, because of proximity and circumstance, ultimately had no choice but to accept English dominance. When the English applied similar measures to the colonies they encountered resistance. Opposition came initially from the elite-dominated assemblies and then from the lower classes. In Ireland, the crown had only to deal with one subservient legislature. In America, by mid-eighteenth century, the crown had to deal with thirteen separate and belligerent legislatures on the mainland alone. In Ireland, all proposed legislation had first to be submitted to the crown before it could even be considered by the Irish Parliament. In America, even in royal colonies, acts were passed by the legislatures without initial approval and then sent to England for confirmation. Assemblies often ignored crown directives demanding that suspending clauses be included in acts to prevent them from going into effect until approved by the crown. Even if the act was ultimately rejected, it would still have been in operation for the year or two it took the ministry to reach its decision.[37]

Despite such leeway, New York colonists came to resent being subjected to an autocratic imperial administration. Nor was it possible to govern colonies or provinces the same way the mother country was governed. This was as true for England in the eighteenth century A.D. as it had been for Athens in the fifth century B.C. Athens itself was a democracy and instituted a democratic form of government within its conquered provinces. But as Thucydides points out in the Mytilenian Debate, "A democracy is incapable of governing others." To enforce its will on subordinate peoples, Athens's colonial administration was tyrannical, since "leadership depends on superior strength." An honest appraisal, said Thucydides, would reveal that any "empire is a tyranny exercised over subjects who do not like it."[38]

Provincials in New York did not like English colonial administration, particularly when it embodied military rule. Many governors recognized that the antagonism and resistance directed at them by provincial assemblies was really aimed at the imperial government they represented. As Governor Robert Hunter commented to New York's assembly, "however your Resentment has fallen upon the Governors, it is the Government you dislike." Distant from the seat of power, elite New Yorkers used their inferior position to gain political sophistication and some measure of home rule. Attempts by the government to limit colonial autonomy led to heightened resistance on the part of the elite, particularly in the assembly. This resistance gave definition to the struggle between privilege and prerogative.[39]

2

This Unsettled and Ungovernable Province, 1710–1719: The Administration of Robert Hunter

> If I have done amiss, I am sorry for't, but what was there left for me to do, I have been struggling hard for bread itself for five years to no effect, and for four of them unpitty'd, I hope I have now laid a foundation for a lasting settlement on this hitherto unsettled and ungovernable Province.[1]

Despite elite dissatisfaction with imperial rule and the presence of internal discord, factionalism, and discontent, it was possible for a governor to seize control of a colony and reduce, if not eliminate, factionalism. Such a feat required a person of extraordinary abilities as well as one who was willing to make concessions and one who appealed to the lower and middling sort. While most governors failed to achieve this balance, an exception, as noted by Cadwallader Colden, was Robert Hunter, who "went through a long administration with more honour and advantage to himself than all his predecessors put together." Hunter's administration was successful, but it was achieved at a high price. Robert Hunter brought peace to New York but lessened the crown's prerogative power while strengthening local privilege.[2]

Hunter was appointed to the joint New York–New Jersey post in 1709 by treasurer Sidney Godolphin, with the approval of John Churchill, duke of Marlborough. The duke, who controlled colonial patronage during Queen Anne's reign, wanted only military men as governors of the provinces. He was familiar with Hunter's abilities since Hunter had served as the duke's aide-de-camp during the War of the Spanish Succession. Marlborough refused to permit economic

Robert Hunter, ca. 1720, attributed to Sir Godfrey Kneller, courtesy of The New-York Historical Society, New York. After leaving New York, Hunter exchanged offices with William Burnet to become comptroller of customs. In 1727 he was named governor of Jamaica and became the only governor in the eighteenth century to secure a permanent revenue.

considerations alone to dictate imperial philosophy. His intent was to expand and control the empire through military might. Hunter shared the duke's imperial philosophy and his dislike of mercantilists.[3]

Hunter's techniques of governance worked well during his nine years in New York. He was able to reduce factionalism and calm the continuing discontent that had characterized New York since Leisler's 1689 rebellion. Hunter achieved relative tranquility by making strategic alliances with key members of New York's elite. His allies included Lewis Morris and Robert Livingston, both of whom Hunter encouraged to run for the assembly. In that body, Morris and Livingston formed the nucleus of a proadministration party that effectively neutralized the opposition. The assembly-based court party grew because of the governor's popular appeal to the masses who comprised the bulk of the voting population and elected to office Hunter's assembly candidates. Hunter's success in wooing voters and controlling opposition elites made his tenure successful.[4]

Hunter's judicious alliances with the colony's landowning elite were natural because of his dislike of merchants. As a landowner and a Whig who had opposed James II in the 1688 Glorious Revolution, Hunter allied with New York's Leislerian-Whig-landowning faction. Hunter's appointive council was comprised primarily of landowners, although he kept some opposition members on the council (and under his control). Two such councillors were the merchants Adolph Philipse and Peter Schuyler. Hunter realized that if Philipse and Schuyler were deprived of their council posts they would run for the assembly and, if elected, would increase dissident strength in that body.[5]

Merchants constituted the majority of the country party during Governor Hunter's administration. Hunter's antipathy toward merchants sprang from his belief that they were concerned only with their own profit and not with the welfare of the colony as a whole. Hunter claimed that New York's merchants were determined to "oppose and obstruct as much as in them lies all Acts for support of Government," despite the fact that they could afford the tax imposed because trade was excellent. Hunter's scorn of merchants was usual in a military aristocrat and landowner, particularly in an era in which the profits accrued from land were regarded as more respectable than income from trade. Land profits were great in New York. During a period when landowning in Great Britain was becoming less profitable because of rising taxes on land, the reverse was true in the colonies. In New York, landowners were realizing substantial profits. These profits increased when the governor decided to force merchants and their customers to bear the brunt of taxation, a practice that continued in New York until the Revolution.[6]

The Church of England was active in New York politics. The Anti-Leislerian-Tory-merchant faction was bolstered in New York by its alliance with Church of England minister William Vesey. This minister, who might logically have been expected to support the crown-appointed executive, instead proved a thorn in Hunter's side, obstructing early attempts at a legislative revenue settlement. Hunter, although born in Scotland and raised a Presbyterian, had joined the Church of England to qualify for a government position because England's 1673 Test Act barred nonconformists from holding official posts. While Hunter's personal commitment to the Anglican Church was not very deep, he favored prosletyzing efforts by the Society for the Propagation of the Gospel in Foreign Parts. Hunter fully recognized the cultural importance of the Anglican Church in uniting people of diverse backgrounds, whether European, African, or Native American, thereby reducing social tensions.[7]

The Church of England in the colonies fell under the dominion of the Bishop of London, since there was no resident bishop. Nonconformists believed that the appointment of such a bishop might well signal the intent of the home government to fully establish the Church of England in the middle colonies. Hence, nonconformists were particularly alarmed by Hunter's purchase of a house for a resident bishop in Burlington, New Jersey. Hunter for a time believed the bishophric would be filled by his friend, Jonathan Swift. Swift, denied high church office because the queen believed him irreverent, contented himself with the deanery of St. Patrick's in Dublin, Ireland. The colonial bishophric remained unfilled, much to the relief of provincial nonconformists, who feared they would be deprived of offices and power with an established church.[8]

As a Whig, Hunter favored representative parliamentary rule and the limitation of executive power in Great Britain. His beliefs did not extend to New York. Hunter did not look kindly on attempts by provincial assemblies to increase their power at the expense of the royal prerogative. Assemblies, for their part, believed they were following the anti-executive tradition established by the English Parliament following the 1689 revolutionary settlement. Hunter believed that to condone the decline of the executive in the province would be to ignore the best interests of the mother country. Like most colonial administrators, Hunter agreed that colonial interests should be subordinate to those of England and that colonies should selflessly contribute to the prosperity of the mother country. As Hunter put it, "it is expected that ye Colonies, now they are grown up, should be a help and of some use to their parent country."[9]

New York's assembly was more concerned with advancing provincial affairs than with furthering imperial interests. By 1710 New York's assembly was already an experienced legislature, insistant on establishing and expanding its privileges. The assembly, said Hunter, claimed "all ye priviledges of a House of Commons and stretching them even beyond what they were ever imagined to be there." Hunter warned the home government that if the provincial "Councill by ye same rule lay claime to ye rights and priviledges of a House of Peers; here is a body pollitick co-ordinate with (claiming equall powers) and consequently independant of ye Great Council of ye realm."[10]

Hunter believed much of the assembly's belligerent determination to secure rights and privileges was due to the unfortunate influence of Puritan New Englanders who migrated to Long Island and New Jersey. Hunter acknowledged that "all the oposion and vexation I have met with in both these Provinces [New York and New Jersey] has been in a great measure owing to those who have come to us from that [New England]." Added to the extremism of New Englanders were the unfortunate characteristics of most New World immigrants, who were often the malcontents of European society. Colonists, Hunter believed, were "generally obstinate, the whimsical & factious who flock hither for elbow room to exert their talents."[11]

Obstinacy was obvious in New York's assembly. That body, led by speaker William Nicoll, claimed the right to set fees, including the amount of the governor's salary, would not let the council amend its money bills, refused to let the crown's representative disburse money, demanded the right to appoint and control the province's London agent, and insisted the governor could not erect courts without its consent. Hunter resisted the assembly's dictates, thereby alienating the assembly by initially adhering to the letter of his instructions. Hunter, the urbane, sophisticated statesman, may also have made all too evident his dislike and disdain of assemblymen, who were largely "Dutch boors, grossly ignorant and rude, who could neither write or read nor speak English." Hunter insisted the assembly vote New York a permanent revenue and that only the queen's receiver general handle the disbursement of the colony's funds. The assembly balked, stating that they would only vote yearly support and their treasurer would disburse funds. Hunter would not accept their terms and consequently was left without a salary and no money for government expenses, which were paid out of his own pocket.[12]

Hunter offered the ministry alternative means by which money for New York's government could be raised without the assembly. He suggested that quit rents be tapped, but acknowledged the present income from these rents was inadequate for government expenses. The rent charged, but rarely paid, was 2s 6d per one hundred developed acres.

Hunter proposed a parliamentary act be passed to tax undeveloped acres as well as developed. This would not only bring the government a substantial income but would also have the welcome side effects of increasing population and reducing extravagant land grants, some of which were twenty to thirty square miles. Landlords wanted large landholdings to attract tenants, but few immigrants would resign themselves to becoming tenants if they could own land of their own in neighboring colonies. These same immigrants might well choose to remain in New York if land became available when landlords were forced to breakup their estates.[13]

Hunter anticipated by fifty-seven years the Townshend Acts when he suggested that Parliament place "an Impost on all goods imported and exported into and from this Province" for the sole purpose of paying the civil establishment. If these measures were not implemented, Hunter suggested that the crown might make the executive independent of the legislature by "defray[ing] the charges of this Government from home."[14]

The Privy Council approved Hunter's recommendations and ordered the Board of Trade to "draw up Heads of a Bill to be laid before the Parliament of Great Britain for enacting a Standing Revenue of what has been usually allowed within the Province of New York, for the support of the Governors there, and the necessary expences of the Government." The act was submitted to Parliament, but that body adjourned before it could be considered. Hunter learned later "that the Revenue-bill was never intended to be passed, tho' prepared by the Lords." Hunter's request to draw his salary out of the province's quit rents was also denied.[15]

The assembly's recalcitrance brought the colony to severe economic distress and by 1711 put the province at military risk. As Hunter reported, "the Officers of the Government are starving, the Forts on the Frontiers in ruine, the French and French Indians threatening us every day, noe publick money nor credit for Five pounds on the publick account, and all the necessary expence of the Government supply'd by my proper credit . . . and noe hopes that I can think of for any remedy here, ffor as to the calling of a New Assembly, I shall either have all the same members, or such others who will returne with greater ffury." Hunter was voted a salary by the assembly in 1711 but continued to pay all government expenses until 1712. The assembly that year voted money for current government expenditures, but Hunter was not reimbursed for past expenses.[16]

Strapped for cash, Hunter moved to establish other sources of government revenue. With the support of his court party and council, Hunter decided to erect a chancery court to collect quit rents, which were several years in arrears. The governor served as chancellor, while the registrar and marshall, who were appointed and paid by the governor, were likely to do his bidding. The assembly balked when Hunter stated his intent and informed him that only they had the right to erect courts in the province. With the support of colonial oligarchs in his court party, Hunter ignored the assembly, erected a chancery court, and began to collect from £300 to £500 a year in quit rents.[17]

The assembly openly defied Hunter in the matter of quit rents and all other measures because they fully realized that he struggled under a political disadvantage. Appointed by the Whig Godolphin ministry, Hunter's position was secure only as long as the ministry endured. The Whigs fell from power in 1710, and Godolphin was replaced as first lord of the treasury by the Tory, Robert Harley. Neither Harley nor any other Tory was interested in alleviating the plight of the Whig governor of New York. Hunter's situation was weakened still further as the Tories strengthened their hold on England's politics. Their power increased when Marlborough was deprived of all his posts in December of 1711.[18]

Although Hunter experienced a marked decline in support he was fortunate in that colonial affairs were not Harley's chief concern. Beset by war and internal problems, it would be several years before the Tories could deal with colonial administrators, even if they were Whigs. In fact, the Tory administration backed the governor in at least one contest with local oligarchs. In 1712 some two dozen slaves set fire to a building in New York City in the middle of the night. They then attacked the mob that came to put out the fire, killing nine people. The incident enflamed white fears of slave rebellions. Before the hysteria ran its course, more than seventy Blacks were imprisoned; several were tried, twenty-seven convicted, and twenty executed, while others were left to rot in jail. Hunter, convinced that many of the convicted slaves awaiting execution were innocent, asked the Queen that they be pardoned. The Tory ministry agreed, and the slaves were pardoned.[19]

In reaction to public fear, in December 1712 the assembly passed an act to reduce the number of slaves in New York. The common perception was the presence of free Blacks caused discontent among slaves and led to rebellion. Manumission was discouraged by requiring owners to pay £200 as security for any slave they wished to free, plus a contribution of £20 a year for their support. Faced with lingering hysteria in New York, Hunter had no choice but to approve the bill. He then advised the Board of Trade not to recommend it for confirmation. The bill was rejected, another victory for the royal prerogative.[20]

Despite such selective support, Hunter was still in danger of being recalled and was thus a tempting target for the assembly. The assembly's defiant actions led Hunter to warn the Tory ministry that if left unchecked, such action might well lead New York to cast off its ties from the mother country. The assembly based its defiance on tradition, or, as Hunter put it, they had "trumpt up an inherent right, declared the powers granted by her Majesty's letters patent to be against law, and have but one short step to make towards what I am unwilling to name." New York and other "Colonies," he warned, "were infants sucking their mother's breasts, but such as, if he was not mistaken, would weane themselves when they came of age."[21]

The assembly based its defiance on principle. They believed that to comply with the governor's demands by "supporting the Government in the manner her Majesty has been pleased to direct" was equivalent to reducing them to "slavery." By the same token, persisting in "their own rash resolutions and practises" was seen by provincials as guaranteeing their "liberty." Hunter complained that the assembly's rhetoric led many "thoughtless people to speak after them."[22]

One of the persons who influenced the assembly in its defiance was the Anglican minister of New York's Trinity Church, William Vesey. The minister disliked Hunter and thought him a threat to the Anglican Church. Vesey wanted a Tory as governor and had in the past allied with Tory governor Lord Cornbury. Vesey backed the assembly's defiant attempt to starve Hunter out of New York. The heights of absurdity were reached when Vesey accused Hunter of prompting the desecration of vestments and prayer books in the church. Hunter retaliated in print with a proclamation in which he none too subtly reminded Vesey that his primary duty as a Church of England minister was to support royal government.[23]

Despite Vesey, Hunter's situation improved dramatically in 1714 when the New York assembly finally agreed to reimburse Hunter for past government-related expenses, which amounted to £5,000. His condition improved even more when the death of Queen Anne in 1714 brought George of Hanover to the English throne and the Whigs back into power.[24]

The next year the New York assembly, still dominated by a substantial mercantile majority, worked out a deal with the governor. A deal was necessary on Hunter's part even though the Whigs were again in power in England. While sympathetic to Hunter, the new ministry was still too preoccupied by internal affairs to deal with provincial problems. Realizing this, Hunter, desperate for money, was willing to compromise, but not to take bribes from the assembly for his approval of an annual revenue bill. Hunter pointed out to the Board of Trade that he had refused "offers of several thousands of pounds for my assent" to such a bill.[25]

What Hunter wanted and received was long-term support. He got that when the assembly voted a five-year revenue. In return, Hunter permitted the assembly's treasurer to handle the disbursement of funds, even though only a year earlier he had warned the assembly that "there are things it will be useless for you to attempt," among them lodging "money for the support of government in any hands but those of the officers appointed by Her Majesty." Hunter well realized his surrender of this key function was a major blow to the royal prerogative he represented. As he half-apologized to the ministry, "If I have done amiss, I am sorry for't, but what was there left for me to do, I have been struggling hard for bread itself for five years to no effect, and for four of them unpitty'd, I hope I have now laid a foundation for a lasting settlement on this hitherto unsettled and ungovernable Province."[26]

Hence, the first significant advances by the assembly against the royal prerogative were made during the administration of New York's most effective colonial governor. George Clinton (1743–53), recognized that the decline of the royal prerogative in New York began with Hunter's 1715 decision to permit the assembly, rather than the queen's receiver general, to handle the disbursement of money. Hunter was forced to this expediency to obtain funds to run the government. The result, according to Clinton, was that "the Assembly continued from time (as occasions offered) in grasping more and more power to the Prejudice of the Royal Prerogative 'till the Kings authority and Power of Assemblys are at last brought to the state they now are."[27]

Another point of contention between Hunter and the assembly was the appointment of a colonial agent in London. The assembly had recently passed "an Act intirely excluding the Governor or Council from having any thing to do with the agent or to make any representations or applications by him." Hunter had not approved this act because he believed the direction of the agent should be his responsibility. This issue was also compromised. The agent was to be appointed by and receive his instructions from both the governor and legislature together.[28]

With these concessions, control of the province was within Hunter's grasp. All that was necessary was to convince the voting population that they should support his assembly candidates. Hunter achieved control of the assembly with the use of the press. Hunter wrote and published a satirical farce, *Androboros*, in which he ridiculed his enemies. Pilloried in this crude, vulgar, and bawdy play were his predecessor in New York, Lord Cornbury, his enemies in the council and assembly, Adolph Philipse and William Nicoll, minister William Vesey, and other prominent Tories. New Yorkers read the play and laughed all the way to the polls. Hunter was able to get most of his landowner candidates elected to the 1716 assembly, breaking the control of the merchant country faction and bringing a victory for the royal prerogative. Hunter's use of satire and the press were lessons in political propaganda that neither court nor country would soon forget.[29]

Hunter's control of the assembly was achieved with the assistance of such well-placed allies as Lewis Morris. Born in New York City in 1671, Morris was orphaned at the age of one. He was raised by an uncle, Lewis Morris, of Barbados. The senior Morris moved to New Jersey in 1674 and died in 1691, leaving land in New York and New Jersey to his nephew. The junior Morris was active in the politics of both provinces.[30]

Morris, as a member of New York's country opposition, had opposed the governorship of Lord Cornbury and actively and successfully worked to achieve the corrupt governor's recall. When Robert Hunter arrived in 1710, Morris formed an alliance with the governor. Elected to the New York assembly, Morris fought four years before he successfully neutralized Hunter's country opposition in that body. As Hunter's legislative leader, Morris fully supported a permanent revenue, the establishment of prerogative courts, and the collection of quit rents. In return for Morris's legislative support, Hunter in 1715 used his patronage power to name Morris as the province's chief justice, even though Morris had no legal training.[31]

Livingston, born in 1654, was the son of a Presbyterian minister in Scotland. He migrated first to the Netherlands and then to Boston and New York, where he married the widow Alida Schuyler Van Rensselaer in 1679, thus allying himself with two of New York's most powerful families. In 1686, Livingston was awarded a patent for 2,600 acres by Governor Thomas Dongan. The acreage constituted the lordship and manor of Livingston.[32]

By 1715, Hunter owed Livingston money for expenses incurred from provisioning more than two thousand Palatines. The immigrants were imported to establish a naval stores program in New York. Hunter could not pay the debt because he had not been reimbursed by the British ministry as promised. Livingston wanted the patent to his manor confirmed. Although the original patent was for 2,600 acres, by 1715 the manor had increased to 160,000 acres even though no new patents were issued. Hunter approved the patent in 1715 and gave the tenants the right to elect a representative to the provincial assembly. In return for this substantial favor, Livingston gave Hunter a formal release for his Palatine-related debts. As the lord of Livingston Manor, Livingston was promptly elected representative and in the assembly gave Hunter his unwavering support. In 1717, following the resignation of William Nicoll, Livingston was elected speaker. Nicoll resigned in frustration when he realized that Hunter and his court party now controlled the majority of the votes in the assembly.[33]

Hunter also controlled the court system and used it to harrass and punish his political opponents. One such instance during Hunter's administration involved Suffolk County representative Samuel Mulford, a Puritan who migrated to Long Island from Connecticut. In 1714 the verbose Mulford drew down Hunter's wrath because he blocked the passage of a financial settlement by attacking Hunter verbally in the assembly chamber. Mulford accurately charged that Hunter controlled New York's legislature, the judiciary, and the militia. Mulford, perhaps taking a lesson from Hunter's own successful use of the press, had the speech published. Mulford enjoyed great popularity not only among his constituents but also among other gullible New Yorkers. Born a New Englander, he used typical Puritan rhetoric about natural rights to justify his continued defiance of Hunter. Appealing to basic fears—whether of Indians (who he recommended slaughtering) or taxes (which he was against)—he told the middling and lower sort exactly what they wanted to hear. This was the case with Mulford's harangue against Hunter. It was read by and influenced voters, who did not want to pay the higher taxes. Voters well realized that the bill would be funded by taxes on mercantile goods and that merchants would pass on the expense to consumers.[34]

Hunter was furious at Mulford for inciting resistance and insisted the assembly expel Mulford from the house. The governor then had his protégé, attorney general David Jamison, issue a writ of attachment for the arrest of Mulford for seditious libel. The charges against Mulford were for "publishing and dispersing a false scandalous and malicious libel containing false and unjust reflections on the Governor and Government of this Province . . . with an intent to raise Sedition amongst the people and in their minds an aversion to both." Mulford was prosecuted not because of his verbal attack in the assembly, a privilege guaranteed to representatives in parliament by English law, but because the speech had been published.[35]

Mulford's case was brought before New York's grand jury, composed largely of merchants who, like their customers, resented Hunter's approval of acts that imposed heavy taxes on them, while lightly taxing landowners. The jury considered the evidence against Mulford insufficient and endorsed the bill *Ignoramus*. Faced with the grand jury's defiance, Jamison moved the case to the Supreme Court. There, Chief Justice Lewis Morris set bail at £500 to guarantee Mulford's appearance.[36]

As in England, Mulford was to be tried by common law procedures before a jury. English libel laws had grown out of government efforts to control the information given to the public and to stop criticism of rulers. All English monarchs since Henry VIII had controlled the press to some degree, usually by the enforcement of licensing, treason, and seditious libel laws. In the sixteenth and early seventeenth centuries, truth was considered a defense against charges of seditious libel in England. This was altered in 1606 by the Star Chamber, an equity court composed of five members of the Privy Council and two judges, whose jurisdiction was breaches of the peace and proclamation, the regulation of trade, and seditious libel. In the case *de Libellis Famosis*, the court established the precedent that truth was immaterial against a charge of seditious libel—that is, sedition, not libel, was the crime, or, more precisely, sedition was libel.[37]

Henceforward, juries in common law courts decided only whether the material had actually been published and circulated and whether it did in fact refer to the people or institutions said to be libeled. Libel was defined as any oral or written criticism of the government, or as Chief Justice Sir John Holt explained in 1704, "To say that corrupt officers are appointed to administer affairs is certainly a reflection on the government. For it is very necessary for all governments that the people should have a good opinion of it. And nothing can be worse to any government than to endeavour to procure animosities as to the management of it; this has always been looked upon as a crime, and no government can be safe without it."[38]

Criticism of the government was not tolerated, but the government in England made no attempt to block publication of potentially seditious or libelous material. Freedom of the press existed, but it was a circumscribed freedom with censorship in the threat of prosecution for seditious libel. Freedom of the press simply meant freedom from prior restraint. The press was free to publish what it pleased and also free to face the consequences of its actions. In the words of Blackstone, freedom of the press consisted solely in laying "no previous restraint upon publications, and not in freedom from censure for criminal matter when published." Those who wrote material considered seditious or libelous could be, and usually were, prosecuted. Libel was defined as any oral or written criticism of the government.[39]

Licensing laws had expired in England, but prior approval for publication was still required in New York in 1710. Hunter's instructions specifically ordered him to see "that no Person keep any press for printing, nor that any Book or Pamphlet or other matters whatsoever be printed without your especial leave & license first obtained." These restrictions, although rarely enforced, were deemed necessary because of the "great Inconveniences [that] may arise by the liberty of printing within the Province of New York."[40]

Although many Britons agreed that the press required some control, the licensing system was dropped in England during the reign of William III primarily because licensing laws proved ineffective in curtailing the publication of seditious material. The remaining controls on the press were the laws of treason and seditious libel. Freedom of the press in England and its colonies simply meant freedom from prior restraint. The press was free to publish what it pleased and also free to face the consequences of its actions.[41]

It was under the English law of libel that Mulford was brought before New York's supreme court, where Lewis Morris presided. Despite Morris's control of the court, public pressure against conviction was so great that on four occasions the jury could not reach a verdict. The jury's failure to convict underscored the fact that, while Hunter controlled the judges, neither he nor any other governor controlled the juries. Mulford was a popular figure, and his peers would not convict him, a significant victory for local privilege.[42]

But if Hunter did not control juries, by 1716 he did control the assembly. In August of 1716, Mulford was reelected to the assembly. The assembly petitioned the governor to drop charges against Mulford so that he could take his seat. Hunter adamantly refused to do so and two months later, Mulford forfeited his £500 security and sailed for England, there to file unsuccessful counter charges against Hunter.[43]

Hunter also dealt expeditiously with vocal merchants in New York when, in 1717, they objected to the passage of a new act that placed still further taxes on trade. The focal point of dissent was the merchant dominated grand jury, which issued statements claiming the taxes were unfair. Hunter had the jury members charged with contempt and brought before the now landowner-dominated assembly. Prior to the establishment of courts, the assemblies in virtually all colonies served as courts of law. They continued in that function for offenses such as seditious libel throughout the provincial period. The assembly had the power to convict and inflict punishment. When brought before the house, the intimidated merchants hastily apologized and explained they had not meant their comments to be contemptuous. When the merchants regained their composure and again protested, Hunter, with Chief Justice Morris's support, silenced them by threatening to prosecute them in the supreme court for sedition.[44]

Hunter, with his court party, achieved success in New York because of an intelligent blending of intimidation, coercion, and compromise. Only the most troublesome members of the opposition were hounded into exile. The majority remained in the province, and a few of these continued to hold profitable posts. Hunter secured needed legislation from the assembly because he was willing to concede some of that body's demands, even if doing so reduced the royal prerogative.[45]

Hunter's methods were successful in that he managed to stifle most opposition in the colony. Even after losing control of the assembly, the country party's insistent complaints to the home government and the personal petitions of several provincials to the ministry convinced Hunter that he should return to England to defend himself in person from the charges of such enemies as Samuel Mulford.[46]

In 1719, on the eve of Hunter's departure, peace reigned for the most part in New York. Hunter addressed the assembly and noted to that body that "the very name of party or faction seems to be forgot" in New York. The assembly, in response, paid Hunter the compliment of telling him, "you have governed well and wisely. . . . We have seen many Governors, and may see more; and as none of those who had the honor to serve in your station were ever so justly fixed in the affections of the Government, so those to come will acquire no mean reputation, when it can be truly said of them, their conduct had been like yours." As for Hunter, he candidly expressed his personal opinion of New Yorkers and his office when he commented that "People think it a fine thing to be a governor. A governor by ———, a Tom Turdman's is a better office than to rake in the dunghill of these people's vile affections."[47]

Despite his unfavorable opinion of New Yorkers, Hunter had achieved a successful governorship, in that he quieted dissent, secured long-term support for government, achieved control of the assembly, and established prerogative courts. Despite his success, the country party, through its control of the assembly, scored a significant victory by having funds dispersed by an officer of their choice, thereby usurping a significant crown function. Hunter's decision to yield to the assembly's demands brought peace to the province, but the practice of making concessions to the assembly, once established, brought more grief to Hunter's successors than many of them could handle.

Achieving the right balance between concession and intimidation was a feat beyond the reach of most colonial governors, including Hunter's successors in New York and New Jersey. These governors were further hampered by a change in colonial administration. Robert Walpole came to power in 1722, following the deaths of leading Whig statesmen, including the duke of Marlborough. With the old guard died the militaristic imperial philosophy they represented. Walpole, while also favoring the expansion of the empire, did not approve of military conquest, but instead favored expansion through trade and peaceful commerce. Walpole's policies discouraged home government interference in peaceful and profitable colonies. After 1722,

New York and other royal colonies encountered administrative indifference and were governed by a series of inept officeholders. Placemen were given New York posts not on the basis of their merit but rather as rewards for their political support of the Walpole ministry. This change in imperial philosophy was immediately noticeable in New York's internal politics and adversly affected Hunter's successor, William Burnet.

3

To Prepare The Way and Alarm the People, 1720–1735: The Administrations of William Burnet (1720–1728), John Montgomery (1728–1731), and William Cosby (1731–1736)

"Satyr was of great service to the patriot Whiggs in the reign of King Charles and King James the second, as well as in that of Queen Anne. They asserted the Freedom of Writing against wicked Ministers . . . they made use of Satyr to prepare the Way and alarm the People against their Designs."[1]

The political and philosophical platform that would carry New York to independence was formed during the administrations of William Burnet, John Montgomery, and William Cosby, all appointed to the joint governorships of New York and New Jersey. This ideological platform was apparent during the landmark 1735 trial of John Peter Zenger for seditious libel; the platform changed little by 1776. New York opposition leaders challenged imperial government when they believed it threatened their traditional liberties, the safety of their property, or their own security in public office. They protested the establishment of prerogative courts and the presumed threat such courts presented to trial by jury. They rejected executive interference with the legislature, believed the exercise of imperial authority was designed to reduce them to slavery, and were determined to protect life, liberty, and property. The primary vehicle used by the elite to carry their message to the people was the press.[2]

The controversy that led to and followed the Zenger trial increased the deep divisions that already existed in the province. Whether members of the court or country factions, the elite needed the support of the bulk of the voting population. This meant the middling and lower sort had to be kept informed of political developments. They also had to be instructed in constitutional principles and their basic rights as English subjects. The efforts of the elite to involve the lower class in political issues so they could lend support to elite programs had the effect of politicizing the masses.

Politicization of the lower and middling sort was well underway when William Burnet arrived in New York. Burnet formed strong alliances with the court party of his predecessor, Robert Hunter. On the advice of such court politicians as Lewis Morris, James Alexander, Robert Livingston, and Cadwallader Colden, Burnet did not call for assembly elections but kept in existence the proadministration, largely landowner body elected in 1716. Burnet's decision caused dissent among country opponents in the council who wanted the governor to call assembly elections so that their side would have a chance to achieve an assembly majority. Merchant councillors Adolph Philipse and Peter Schuyler questioned "whether the Assembly could be continued legally. . . . The argument which prevailed with Mr. Burnet to continue the same Assembly was this. He was assured that the members of that Assembly would readily grant the support of government for five years," which they promptly did.[3]

Burnet's refusal to call new assembly elections mobilized the predominantly merchant country opposition party. The country party's ire was further raised by an act, passed by the landowner-dominated assembly in 1720, that banned the highly lucrative Albany-Montreal fur trade with the French enemy. The act was strenuously opposed by Stephen DeLancey and other New York merchants, who had profitably engaged in the French trade for decades, whether or not England and France were actively at war. Their complaints met a sympathetic audience in England where mercantile imperialism prevailed.[4]

Although the DeLanceys adhered to a Tory philosophy in government, their attitude toward commerce was decidedly Whiggish. The theory of commercial imperialism to which the DeLanceys and other New York merchants were committed was that of the Whig first lord of the treasury, Robert Walpole. In 1721, Walpole had succeeded the earl of Sunderland as head of the treasury. Although Walpole was named treasurer, Sunderland retained his influence on the king until his unexpected death on 19 April 1722. Walpole seized full power after the June death of the duke of Marlborough. Walpole's view of commercial empire replaced Marlborough's commitment to expanding the empire through military might. Under Walpole, foreign and domestic trade were the ministry's most important considerations. A tranquil, peaceful international environment had to be maintained so that trade could flourish. Walpole believed that if trade prospered, so would the nation.[5]

In 1724, Walpole moved to tighten his control over the ministry by easing southern secretary Lord Carteret out of office. Carteret was replaced by Thomas Pelham-Holles, duke of Newcastle, who now controlled colonial patronage. Newcastle, much criticized as being overly cautious and incompetent, was nevertheless a painstaking and long-lasting administrator. Typical of the opinion many contemporaries had of the duke was a comment by Lord Hervey. Hervey noted that his conversation with another person was interrupted by the "Duke of Newcastle, who made his entry with as much alacrity and noise as usual, mightily out of breath though mightily in words, and in his hand a bundle of papers as big as his head and with little more in them."[6]

The duke may have lacked intelligence, but he proved a political survivor. He served as southern secretary, with responsibility for the colonies, from 1724 to 1748, then northern secretary from 1748 to 1754, then as first lord of the treasury or prime minister from 1754 to 1756, and finally shared power with William Pitt from 1757 to 1762.[7]

As his career began, Newcastle, ever the political opportunitist, supported Walpole's commitment to promoting trade. The new emphasis on trade reflected changing economic conditions in England. The rise of capitalism disturbed the traditional order of society since it brought to prominence a new social class. Despite rapid economic change, the belief persisted in England that wealth acquired through trade was less acceptable than wealth acquired through land. Hence the nouveau-riche commercial class bought land to acquire respectability. Land was available for purchase because rising prices were devastating to small landowners on static incomes. Many of these landowners were unable to pay the high taxes necessitated by a large public debt, which reached £54 million in 1720. When owners were forced to put their land on the market, it was bought by a relatively small number of wealthy entrepreneurs. The loss of property by small landowners was thus seen by country politicians as limiting liberty and freedom, secured only by the ownership of land, to an increasingly smaller segment of the population. In the words of Harrington, "the inexorable law of politics is that all who have a share of property have a share of power, because dominion follows property." Colonists in New York and other colonies shared this view of the sacredness of property.[8]

In 1723, the Whig ministry sought to tighten the English elite's control of property, and hence their own liberties and freedoms, by the passage of the Black Act. Aimed primarily at poachers, the act also addressed those who were "maliciously killing or maiming cattle; cutting down trees . . . ; setting fire to any house, barn, haystack, etc.; maliciously shooting at any person; sending anonymous letters demanding 'money, venison, or other valuable things'; and forcibly rescuing anyone from custody, who was accused of any of these offences." A broad interpretation of the act shows that there were between 200 and 250 offences for which the death penalty could be applied. The property of the elite in England was thus secured by their manipulation of the law.[9]

Taking their cue from the English upper class, New York's elite, both landowners and merchants, also tried to manipulate the law to their own social and economic advantage. Manor lords, for instance, attempted to control their tenants as tightly as did their counterparts in England. The landowners remained influential because Burnet, like Hunter, allied with them.[10]

To strengthen landowner control and reduce merchant opposition even further, Burnet, against the advice of former Governor Hunter, in 1721 dismissed merchants Adolph Philipse and Peter Schuyler from their council seats where they were relatively harmless. He appointed in their place Cadwallader Colden and James Alexander, both Scots-born and both former political allies of Robert Hunter. Alexander, a supporter of the Old Pretender when he invaded Scotland in 1715, was exiled for his role in that rebellion. He was sent to New Jersey by his patron, the duke of Argyll. In New Jersey, he was befriended by Robert Hunter, who named him receiver general of that province, recorder of Perth Amboy, and deputy secretary of New York. Cadwallader Colden, son of a Scots Presbyterian minister, was educated at the University of Edinburgh and trained as a physician. He emigrated to Philadelphia in 1710 where he worked as a physician and as a merchant. He returned to Scotland in 1715, leading his future political enemies to charge he had supported the Old Pretender. Colden consistently denied these charges, and he returned to Philadelphia in 1716. Colden visited New York in 1718 and met Hunter, who urged him to move to New York permanently. Colden agreed, and Hunter, in 1720, had him named to the profitable post of surveyor general, a post Colden kept in the family even after his retirement.[11]

With the support of Alexander, Colden, and other court party members, Burnet continued to pack the council with his allies. On the 1722 death of councilor Caleb Heathcote, Burnet named Lewis Morris's son, Lewis, Jr., in his place, and in 1724, Burnet nominated Robert Livingston's son, Philip, to the Council. Thus, Burnet had a solid court majority in that body and in the assembly, where Robert Livingston continued as speaker of the house.[12]

Burnet had overplayed his hand. Much to his surprise, the tide turned against him in 1725 because of events he had set in motion with the dismissal of Philipse from the council. On losing his post, Philipse ran for the assembly in the special election called after the 1722 death of Westchester representative Joseph Budd. Three more special elections were held in 1725 following the deaths of three other members. Elected in their stead were three Philipse allies, Richard Merrill, Benjamin Hicks, and Stephen DeLancey. With their support, Philipse was voted the speakership of the house in place of Robert Livingston, who was forced to resign that year because of illness.[13]

Burnet, disgusted with the turn of events, refused to administer the oath of office to representative Stephen DeLancey on the grounds that DeLancey was an alien. The French-born DeLancey fled his native land after the 1685 revocation of the Edict of Nantes. He had resided in New York since 1686 and was naturalized by a 1715 act. Whigs in both England and New York favored naturalization as a way of building voter support. Tories, on the other hand, deplored naturalization, wanting to keep England for the English. Part of the Tory attitude was prompted by the often unscrupulous use made by Whigs of immigrants in Great Britain. During the Walpole ministry, for instance, a Scottish politician reported of "a forreigner unnaturalized—good Voter, if for us; no Voter if against us."[14]

The Whig Burnet might also favor naturalization in England or Scotland, but not in New York where votes of aliens could be used against him in assembly elections. He turned the DeLancey matter over to Chief Justice Morris for a decision. The assembly was furious that the chief justice should presume to judge the qualifications of its members. Morris's favorable decision, made under pressure, did little to ease their collective anger. The assembly in September 1725 ignored Morris and unanimously voted that DeLancey should take his seat. DeLancey's bitterness at the chief justice and other members of the court party remained for the rest of his life. More seriously for Burnet, his actions, and those of Morris, caused formerly neutral representatives to swing to the Philipse-DeLancey side. The royal prerogative suffered as local privilege reasserted itself with an overt attempt by the assembly in 1725 to weaken the power of the governor by voting only a two-year revenue instead of five-year support as they had in the past.[15]

With an active and angry country majority in the assembly, Burnet's administration was no longer troublefree, as the assembly opposed such imperial measures as the establishment of a chancery court. The Philipse-DeLancey assembly based its legal opposition to this court on the fact that the governor had established it without the authority of the assembly, as called for in New York's 1691 Judiciary Act. This was an about-face for Philipse who, as a member of the council during Robert Hunter's administration, had supported the establishment of the chancery to collect delinquent quit rents. The chancery was also a prerogative court that sat without a jury and with the governor as the sole judge. The combination of constitutional principles with an unwanted tax made the chancery one of the most hated courts in the province.[16]

Philipse's opposition to the chancery led Burnet's court party to attack Philipse anonymously in print, mercilessly ridiculing him and calling him "Ape," from his name, A[dolph] P[hilips]e. The widely circulated pamphlets were so virulent that James Alexander, after asking Cadwallader Colden to write "a 3d & 4th Letter to Ape," advised Colden that "there should be rather more reservedness of Epithets, no passion but clear truth & reason well painted" in future essays.[17]

The use of the press in New York to discredit and humiliate opponents paralleled practices in England where voters were inundated with both pro- and antiadministration political pamphlets and newspapers. The country party took the offensive, with its targets Walpole and his regime. Whig and Tory country opposition members saw Walpole as corrupt and unprincipled. They detested him and the new economic order he represented, with its emphasis on trade and profit. Old values seemed forgotten in England during the Walpole era.[18]

The leading spokesmen for the Tories was Lord Bolingbroke, who published anti-Walpole essays in *The Craftsman*. The leading radical Whig writers were John Trenchard and Thomas Gordon who wrote "Cato's Letters" and the "Independent Whig." The philosophy of both country Tories and country Whigs was quite similar in that both defended traditional English freedoms while attacking patronage, the new economic order, standing armies, and unlimited power. In numerous essays, Walpole and the ministry were viciously satirized by the country opposition who believed that the press, using "the lash of satire," was a check on despotic rulers. Attacks in print might "awaken his [the ruler's] conscience, and if he has no conscience, rouse his fear by showing him his deserts, sting him with the dread of punishment, cover him with shame, and render his actions odious to all honest minds."[19]

The opposition authors argued that a necessary function of the press was to expose "the exorbitant crimes of wicked ministers." Trenchard and Gordon in their essay on freedom of the press pointed out that

"Satyr was of great service to the patriot Whiggs in the reign of King *Charles* and King *James* the second, as well as in that of Queen *Anne*. They asserted the Freedom of Writing against wicked Ministers . . . they made use of Satyr to prepare the Way and alarm the People against their Designs." The authors said that "if Men in Power were always Men of Integrity, we might venture to trust them with the Direction of the Press, and there would be no Occasion to plead against the Restraint of it." Since this was not the case and since those in power "have Vices like their Fellows, so it very often happens that the best intended and the most valuable Writings are the Objects of their Resentment, because opposite to their own Tempers or Designs."[20]

Walpole countered opposition attacks by publishing prominristry propaganda in his own paper, *The London Journal*. The seriousness of the threat presented to the ministry by the opposition press is evident from the amount of money Walpole paid to writers and printers over a ten-year period, with some £50,000 expended from the public treasury.[21]

Walpole also countered propaganda by bringing charges of seditious libel against opposition printers. A particular target was Bolingbroke's newspaper, *The Craftsman*. The paper, edited by Nicholas Amherst and printed and published by Richard Franklin, was started by viscount Bolingbroke in 1716. Bolingbroke provided financial support and submitted anonymous articles. Other anonymous contributors, who acted from principle or spite because they had not received suitable rewards from the Whig ministry, were Jonathan Swift, Alexander Pope, and John Gay. Walpole was annoyed by the newspaper's attacks, but the various suits he brought against Franklin usually failed. When the printer was arrested, Bolingbroke simply put up bail, and the paper quickly resumed publication.[22]

In New York, Burnet's old court party found ample opportunity to criticize government following Burnet's 1728 transfer to the governorship of Massachusetts. Burnet's successor in New York was John Montgomery, appointed at the order of George II whom he had served as groom of the bedchamber. Montgomery allied with the country mercantile opposition who were pleased when, in 1729, the sympathetic Walpole ministry overturned the 1720 New York act barring the fur trade between Albany and Montreal. Montgomery further sought to placate local interests by refusing to take the oath as chancellor or to erect a chancery court, thus further weakening the royal prerogative.[23]

Unlike Hunter and Burnet, Montgomery allied with the Philipse-DeLancey mercantile faction, who now formed the court party. This alliance justifiably alarmed Morris, Alexander, Colden, and their allies, who now constituted the country opposition party. In the assembly election, the popular appeal of the merchant faction was again evident. Landowners lost seats, perhaps the most unsettling loss being that of Lewis Morris, who ran from Westchester County. Morris, however, retained his position as chief justice.[24] Their fears of being excluded from the source of power increased as the new country party lost their former monopoly on offices when the governor extended favors to the Philipse-DeLancey faction. An early sign of this favor was Montgomery's appointment of Stephen DeLancey's son James to the council and as puisne judge on the supreme court.[25]

James DeLancey was admirably suited by birth and training to take a leading role in the colony's fortunes. Born in New York in 1702, James was sent to England to be educated at Corpus Christi College in Cambridge. His tutor there was Dr. Thomas Herring, later archbishop of York and, in 1747, archbishop of Canterbury. DeLancey, throughout his life, maintained close ties with Herring, who proved to be a very effective patron in England.[26]

DeLancey returned to New York in 1725, after studying law at Lincoln's Inn and was admitted to the New York bar. Despite DeLancey's highly respectable legal education, William Livingston, a perennial political enemy, consistently and inaccurately charged in print throughout DeLancey's life that DeLancey was not trained as an attorney. DeLancey, born to one of the most powerful, prestigious, and wealthy families in New York, further secured his financial and social position through his marriage to Anne Heathcote. This marriage allied him with one of the richest and most influential families in England and America. The first sign of the favors that would accrue to DeLancey, because of these connections and because of his innate ability, were his appointments by Montgomery to the council and the supreme court.[27]

While the governor was willing to favor DeLancey, he did nothing to defer the assembly's continued anger at Lewis Morris. With Montgomery's approval, the assembly reduced Morris's salary as chief justice from £300 to £250 per year. Lewis Morris, Jr., in the council objected to the decrease of his father's salary. The younger Morris's written protest to the governor "concluded with these words, Arbitrary illegall & unwarrantable. . . . Upon reading them, his Exy Coloured as well he Might. . . . His Excellency Expressed himself in a great deal of passion, that Never man in his place had been so . . . used, to be charged with the breach of his Commn Instructions, his oath with acting illegally unwarrantably & arbitraryly." Morris, Jr., apologized for his insults, but the governor suspended him from his council post.[28]

William Cosby, appointed after the 1 July 1731 death of John Montgomery, quickly allied with Montgomery's court party. Cosby was

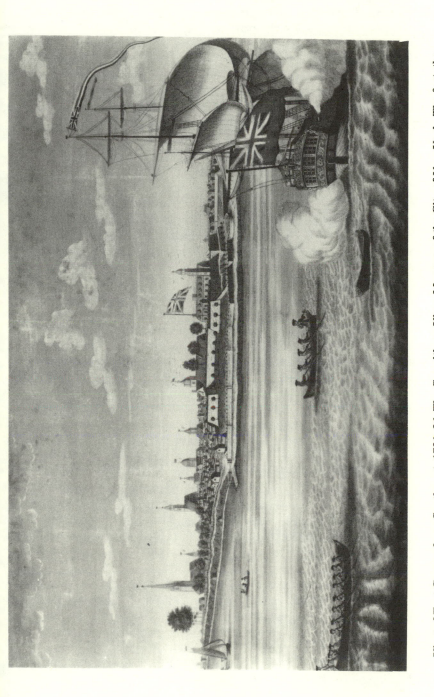

View of Fort George from Southwest, 1731–36, The Carwitham View, Museum of the City of New York. The fort, the official residence of William Cosby and other New York governors early in the eighteenth century, housed regular British troops. It was partially destroyed by fire in 1741.

named to the New York-New Jersey governorship because of his influential connections within the ministry. Related to southern secretary Thomas Pelham-Holles, duke of Newcastle, Cosby had already accepted the governorship of the Leeward Islands and was actually "fallen down the River to go to his Government, but on the News of Mr. Montgomeries death, he returned to London and chose this [New York] government." He chose the New York–New Jersey governorship because he knew it to be more profitable than the Leeward Islands, and Cosby needed the money. As governor of Minorca, Cosby had illegally appropriated a shipment of snuff from a Portuguese merchant. Tried in London on the complaint of the merchant, Cosby was ordered to pay £10,000 in damages.[29]

That Cosby and all other governors came to New York to make money was obvious to provincials as was the fact that he had gotten the appointment to New York, not on the basis of merit, but rather because of his connections with Newcastle. Cosby was looked on by provincials with particular suspicion because word preceded him of his greed in Minorca.[30]

The suspicions of New York oligarchs about Cosby's excessive greed were confirmed shortly after the governor landed. Cosby, like Burnet, kept in office the agreeable merchant assembly elected in 1728 during Montgomery's administration. He also allied with the merchant faction, as had his predecessor. The assembly proved willing to accept royal authority and voted five-year support, but some members balked at giving Cosby a present of £1000. Instead they voted the governor only £750. Cosby invited those assemblymen who opposed the £1000 gift to dinner. "After Dinner he Damn'd them & askt them why they did not make their Present in pounds shillings & Pennies." The assemblymen got the message; the next day representatives voted to increase Cosby's present to £1000.[31]

Cosby, with the support of his court party, also tried to collect money from Rip Van Dam, who, as senior councilor, had been head of government from Montgomery's death on 30 June 1731 until Cosby's landing on 1 August 1732. Cosby's instructions authorized him to take half the salary and half the money from perquisites and fees that Van Dam had received during that period. Van Dam, with the backing of the country faction, refused to pay.[32]

Cosby sued Van Dam for the money, but he realized he had little hope of obtaining a favorable verdict from a New York jury in a common law court. Nor could Cosby bring a case concerning himself before the chancery where he presided as chancellor. Cosby passed an ordinance giving the superior court judges the power to judge the case "in Equity as in the Exchequer in England." The case was brought before the court on 9 April 1733 with James Alexander and William Smith representing Van Dam. Chief Justice Morris "pulled out of his pocket and read a long argument against the Jurisdiction of the [Supreme] Court to try Causes in Equity and against the Kings Authority to erect Courts of Equity." The other two judges, James DeLancey, son of Stephen DeLancey, and Frederick Philipse, son of Adolph Philipse, understandably disagreed with Morris's position.[33]

Cosby was angered by Morris's decision that the Supreme Court did not have jurisdiction over equity causes, particularly because he realized that Morris had not acted solely out of consideration for legal niceties, but rather to frustrate Cosby and to serve Morris's own interests. Morris, as senior councillor in New Jersey, acted as governor of the province after Montgomery's death. If Cosby won his case against Van Dam, the governor would file a similar request with Morris for half of the salary he received in New Jersey. Morris won a victory for Van Dam (and himself), but paid a price. In August of 1733, Cosby dismissed Morris as chief justice of New York and appointed James DeLancey in his place. This action split the colony into those who supported the governor's action and those who did not, with Morris becoming the focal point of the opposition.[34]

The country party's ire was further raised by Cosby's determination to establish a chancery court. Just as Philipse and DeLancey, now members of the court party, supported policies they had previously condemned, so the country oligarchs now opposed practices they had previously supported. As court politicians, Alexander, Morris, Sr., and Jr., Colden, and Robert and Philip Livingston supported Hunter and Burnet when those governors used the chancery court to collect quit rents, dismissed dissenting officeholders, used the court system to punish their opponents, and awarded land grants to favorites. Colden in particular had strongly supported the establishment of a chancery court in New York in 1727 during Burnet's administration. Doing an about-face during Cosby's administration, Colden even more strenuously objected to the governor's attempts to establish a chancery court without the approval of the Assembly. He stated that "Erecting or exercising in this Colony a Court of Equity or Chancery . . . without consent in the General Assembly is unwarrantable & contrary to the Laws of England & a manifest Oppression & Grievance to the Subjects & of perniceous consequence to their Liberty & Properties." His inconsistency was brought to Colden's attention by Board of Trade secretary Alured Popple, who noted that he "cannot help being Surprize'd that you who was so strenuous for it as appears by the Minutes of Council of the 5th of Decemr 1727, should now oppose the holding of that [Chancery] Court." Popple believed Colden's vocal and persistent opposition to the Court was the main stumbling block to his reestablishing good relations with the governor.[35]

Cosby's campaign against the opposition extended to challenging land investments. Throughout New York's provincial history, no other single issue, not even taxation or the collection of quit rents, alarmed New York oligarchs as much as did any threat to landholdings. Discontent was stirred among the country party when Cosby permitted the Mohawks to burn a deed that gave Albany one thousand acres of the tribe's lands. Cosby, acting from imperial motives, argued that the Indians were led to believe that deeding the land to Albany would ensure that it would be saved for them. Since this was not the case, Cosby feared the deception would drive the Mohawks to ally with the French in Canada.[36]

Another area in dispute was a tract of land called The Oblong, recently ceded by Connecticut to New York. Colden, Alexander, Morris, William Smith, and Philip Livingston, along with councillor and city recorder Francis Harrison, formed a company to secure title to the land, which was granted by Montgomery in May 1731. Prior to that date, Harrison despaired of getting a legal title to the tract through the governor and applied for a royal patent. The royal patent was granted, and the result was that two rival companies claimed ownership of the same tract of land. After Cosby arrived in New York, Harrison persuaded the governor to join the company holding the English title. With the governor's backing, Harrison in 1735 brought a suit before the governor in chancery to vacate Montgomery's grant. The opposition was further alienated by Cosby's decision to take a one-third share of all land grants, because, as he complained, "the profitts of his Governmt were so inconsiderable that he was Obliged to make the most of everything." [37]

The ministry was informed of the turmoil in New York by numerous opposition petitions and letters, which charged, among other things, that Cosby had altered land titles, dismissed judges, and erected courts without the approval of the legislature, thereby threatening trial by jury. In reality, Cosby had dismissed only one judge—Morris—and erected only one prerogative court—the chancery—and altered only one land title—the Albany Deed. By deliberately exaggerating Cosby's presumed misdeeds, the country party hoped to secure the recall of the governor. The country party also proved they were effective propagandists, but not effective enough because the ministry did not respond, perhaps because it was distracted by problems of its own.[38]

The ministry's distraction was partially caused by the fact that Walpole, in 1733, made one of the few political blunders of his career in trying to extend the excise tax to salt, tobacco, and wine. His intent was that the burden of taxation would fall equally on the poor as well as the rich by reducing taxes on landowners. Walpole was surprised by the negative public reaction to the tax. Country Tories and country Whigs quickly mobilized against the excise. Walpolean placemen reported that signs were displayed at race tracks, "lest the people shou'd forget what they were to cry out against, the Faction had taken care to stick up, No Excise, in great capital letters upon the race post. A very low, mean Artifice." Country politicians traveled to "several parts of the Country in a Body, inflaming the people with the Cry of the Excise, Standing Armys, and every thing that they think will serve their Turn."[39]

What surprised Walpole and other Whigs was that opposition to the excise was not confined to the lower classes, who predictably took to the streets in protest. Most vociferous in their objections were the very upper class landowners the act was designed to help. The rationale of landowners was that because the excise would reduce their obligations, it might also prove a threat to their oligarchic privileges. Walpole capitulated and withdrew the bill from Parliament.[40]

Neither was opposition to the ministry's governor in New York confined to one class, as Cosby was to discover. New Yorkers of all ranks objected to Cosby's high-handed methods and autocratic mannerisms. The governor's attitude was particularly offensive in a relatively egalitarian society such as New York where even the wealthiest resident had started life with very modest means. Word quickly spread that, soon after his arrival, Cosby ordered the whipping of a yeoman farmer whose wagon had failed to promptly yield the right of way to the governor's carriage. News of this incident and similar actions by the governor were quickly spread by the country faction. As a result, by November 1733 James Alexander reported that Cosby had "given more Distaste to the people here than I believe any Governour that ever this province had during his whole Government. . . . He has raised such a Spirit in the people of this province . . . they will give the world reason to believe, that they are not easily to be made Slaves of nor to be governed by Arbitrary power."[41]

As in England, the general population's dislike of the governor and government was spurred by economic as well as ideological factors. New Yorkers resisted the establishment of chancery courts, for instance, not only from principle but also because they could not easily pay the quit rents the court was designed to collect. The province suffered from an economic depression. As Cosby pointed out, most of the province's economic problems resulted from Bahamanian shippers taking away New York's carrying trade. Not only did New York shipowners suffer, so also did merchants, farmers, seamen, and shipbuilders. New York's export trade of wheat also declined. The fault lay chiefly with farmers themselves who did little to ensure the consistent quality of their grain. While virtually none of the economic distress was Cosby's fault, he nevertheless was held responsible as governor.[42]

Economic hardship helped the opposition to raise "a spirit" of discontent in the colony. Petitions could be ignored by the home government, but an angry and volatile populace signaled that the executive was weak and inept. Such discord might well prompt the ministry to recall the governor. To keep the public aware of the governor's misdeeds, the country party stepped up its use of the press. Through this medium, the opposition could inform New York's public of political issues. Their purpose was to ensure voter support for their candidates in the event Cosby should call an assembly election. Cosby also took pains to get public sympathy since he too needed voter support in the event of an election. The governor's side of the issues was brought to public attention through the pages of the official government newspaper, *The New York Gazette*, published by William Bradford.[43]

Since Cosby monopolized the colony's only newspaper, the opposition established *The New York Weekly Journal* printed by John Peter Zenger, to carry their side of the issues to the public. The German-born Zenger had arrived in New York with his widowed mother in 1710, travelling on the same fleet that brought Robert Hunter to the province. The Zengers were part of more than 2,000 displaced Palatines sent to New York by the English ministry to start a naval stores project. Zenger was one of about seventy-three destitute children who were apprenticed soon after arrival. Zenger, on 16 October 1710, was indentured to the printer William Bradford.[44]

Zenger was an experienced printer when New York's country opposition decided it needed a vehicle for its propaganda. Although *The New York Weekly Journal* was printed by Zenger, most articles and essays were either written by the opposition and were published anonymously, or were reprinted from the opposition press in England. Particularly popular were selections from Trenchard's and Gordon's "Cato's Letters," including their essay on freedom of the press, which appeared in two installments on 12 and 19 November 1733. New Yorkers knew that "the loss of liberty in general would soon follow the suppression of the liberty of the press; for as it is an essential branch of liberty, so perhaps it is the best preservation of the whole." Indeed, they were warned against any attempt to restrain the press, since even mild censorship would mean the end of liberty and the beginning of slavery. Later issues expressed concern "for the security of our lives, liberty, and property," all threatened by the governor, and again voiced the fear that "SLAVERY is like to be entailed on them and their posterity."[45]

Prerogative courts, like the exchequer, were also attacked in the *Weekly Journal*, where they were "condemned by every man/that's fond of liberty." The chancery also came in for criticism when the assembly, at the urging of the Morris faction, passed a resolution in October 1735 that such a court "under the Exercise of a Governor, without Consent in General Assembly, is contrary to Law, unwarrantable, and of dangerous Consequence to the Liberties and Properties of the People."[46]

The *Journal* also carried current news. Its first issue reported the October 1733 election to the assembly of the displaced chief justice, Lewis Morris, Sr. Morris ran for the assembly from Westchester County in a special election called after the death of William Willet. The governor's candidate, backed by Philipse and the merchant faction, was William Forster. At the election, where votes were cast orally, James DeLancey appeared personally to lend the prestige of his office to Forster; it was in vain.[47] Morris had campaigned on a platform of "No Excise," while Morris's supporters carried banners bearing the English opposition motto of "King George, Liberty and Law." By the use of such slogans, Morris directly linked his cause with that of opposition country Whigs and country Tories in England and, by implication, linked Cosby with the corrupt Walpole. Victorious, Morris arrived by boat in New York City from Westchester and was saluted by the firing of guns from merchant ships anchored in New York Harbor. An enthusiastic crowd greeted Morris on landing and escorted him to a local tavern for a victory celebration.[48]

A year later, Morris put up a slate of candidates for the New York City Common Council and was gratified when all but one were elected. This led to the publication of poems in the *Weekly Journal*, praising lower and middling class voters, or the "good lads that dare oppose/all lawless power and might...." The poet continued that

> Your votes you gave for those brave men
> who feasting did despise;
> And never prostituted pen
> to certify the lies
> That were drawn up to put in chains,
> As well our nymphs as happy swains;
> with a fa la la.[49]

Morris's victories were an indication of the popularity achieved by the opposition through their propaganda campaign against Cosby. After the election, Morris initiated a two-pronged attack on the governor. In the assembly, Morris harrassed the governor by making "bold and presumptious attempts . . . against his Mayty's authority to establish Courts," tried to pass a bill to permit the assembly to hire a London agent over whom the governor would have no control, and in other ways sought assiduously to increase local privilege while reducing the imperial authority Cosby represented in New York. On the other hand Morris published in the *Journal* "false and scandalous libels" against Cosby. Morris, along with other opposition leaders, legitimized his harsh criticisms of Cosby by placing himself in the role of defender of liberty. Week after week, the *Journal* criticized the governor's tyrannical administration, emphasizing the same complaints the opposition previously voiced to the ministry. Under Cosby, opposition leaders wrote, New Yorkers saw "men's deeds destroyed, judges arbitrarily displaced, new courts erected without consent of the legislature, by which it seems to me trials by juries are taken away when a governor pleases." Cosby was well aware that Morris and other country party members were engaging in a "paper war" to expose him "to the censure of a mob."[50]

Opposition oligarchs gave Cosby a troubled regime, but Cosby remained in control of the colony, so opposition efforts were largely in vain in spite of the fact that Lewis Morris, Sr., went to London in November 1734 to secure Cosby's recall. Morris's intent was to regain his office of chief justice, and defend himself and other opposition leaders against Cosby's countercharges. Morris claimed that any "honest and bold man who Strickly adheres to his duty [was] Obnoxious to the Governour who would be free from all restraints in the pursuits of Wealth."[51]

Morris's mission was ineffective. He was ignored by the ministry and led on by Walpole's opposition to whom he next appealed. He not only failed to secure Cosby's recall, his fortune was depleted by London's high cost of living. The Privy Council saw no reason to restore Morris to his post as chief justice, much less to remove Cosby as governor. Morris left London in July 1736, poorer but wiser, disillusioned with imperial government, and disgusted with the venality of English politicians. Corrupt or not, the ministry had simply shown it would support its appointed governor.[52]

The Board of Trade, if not the ministry, supported the governor when he asked permission to eject opposition leaders James Alexander and Rip Van Dam from the council in June 1734. Van Dam was particularly odious to the governor. Not only did he challenge the governor's right to fees, he was also a leading polemicist for the country faction. Cosby was well aware of Van Dam's literary activities. As he noted to the Board of Trade, several court councillors objected to Van Dam's presence because of "the open and scandalous aspersions he had thrown upon them in printed libels and papers industriously dispersed in the Province."[53]

Despite such support from the home government and its failure to act on Morris's charges, Cosby's popularity in New York continued to decline among the general population, largely due to the efforts of the opposition, whose appeal was made directly to the masses. In their *Weekly Journal* propaganda, the elite noted that it was "the industrious poor" who were "the support of any country." As for the pretensions of the governor and his cronies, or "people in Exalted Stations," who looked down on "the Vulgar, the Mob, the herd of Mechanicks," the writer pointed out that "there are many among them [the poor] of equal if not superior knowledge." No one, including the king or his appointed governor, was above the law. As the opposition noted, no person *"can commit a crime with impunity."* The lower and middling sort had a voice in government, just as did the elite, because the Assembly was elected to "represent the whole province." Such rhetoric, which stressed natural worth and claimed that it was more important than inherited wealth or privilege and emphasized an equality under law, was read and understood by voters of all classes.[54]

Although the opposition was successful in its efforts to rouse the masses, they were not able to secure the governor's recall. They did, however, prevent him from stifling the opposition press. The opposition attacks on Cosby grew so vicious that the governor responded through the press and the courts, much as did Walpole to similar attacks in England. Cosby used the pages of the *Gazette* to bring his side of the dispute to the public. When the opposition continued its attacks, Cosby brought charges of seditious libel against the printer Zenger, the only person he could directly identify as being connected with the *Journal.* Cosby had Zenger charged, but, like Hunter with Mulford, he could not secure his conviction for seditious libel because local sympathy lay with Zenger as it had earlier lain with Mulford.[55]

Zenger, arrested in November 1734, was by his own admission "not worth forty pounds (the tools of my trade and wearing apparel excepted)," but despite this, Chief Justice DeLancey set bail at £400. Zenger could not raise the money, and his patrons in the country party did not choose to do so. Zenger remained in prison for eight months and became a symbol of the governor's tyranny. He was tried for seditious libel in August 1735.[56]

In England and New York, once a writer or printer was accused of seditious libel, he faced a stacked deck. It was not necessary to call a grand jury to indict: the attorney general presented the facts to the court, and the court decided the guilt. A warrant was then issued, and the person was arrested and tried. The jury was not asked to determine guilt; that had already been predetermined. They were only asked to judge whether the material had actually been published and whether it did in fact refer to the people or institutions said to be libeled. Defendants could not escape conviction by proving the truth of their published statements. In fact, truth rendered the offense more serious. Feelings about truth as a defense began to change in the English speaking world at midcentury partially as a result of the Zenger trial.[57]

The jury at Zenger's trial was composed of his peers, all of whom had been sensitized against Cosby by opposition propaganda. Attorney General Richard Bradley instructed the jury not to decide whether the material in question was seditious or not, only judge whether or not it had actually been published. Bradley further argued that, as in English practice, truth was no defense against libel.[58]

Defense attorney Andrew Hamilton, who took over Zenger's defense when country leaders James Alexander and William Smith, Sr., were disbarred by Chief Justice DeLancey, argued that truth was an adequate defense against libel. *"Truth,"* said Hamilton, "ought to govern the whole Affair of Libels." This idea did not originate with Hamilton, but had been forwarded in England as early as 1712 by Whig writer Joseph Addison. In the 1720s, Trenchard and Gordon, writing under the pseudonym "Cato," had further popularized the concept of truth as being an adequate defense. The Cato essays had been reprinted in Zenger's paper and were widely read in New York, probably by the men who comprised the jury. The jurors hated the governor. Hence, as James Alexander reported, they took only "a small time" to reach their verdict. Contrary to English custom regarding seditious libel, they rejected the concept of preassumed guilt and found Zenger not guilty because the statements published about Governor Cosby were true. On hearing the verdict, "there were three huzzas in the hall which was crowded with people."[59]

The most immediate impact of the Zenger case was that it discouraged royal governors from charging printers or authors with seditious libel because of the obvious difficulty in securing a verdict of guilty "contrary to the general bent of the People." As Attorney General Bradley observed following the Zenger verdict, "it is but too manifest that juries here very rarely find for the King tho' the charge be never so well supported by evidence." Printers and authors were prosecuted for seditious libel after 1735, but most of those prosecutions were initiated by provincial assemblies, not by governors.[60]

The long-range impact of the Zenger case was eventually a reinterpretation of freedom of the press in England and America, primarily due to the efforts of James Alexander, who published in 1738 a widely read account of the trial. The law that governed seditious libel and official attitudes toward the press remained essentially unchanged during most of the eighteenth century. Libertarians continued to believe that it was necessary to criticize a bad government but treasonous to criticize a good one. The Zenger verdict by itself did not immediately establish a precedent, but, because of James Alexander's efforts, juries increasingly began to insist that they be permitted to judge the facts of the case, and truth was eventually accepted as a defense against libel.[61]

The Zenger trial involved the lower and middling sort in the political process because of direct appeals by the elite who needed their support whether at the polls or in the courtrooms or in the streets. The elite, through these appeals, instructed the middling and lower sort in constitutional principles and their basic rights as English subjects. The result was that the lower classes became actively involved in the political process. Their support was acknowledged by the elite, occasionally in bad poetry:

> Our country's rights we will defend,
> like brave and honest men;
> We voted right and there's an end,
> and so we'll do again. . . .
>
> Though pettifogging knaves deny
> us rights of Englishmen;
> We'll make the scoundrel rascals fly,
> and ne'er return again.[62]

The constitutional principles that would eventually be used to justify revolution were laid out and defined by New York's elite in the 1730s. Modeling their rhetoric on British opposition writers, New York's elite verbalized their opposition to arbitrary rule and defended such basic rights as that to trial by jury and freedom of speech and the press. Constant appeals by the elite to the lower and middling sort led to the politicization of those groups. Also initiated was the process of democratization, an effect unlooked for and unwelcomed by the elite. Once begun, these processes did not—perhaps could not—stop. In time, the program of the elite to heighten public awareness primarily through the use of the press, raised a confident, articulate, and popular force that would be increasingly difficult to control.

The press represented the weapon of choice for local oligarchs in their ongoing struggle against the crown's prerogative power. Through its use, the country party advanced local privilege with Van Dam's defiance of Cosby, the Zenger acquittal, Morris's election victory, by winning control of the New York City common council, and by the assembly resolution against chancery courts. The prerogative held its own as far as tangible achievements, with Cosby obtaining long-term support from the assembly, over which he retained control as he did the council. Prerogative power was also upheld when the Walpole ministry refused to be swayed by provincial complaints and continued to support Cosby. Intangibly, the appointment of a corrupt, overly greedy governor, with neither the personality nor the ability to govern wisely, increased provincial disrespect for British authority. William Cosby, only one in a series of inept governors, damaged imperial relations and, in the long run, weakened the royal prorogative.

4

Obstruct All Parts of Government, 1735–1753: The Administrations of George Clarke (1736–1743), George Clinton (1743–1753), Sir Danvers Osborn (1753)

No Govr ever departed from the prerogative in one instance, but he raised in the Assembly a confidence to attack it in another, which as constantly brings on contests, which again create animosities, which in the end obstruct all Parts of Governt.[1]

By the late 1740s, James DeLancey emerged as an outstanding country opposition leader in New York. Most politicians joined the country party because they had been excluded from the court party. This was not the case with DeLancey, a member of the court party who became an opposition leader by choice. During George Clinton's administration, DeLancey received numerous posts and favors from the governor until the two men finally broke. After the break, Clinton acknowledged that DeLancey was the most powerful man in New York, controlling the courts, the council, and the assembly. As head of the country opposition, DeLancey led the assembly in its increasingly sophisticated efforts to enhance its hegemony and reduce the power of the royal governor. These efforts were largely successful because of Clinton's ineptness and DeLancey's political astuteness.

DeLancey, with strong emotional, economic, and familial ties with England, whose family during the Revolution were Loyalists, and who was himself a Tory in political philosophy, was, nevertheless, as intent on furthering local privilege and reducing prerogative power as any Whig in New York. His attitude was not considered exceptional or unusual at the time. DeLancey was loyal to the crown (so were the Livingstons), but he was also a supreme realist. His primary concern was to further his own (and his family's) prestige, power, and influence. If, after he had gotten as much from the governor's favor as he could reasonably expect, his interests would be better served by moving to open opposition, then so be it. The Livingston Whigs acted similarly. As Patricia Bonomi perceptively observes of DeLancey, "he was one of a rare breed of eighteenth-century Englishmen—a true Anglo-American—whose bonds to the mother country and to the colony of his birth exerted such nearly equal pull that his personal ambitions were best served when both worlds were in balance."[2]

James DeLancey's rise to political prominence began during the administrations of John Montgomery and William Cosby. Named chief justice by Cosby in 1733, DeLancey allied with Cosby's successor, George Clarke. Clarke's claim to the governorship was disputed by Rip Van Dam. The controversy between Clarke and Van Dam started in 1736, even before Clarke became acting governor. Cosby, still not having heard from the ministry about his request to oust senior councillor Rip Van Dam, did so on his own authority. Cosby's intent was to prevent Van Dam from again becoming acting governor should Cosby die. The next most senior councilor was George Clarke. On Cosby's death later that year from tuberculosis, Clarke announced that he was in charge of the government. Clarke's right to rule was immediately disputed by Van Dam, and the result was a virtual civil war in New York. The country (predominantly landowning) party, which included James Alexander, backed Van Dam's candidacy, while the court (predominantly merchant) party, which included James DeLancey, backed Clarke. Both Van Dam and Clarke acted as chief executives, with each nominating different slates of officers for New York City. Lewis Morris, Sr., returned from England in October 1736 to back Van Dam, particularly since Van Dam promised to eject DeLancey as chief justice and restore Morris to that post.[3]

The country faction appealed for support in their campaign against Clarke to the lower and middling sort through the pages of Zenger's *Weekly Journal.* They were successful, and the mobs took to the streets in support of Van Dam. Clarke prepared for armed conflict by ordering supplies for the garrison at the fort. A full-scale civil war in New York was averted only when word arrived from the English ministry later that same month confirming Clarke as president of the council and therefore as acting governor and bolstering the royal prerogative.

The ministry's stance also assured that Clarke's ally, James DeLancey, would continue as chief justice.[4]

Turmoil arose again in 1737 when Clarke faced a defiant assembly. Elections had not been held since Montgomery's administration. The composition of the formerly agreeable assembly had changed through death and retirement. By the time Clarke came to office, representatives were no longer eager to please the governor and were, in fact, characterized by "seditious spirits." They voted Clarke only half the salary paid to Cosby and demanded the right to make money appropriations independently. Faced with defiance, Clarke dissolved the assembly.[5]

That election, the first in nine years, created intense interest, particularly in New York County where eight hundred votes were cast out of a total county population of only ten thousand. As Cadwallader Colden noted of the election, "Such a strugle I believe was never in America and is now over with a few bloody noses. . . . The sick the lame and the blind were all carried to vote they were carried out of Prison and out of the poor house to vote such a strugle I never saw and such a hurraing that above one half of the men in town are so hoarse that they cannot speak this day the pole lasted from half an hour after nine in the morning till past nine at night there was upwards of 800 persons poled."[6]

New York's election law permitted any adult white male with a £40 freehold, tenants on manors with lifelong leases, and freemen in Albany and New York to vote. While prisoners might well have qualified, poor house residents probably did not. Hence, Colden's statement implies that many voters were not legally entitled to cast a ballot.[7]

Legal voters or not, the population voiced its opinion of the court and country factions at the polls and came down strongly for local privilege at the expense of prerogative. Opposition leaders James Alexander and Lewis Morris, Sr. and Jr., were elected, with the latter voted speaker of the house. Much to the delight of the country party, the numerous New York County voters that turned out elected a slate of opposition candidates.[8]

Lewis Morris, Sr., left New York politics that same year. While Morris was in England, the ministry tentatively offered him the governorship of New Jersey, which in the future would be separated from the New York governorship. The post was formally offered in September 1737, and Morris accepted the office despite his irritation over being badly treated by the ministry. In fact, Morris did another ideological turnabout as chief executive. A court party leader under Hunter and Burnet, then a leader of the country opposition against Montgomery and Cosby, Morris, as governor of New Jersey, became zealous in promoting the royal prerogative and stifling assembly opposition.[9]

In New York, the country party also did a turnabout. With a strong majority in the house, the opposition now allied with the governor and became the court party and factionalism subsided. Clarke was not a strong executive. In fact, he was interested only in making money and biding his time until he could return to England with the fortune he amassed in New York. Consequently he was more concerned with establishing order in the colony than with maintaining the royal prerogative.[10]

Clarke achieved tranquility in the province by making concessions to the assembly. To ensure that no governor again keep a compliant assembly in existence indefinitely, as had Burnet and Cosby, the assembly passed and Clarke approved a triennial bill. In 1738, a new assembly again voted only one year support, and Clarke again gave "way to the Assemblys demands" and accepted it, further sacrificing the royal prerogative. In the 1739 elections, the court party lost control of the speakership, with Adolph Philipse replacing Lewis Morris, Jr. The opposition also lost control of the New York City delegation. The old Cosby faction was again in control, but it made little difference to Clarke.[11]

In 1739, Clarke was again hopeful that he could persuade the assembly to grant "a Revenue for a Competent number of years . . . but all in vain they remained inflexible." Knowing of the growing enmity between England and Spain, the assembly took advantage of Clarke who needed money to "put the province in a posture of Defence." The assembly voted and Clarke accepted yearly support because money for defense was badly needed. As Clarke told the Board of Trade, New York had "an old fort of very little defence cannon we have, but the carriages are good for little, we have ball but no powder, nor will the board of Ordinance send any on pretence that a large quantity was sent in 1711 for the Canada expedition which is 27 year agoe, much of it as for many years been trodden under foot in the magazine the barrells having been rotten."[12]

Clarke's capitulation brought him peace of mind. As Clarke told the Board of Trade, "I never knew the province in greater tranquility than it is at present." His surrender caused opposition writers to lay down their pens. Clarke happily reported that "even the press is silent for we have not had one seditious or political paper since the election." Having decided to placate the assembly, the remainder of George Clarke's tenure as lieutenant governor was relatively uneventful. His achievement was similar to that of Robert Hunter, who had also used conciliation and compromise in New York. The difference was that Hunter was willing to make personal financial sacrifices to support the royal prerogative, going without a salary and paying government expenses out of his own pocket. Clarke was never willing to make that sacrifice. Lord de la Ware was appointed New York governor in 1737, but never left England, so Clarke continued to enjoy the prestige and the profits of the office.[13]

The guiding force for the assembly was now Chief Justice James De Lancey. As noted by Stanley Katz, "DeLancey gained control of the lower house during the Clarke administration and retained it until his death," this control being "the main source" of DeLancey's power in New York. DeLancey gained control because his popularity continued to rise. According to William Livingston, the chief justice was much admired because of his "affability and ease; his adroitness at a jest, with a shew of condescension to his inferiors." DeLancey's winning personality was also aided by "his influence as chief justice, and a vast personal estate at use, all conspired to secure his popular triumph."[14]

Clarke, like DeLancey, enjoyed personal popularity, primarily because his regime brought political calm to the province. This tranquility was disturbed in 1741 by what Clarke perceived to be a major plot on the part of Roman Catholics to raise terror in New York. Suspicions of a Catholic plot followed numerous fires, including the burning of the fort and chapel on 18 March 1741. Clarke concluded the fire was not accidental but part of a "horrid conspiracy to burn it [the fort] and the whole Town." Slaves were suspected of setting fire to the buildings when several were seen running away from the conflagrations. After investigation, it appeared that the slaves were instigated by "a Romish Priest," who, with the assistance of Catholic laymen in New York, incited the slaves to rebellion. Wholesale arrests of blacks and whites followed, with twenty-one whites and one hundred and sixty slaves jailed. Of these, thirteen blacks were sentenced to be burnt while eighteen were hanged and seventy-two transported.[15]

Clarke's suspicions ran rampant because Great Britain was fighting the Catholic enemy in the War of Jenkins' Ear, which began in 1739 and, by 1740, had expanded into the War of the Austrian Succession. Controversy over England's involvement in a war with Catholic Spain caused a split in the Whig ranks. Walpole and his followers were anti-war, while his opponents wanted an all-out war effort. The resultant division in the ranks of the Whigs brought an end to the twenty-year administration of Robert Walpole. Walpole's amazing career as prime minister had endured primarily because of his ability to control the House of Commons. During his administration, the percentage of placemen in that body rose from less than one-quarter in 1700 to more than one-third by 1740. The Commons so consistently voted the ministry platform that country Whigs and Tories complained that body no longer functioned independently. Nevertheless divisions caused by the war led to open opposition in Commons to the prime minister, even among formerly loyal representatives. Walpole resigned as first lord of the treasury and chancellor of the exchequer on 1 February 1742.[16]

Walpole's posts were given to Lord Wilmington, but Wilmington died in 1743. He was succeeded in the treasury and as prime minister by Henry Pelham, younger brother to the southern secretary, the duke of Newcastle. The next year France and England declared war on each other. The War of the Austrian Succession now spread to America where it was known among English colonists as King George's War. In America, the war would be waged primarily in those colonies closest to French Canada, particularly New York, making good leadership in that colony vital to the interests of Great Britain.[17]

Good leadership was not offered to New York. The selection of Clarke's successor in New York was made by Newcastle. His choice for New York was Admiral George Clinton, the younger brother of the earl of Lincoln, who was married to Newcastle's sister. Clinton, after a twenty-five year career in the Royal Navy, was heavily in debt. He was given the post not on the basis of his ability or his character, since both were weak, but on the strength of his family connection with Newcastle.[18]

Clinton arrived in New York in 1743. Like most royal governors, Clinton was ignorant of the internal provincial political system, but realized the necessity of forming alliances with the local elite. Clinton sought out the person he thought would be most knowledgeable of New York's politics. He chose the chief justice of New York, James DeLancey, who, as Clinton realized, was "posesst of a plentifull Estate, he has numerous Relations and others of the principal Inhabitants of the Town attached to him by long habitude; he is of His Majestys Council for this Province and Chief Justice of it; it seems reasonable for me to expect that this Gentleman was likely to be most useful to me from his personal interest and knowledge in the Law and other affairs." Clinton underestimated DeLancey, a consumate politician skilled at wooing the masses. DeLancey inspired deep loyalty from his followers and even deeper hatred from his enemies.[19]

To solidify DeLancey's power base as his aide, Clinton appointed four of DeLancey's closest friends to the seven-man council: Daniel Horsmanden, Joseph Murray, Stephen Bayard, and Admiral Peter Warren, DeLancey's brother-in-law. DeLancey already controlled the assembly, with a majority of that body loyal to him, and, as chief justice, he controlled the courts. By giving DeLancey control of the council as well, Clinton secured him in power. By doing so, Clinton badly miscalculated because DeLancey used his position to further expand his importance while diminishing that of the governor. DeLancey's

George II, 1733, by T. Hudson, National Portrait Gallery, London. Far more interested in his principality of Hanover than the North American colonies, the king took little interest in New York affairs. His ministers turned attention to the colonies only when they were threatened by external forces, as they were during King George's War.

rise began shortly after Clinton convened his first assembly. Clinton, aware of the assembly's growing political sophistication and its long-standing struggle for power with the royal governors, eagerly sought DeLancey's advice on how to get along with the assembly. One of Clinton's instructions was to secure a permanent revenue from the assembly. In December 1743, when Clinton called his first assembly session, DeLancey advised Clinton that securing a permanent or even a long-term revenue was impossible. As Clinton later recalled, DeLancey "perswaded me that the Assembly had come to a resolution not to grant the support of governt for longer than one year at any one time, and that it would be needless to attempt to gain it for a longer time." Clinton followed DeLancey's advice and accepted the one-year revenue that the assembly offered, getting in return a handsome salary of £1,560 per annum.[20]

Clinton's total capitulation to DeLancey and the assembly on the revenue issue left little doubt in the minds of New Yorkers that the real source of effective power in the province was not the governor but the chief justice. Clinton unwittingly further weakened his own position on 13 September 1744, when he gave DeLancey a new commission for the chief justiceship during good behavior, instead of at pleasure, thereby assuring him the office for life.[21]

Clinton's unstable personality caused him either to be deeply attached to subordinates or to abhor them. One person who incurred Clinton's animosity was Philip Livingston. Clinton's initial hatred of Livingston may have been inspired by James DeLancey, whose loathing of the Livingstons was fully reciprocated. The Livingstons, who rivaled the DeLanceys in wealth and influence, had acquired the manor through the efforts of Philip's Scottish-born father, Robert. Comprised of some 160,000 acres, it was the third largest manor in New York. Most of the acreage had come from illegal Indian purchases made by Robert. Philip Livingston, Robert's son and heir, continued to acquire land along with political offices. He was councillor, secretary of Indian affairs, and clerk of the common pleas and peace in Albany and Albany County. The disposition of these and other profitable posts was at the discretion of the royal governor.[22]

Clinton may also have been influenced in his negative attitude toward Philip Livingston by William Johnson, a nephew of Admiral Peter Warren and the manager of Warren's lands on the Mohawk and Schoharie rivers. Clinton, realizing Johnson was knowledgeable about Indian affairs, named Johnson as Indian agent and ordered him to recruit as many Iroquois as possible to fight with the English in King George's War. During the course of the war, Johnson came to despise Albany traders, including Philip Livingston. Much to the outrage of

Livingston, Johnson refused to purchase war supplies from them, turning instead to New York City merchants.[23]

Johnson's critical view of Albany traders was also shared by Cadwallader Colden. Colden, who became Clinton's chief advisor after DeLancey broke with the governor, was aware that Albany Indian traders, such as Philip Livingston, dealt unethically with the Indians. Livingston, as secretary for Indian affairs, did nothing to stop such practices as selling Indians supposed casks of rum that really contained nothing but water, or holding Indian children captive for their parents's debts. In addition, Livingston had Dutch blood, and Colden disliked what he considered Dutch ethnic traits. As Colden noted, the first Dutch settlers had a "Scandalous attachment . . . to the getting of Money," while ignoring his own pursuit of profit. In Colden's opinion, it was the same kind of men who had the "management of our Indian affairs." As a result of unethical treatment by Albany's Dutch, "The Indians . . . will on no occasion trust an Albany man."[24]

Philip Livingston was himself guilty of unethical practices. In 1730 he bought from three drunken Mohawk Indians 8000 acres of land on the banks of the Mohawk River. This land included the tribe's village of Canajoharie as well as the land the Indians used for planting. The Mohawks' sober compatriots were outraged when they learned of the sale. Well aware of the risks involved, Livingston waited three years to have the tract surveyed and then had it done secretly by moonlight.[25]

In the instance of the Canajoharie tract and in other cases, Philip Livingston, as had his father before him, proceeded contrary to the usual practice in New York for buying land. The standard procedure was for the prospective buyer to petition the governor in council for a license to buy certain land from the Indians. If the council approved, a license was granted. After the purchase, the prospective owner asked for an order to survey the property to obtain a patent. When the survey was completed, the purchaser obtained certificates from the provincial secretary and the receiver and surveyor generals. These certificates were turned over to the attorney general, who issued a patent.[26]

New York's landlords often sidestepped this procedure, as had Philip Livingston. On learning that Surveyor General Cadwallader Colden was against granting him and his recently acquired partners the patent for the Canajoharie tract because much of the land was already patented to others, Livingston tried unsuccessfully to go over Colden's and Governor William Cosby's heads to obtain a patent directly from the king, raising great indignation among colonial bureaucrats who were thus deprived of their fees. A patent was finally issued for the tract, but Livingston's ownership was a constant source of outrage to the Mohawks, who repeatedly petitioned New York's governors that "the said Patent may be broke, it haveing never been bought . . . or paid for."[27]

Livingston, like many other Albany traders, was also guilty of selling weapons to the Indians allied with the French in Canada, who "went directly from Albany to murther in a most cruel and barbarous manner the People of New England." When so charged by Massachusetts officials, Philip Livingston claimed not to remember whether he had traded with the French Indians. Livingston's actions are yet another example of the short-sightedness of the elite and their pursuit of their own profit at the expense of imperial interests. Livingston, as imperial-minded as Clinton, could not resist cheating the Iroquois of land or selling weapons to French-allied Indians. To accomplish his ends, he flaunted laws and looked for legal loopholes, both of which lessened respect for the royal prerogative and encouraged other New Yorkers to do the same.[28]

Clinton, not above making a profit himself, even if at the expense of the royal prerogative, was outraged at reports that Livingston was arming the enemy. Clinton's ire was further raised when he learned of Livingston's illegal purchase of the Canajoharie tract. The sale infuriated the Iroquois, and Iroquois support, or at least neutrality, was vital to Great Britain as they continued to war against the French. Livingston, as secretary of Indian affairs, had abused his position to steal land from the Indians. Clinton feared that because of this and similar incidents by other speculators, the Iroquois would fight for the French. Clinton decided the Livingstons were "a vile family," neither the first nor last New York governor to arrive at a negative assessment of the Livingstons. A year later Clinton requested the home government to relieve Philip Livingston of his post as secretary of Indian Affairs.[29]

Clinton's concern that Livingston and other Albany traders would alienate the Iroquois was valid. To secure the allegiance or neutrality of the Iroquois, Clinton in June 1744 met with sachems in Albany. The sachems had little interest in whether France or England triumphed; their concern was the fur trade. In an effort to control this trade, the Five (later Six) Nations of the Iroquois had in the seventeenth century embarked on wars of conquest against other Indian tribes. Their victories gave them hegemony over an extensive territory in the Ohio and Mississippi river valleys ranging from the Carolinas north to the Great Lakes. The tribes, whose home territory spanned present-day New York State from the Hudson River to Niagara Falls, were the Mohawk, Oneida, Onondaga, Cayuga, and Seneca. The Tuscarora, an Iroquois-speaking tribe, were added to the League in 1714, after their attacks on white settlers led to their being driven out of North Carolina.[30]

The strategic location of the Iroquois between the French in Canada and the English in New York gave them the key to the North American continent. Their allegiance was crucial to both the English and the French. Clinton wanted the Iroquois to ally with the English, and the Indians grudgingly agreed that they would fight the French in the event of a French attack. But only a year later Clinton reported that most of the Iroquois "are gone to Canada" to fight against the English. Part of the Iroquois's disenchantment with the English was caused by widely circulated rumors that the colonists were planning to massacre the Mohawks. Clinton met with Iroquois sachems in October of 1745 to calm their fears. He again obtained promises from the Iroquois that they would fight the French if the French attacked the colonies.[31]

Several Iroquois sachems could not bring themselves to make even this half-hearted promise of assistance. At the same time Iroquois sachems were meeting with Clinton in Albany in 1744, other sachems were in Lancaster, Pennsylvania, meeting with commissioners from Virginia, Maryland, and Pennsylvania. At this meeting, the Iroquois promised only to remain neutral during the war. The treaty signed at Lancaster also led indirectly to still another, and this time decisive, war between France and England. By the terms of the treaty, the Iroquois unwittingly ceded to Virginia all their claims to land within Virginia's boundaries. The Iroquois believed they were giving up only the Shenandoah Valley, not realizing that Virginia claimed land from sea to sea. Within months of the treaty, Virginia approved grants in the Ohio Valley for three hundred thousand acres. The resultant movement west by Virginians was bitterly resented and resisted by the French, who had similar claims to the Ohio Valley, and by the Iroquois, who still believed the land was under their hegemony.[32]

England's intent was to drive the French not only from the Ohio Valley but from the continent. Clinton himself wanted to take an active military part in this task and asked to command the fleet that, in 1745, successfully attacked the French fort at Louisbourg on Cape Breton Island. Clinton was passed over in favor of DeLancey's brother–in–law, Peter Warren, and it was Warren who was knighted and enjoyed the glory of the conquest. Clinton, as early as 1745, was desperate to leave New York and its problems. He begged Newcastle for the command of any ship that would take him back to England. Not only was the assembly recalcitrant but, because of the abominable climate, Clinton and his family also were in poor health. In addition, Clinton claimed the profits from the office had "fallen far short of what it was represented."[33]

Clinton's rampant but ineffectual imperialism toward French Canada was not shared by James DeLancey, whose family had made a handsome profit from trading with the French and who feared the results of an ill-considered attack on the French and their Indian allies. This fundamental difference in philosophy may well have driven the two men apart. The break may also have occurred because Clinton became resentful of DeLancey's power over the assembly. According to Clinton, the root of the problem was the financial dependence of the governor on the assembly. That body used its control of the purse strings to reduce "the power of the Crown." The assembly members were "of such levelling principles, that they are constantly attacking it's prerogative, so that nothing but a Governour's independence, can ever bring them to a just sence of their duty." Clinton, like Hunter, recommended that Parliament "take cognizance of their disobedience and indolence, and enjoin them to a more submissive behaviour." DeLancey, as he worked to increase the power of the assembly, was at odds with the governor.[34]

In retrospect, Clinton claimed he had long been suspicious of DeLancey's ambition. Clinton claimed "it was not long before I perceived, that under this mask of Friendship to me, he [DeLancey] was establishing his own interest, and only serving his own immoderate thirst after power." According to Clinton, DeLancey's intent was to effect the "alteration of the Constitution of Govert, by putting the Administration absolutely in the hands of a Faction . . . entirely dependent on him." DeLancey, Clinton said, urged Clinton to accept yearly support from the assembly, because he desired that "all other Governours after me should be in a continual dependance on the Assembly, or more proper the faction, which in this Country always governs, and directs the Assembly."[35]

In 1746 DeLancey broke with Clinton. Whatever the underlying reasons for the break, it was apparently initiated by DeLancey who deliberately instigated a quarrel while dining with the governor. William Smith, Jr., reports that "the altercations ran so high that Mr. Delancey left the table with an oath of revenge, and they became thenceforth irreconciliable foes." Over the years, DeLancey had carefully cultivated a broad popular base that permitted him to control assembly elections and hence the assembly. In addition, as chief justice, he controlled the courts and a majority of the members of the governor's council were loyal to him. DeLancey no longer needed the governor.[36]

Clinton, in letters to the Board of Trade and secretary of state openly accused DeLancey of undermining his authority. Clinton was right in that Delancey had deliberately worked to weaken the governor. In truth, Clinton was undermined not so much by DeLancey as by his own stupidity and lack of political finesse. A governor who controlled neither his own council nor the assembly nor the courts was severely hamstrung.[37]

DeLancey used his relationship with the governor successfully. Clinton, by giving DeLancey lifetime tenure as chief justice, ensured DeLancey was one of the most powerful men in New York. As William Livingston noted of DeLancey, "Of all provincial affairs he is the uncontrolled director. As chief justice, great is his interest in the counties; with that interest he commands elections; with his sway in elections he rules the assembly; and with his sovereignty over the house controls a governor." Clinton, too, was aware of DeLancey's power. As he told London officials, even if he were to remove DeLancey from the council his power would be unaffected as long as DeLancey retained his chief justiceship, "for while that continues his influence over the Members of both the Council and Assembly and over great numbers of the Officers of Govert would continue." The influence of the chief justice was in fact as far reaching as his enemies claimed, touching every landowner and merchant in the province. As Colden noted, "no man that has any Property can think himself independent of the Courts of Justice. . . . There are in this Country numbers of Lawyers who's bread & fortune depend on the Countenance of a Chief Justice." This control gave DeLancey as much power as formerly was wielded by "the Popes . . . in the days of Ignorance." There were a few assembly members who opposed DeLancey, but, as Clinton noted, DeLancey's opponents were so afraid of the chief justice that they simply refused to attend assembly sessions.[38]

DeLancey managed to have his candidates elected to the assembly in elections held in 1743, 1745, 1747, 1750, and 1752. In the 1752 body, the votes of twelve of twenty-seven members were directly controlled by DeLancey. Of the remaining representatives, Robert Livingston, Philip's oldest son, was the only assemblyman "neither connected with Mr. Delancey nor in the sphere of his influence." DeLancey's assembly victories were made relatively easy because Clinton had deprived himself of allies in that body. He had, for instance, alienated the politically powerful Livingstons. In 1747, Clinton charged inaccurately that Philip Livingston favored neutrality toward the French, a charge better directed at James DeLancey. Clinton claimed that Philip Livingston "has abandoned his Country, neglects his Office and supports the neutrality." He again requested that the home government dismiss Livingston from his office as Indian secretary, his council post, "and all other employments in this Province."[39]

Clinton's attempts to drive Philip Livingston from his offices cost him the assembly vote of Philip's son Robert, who represented the Manor, as well as the votes of other Livingston allies in the assembly. The Livingstons were further alienated from Clinton following Philip's 1749 death when the governor continued his vendetta against the family. Clinton saw that none of the government posts that Livingston had held were passed on to any of his sons. One of Philip Livingston's posts, clerk of the peace and common pleas for the city and county of Albany, was given to Cadwallader Colden's son, John. It was a lifetime appointment, with the salary and perquisites being paid to Cadwallader Colden for the duration of his life.[40]

DeLancey was successful in getting his candidates in office because of his popular appeal. DeLancey's popularity contrasted dramatically with that of the governor, a man who "in a province given to hospitality," chose to socialize with a small circle of friends and "his bottle." Clinton seldom left Fort George, consequently "many of the citizens never saw him," since he even failed to attend church. As William Smith, Jr., noted, Clinton's "manner of living was the very reverse of that requisite to raise a party or make friends."[41]

In addition to the governor's lack of personal popularity was the knowledge that his tenure was limited. Eventually Clinton would return to England, but DeLancey was in New York for good. To vote against DeLancey candidates took courage since those voters would be "exposed to the resentments of an evidently malicious faction headed by a man of violent passions & unforgiving principles and Chief Justice of this Province for life . . . & whose authority may be of the most detrimental consequences to them and their familyes."[42]

Clinton accurately but belatedly realized that James DeLancey was "insatiable in his persuit of power" and controlled a "Government within a Government." DeLancey did exactly that. DeLancey's position was further strengthened in 1747 when, thanks to his brother–in–law, Sir Peter Warren, he received a commission as lieutenant governor of New York. Ironically, news of DeLancey's commission arrived in the same letter to Clinton as did word that Clinton's long-awaited leave of absence had been approved. Clinton was free to return home, but if he did, DeLancey would be acting governor. Clinton could not bring himself to leave.[43]

Clinton was appalled when he received DeLancey's commission and claimed that most New Yorkers were also "greatly moved with dislike to it, as thinking that he [DeLancey] and his family had engrossed already too much power." Clinton's assessment of DeLancey's appeal was wrong. The new lieutenant governor retained his popularity with New Yorkers until his death. It was, in fact, Clinton who increasingly alienated colonists, thus making it impossible for him to govern effectively. Clinton ignored this and chose to believe that DeLancey was successful solely because of his English connections. As Clinton told Newcastle, DeLancey "presumes on the personal interest which he pretends to have with the Archbishop of Canterbury and Sir Peter

Warren, & which he had the assurance to tell me to my face was better than my interest."[44]

The governor's "interest" was in fact substantial, but his patron Newcastle was preoccupied by European events and often ignorant or misinformed about New York's internal affairs. Then, too, Newcastle might have been irritated with Clinton's constant complaints and chosen to ignore his kinsman. From New York, Clinton continued to solicit Newcastle and the Board of Trade to have DeLancey's commission as lieutenant governor revoked. Clinton was aware that, with the lieutenant governor's commission DeLancey's ambition would know no bounds. As Clinton noted, DeLancey "makes all men affraid of the power he has by this office, and of his resentment, and to which every man in this Province may in some way or other be subjected. . . . if the administration should come into his hands, no relief can be had when the powers of Governour & Chief Justice are united in the same person."[45]

The prospect of unrestrained power in DeLancey's hands alarmed Clinton, particularly when he saw at firsthand how effectively DeLancey led the assembly based opposition. Under DeLancey's direction, the country party in the assembly gained ground in its perennial struggle with royal governors for power. It usurped the governor's nomination of officers and the responsibility for mustering and paying militia. The assembly assumed control over repairing and building the province's fortifications and refused to permit the Council to amend its money bills. In addition, the assembly authorized payments directly without the governor's warrant.[46]

Clinton realized that the assembly wrested the loyalty of officeholders from the governor because only the assembly had the power to authorize payments. The governor had no control over the disbursement of funds and thus was not in a position "to reward any one person, while at the same time the faction is enabled to give liberally to all those who assist in opposition." The assembly also voted salaries only to specific officeholders, not the office, in an effort "to deprive the King of the appointment of Officers," since the assembly would not pay officeholders of whom it did not approve.[47]

The assembly, at DeLancey's orders, "opposed every measure which I took for the security of the Province," said Clinton, and only voted money for military expenses "by tacking clauses derogatory to His Majesty's authority to all the money Bills for paying the troops." In the case of the colony's London agent, for instance, the assembly had tacked the appointment of Robert Charles, who was also secretary to DeLancey's brother–in–law, Sir Peter Warren, on an appropriations bill. Clinton needed the money and approved the bill. Clinton and all subsequent royal governors lost control of agents when Charles was instructed by the assembly "to follow Sir Peter Warren's directions in every thing." Clinton asked the Board of Trade to reject Charles's appointment, since Charles was accountable only to the assembly and not the governor and council. The Board pointed out to Clinton that since he had approved "the Act, whereby Mr. Charles is appointed Agent, we must look upon his appointment as good."[48]

The assembly's desire to increase its power was not new but had been evident as long as there was an assembly in New York. Clinton, in tracing the increase in assembly power, stated that body's first dramatic victory over the royal prerogative occurred during the administration of Robert Hunter. He detailed how, in 1715, Hunter, who had been without a revenue and without assistance from the home government, agreed to permit the assembly's agent rather than the crown's receiver general to disperse funds. Clinton believed that since that date, the assembly "continued from time (as occasions offered), in grasping more and more power to the Prejudice of the Royal Prerogative."[49]

Clinton neglected to mention that, although Hunter had made concessions to the assembly, the assembly, in turn, made an important concession to him in granting long-term support. Clinton also failed to mention that the other issues for which the assembly struggled were points of contention between virtually every assembly and every governor for more than fifty years, but not all previous governors had given up as easily as had he. Clinton concluded that "it is no way in the Power of a Governor to support the Kings authority, against the Power of a Faction [the DeLanceys] which has by so many ways & for so long a time been gathering strength in this Province."[50]

Clinton was partially correct in that it was impossible for an incompetent governor, such as himself, to gain control of the province from a person as politically astute as DeLancey who consistently outmanuveured him. Other governors with more political acumen had not surrendered the royal prerogative as cheaply as had Clinton. Clinton's weakness, and that of many preceding governors, caused an "unmeasurable increase of popular power by which the proper Ballance of power essential to the English Constitution is entirely distroy'd." Colden and others believed this was "wholly owing to the Governors having no subsistence but from the Assemblies." If the situation were permitted to continue, the now mature colonies would break away, as Hunter and other royal observers had long predicted.[51]

Faced with this usurpation of power, Clinton urged the home government to take steps to discipline the assembly "and enjoin them to a more submissive behaviour to His Majty's Royal orders and instructions." Clinton wanted a letter from the ministry "signifying His Majestys approbation of my conduct, or displeasure of theirs [the

DeLancey faction]," but such a letter was not forthcoming. Newcastle and other English officials were distracted not only by the ongoing War of the Austrian Succession but also by Charles Edward Stuart's 1745 invasion of Scotland.[52]

Without help from the ministry, Clinton grew exasperated by what he perceived as a DeLancey-led local rebellion. Clinton requested that Massachusetts governor William Shirley report to the ministry on the activities of New York's country opposition. Shirley, after reviewing the assembly's actions, reported to the home government "that the Assembly seems to have left scarcely any part of His Majesty's prerogative untouched, and that they have gone great lengths towards getting the government, military as well as civil, into their own hands."[53]

DeLancey's political control extended to both houses of the legislature. To demonstrate to the ministry DeLancey's influence on the council, Clinton cited an incident that occurred when the governor had gone to Albany in 1746 for a conference with the Iroquois. During his absence from New York City, DeLancey called a council meeting "and exercised acts of Government . . . and neglected even to acquaint me with their proceedings." To rid the council of DeLancey's influence, Clinton requested that James DeLancey, Daniel Horsmanden, and Stephen Bayard be suspended from the council. To increase the effectiveness of the governor in the future, Clinton urged, as had Hunter, that he be made financially independent of the assembly and urged the ministry to pay royal officials from the province's quit rents.[54]

To solidify their power base, DeLancey and his allies attacked Clinton in print and in public, while the assembly rewarded the authors by tacking "the payment of the Forces" to a bill that authorized a payment of "one hundred and fifty pounds to Daniel Horsmanden for his publick services." As Clinton reported, these public services consisted of writing "scandilous libells that have been published against me and my Administration, of which none doubt of his being the Author."[55]

Clinton's new favorite was Colden, to whom the governor offered the lieutenant governorship, if and when he got DeLancey's commission recalled. Colden was also the object of both written and personal attacks, as the DeLanceys "endeavoured to expose his person to the mobb, throwing out the vilest slanders upon him, and even threatned [him] with death." The DeLanceys' vicious attacks on Colden show that family feelings played little or no part in New York politics. Colden's daughter Elizabeth was married to Peter DeLancey, "one of the late Mr. [Stephen] DeLanceys son," making her the sister–in–law of James DeLancey.[56]

Most outspoken in insulting Clinton and Colden was Oliver DeLancey, James's younger brother. Oliver said forthrightly, *"The*

Cadwallader Colden, n.d., by John Wollaston, The Metropolitan Museum of Art, Bequest of Grace Wilkes, 1922 (22.45.6). Colden's long life spanned almost the full gamut of New York's eighteenth-century colonial experience. A distinguished physician, successful merchant, competent bureaucrat, respected natural scientist, and dedicated administrator, Colden lacked the ability to govern effectively.

Governour . . . is a damnd Rogue a damd . . . fellow, the worst Governour that ever was in this Province . . . the Governour . . . is an Arrant Villain Scoundrel and Rascal. " The younger DeLancey lacked James's restraint and polish. He indulged in tavern brawls, berated councilmen and New York City mayor Edward Holland, insulted a newly arrived Jew in the man's own home, and attacked strangers on the street with impunity. Victims were reluctant to press charges against the chief justice's brother. Even the governor was reluctant to do so. Clinton, along with other victims, realized the colony's attorneys would not prosecute the brother of the chief justice. In 1749, Oliver DeLancey was finally charged with seditious libel for statements against the governor when William Smith, Sr., and James Alexander agreed to take on the prosecution.[57]

Clinton in 1748 formally suspended DeLancey allies Daniel Horsmandan and Stephen Bayard from the council and appointed his own supporters in their places. His decision to alter the council and to take a stand against Oliver DeLancey reflected changes in imperial administration that began in 1748 with the signing of the Treaty of Aix-la-Chapelle to conclude the War of the Austrian Succession. Internal peace was guaranteed in Great Britain with the passage of two parliamentary acts designed to destroy Scottish culture and the power of clan chiefs. Attempts were made by George II's son, William Augustus, duke of Cumberland, the victor in Scotland, to extend similar imperial control to the colonies. This was to be effected by the elevation of Cumberland's friends to high office. One such appointment was that of John Russell, duke of Bedford, who, much to Newcastle's dismay, succeeded him as southern secretary when Newcastle moved to the northern department in 1748. Yet another change of personnel occurred following the 1748 death of John Lord Monson, president of the Board of Trade. Bedford's choice for president of the Board was another of Cumberland's cronies, George Montagu Dunk, second earl of Halifax.[58]

As president of the Board, Halifax responded to complaints made by Clinton and other governors of rising provincial autonomy. Halifax did his best to stem that tide by preparing reports on troublesome colonies and recommending that the ministry take immediate action to bring the colonies back in line. The ministry failed to respond.[59]

Changes in colonial administrators did not help Clinton because there was little change in colonial administration. The ministry was slow to deal with Clinton's problems, despite numerous and detailed letters written by Clinton about his problems in New York. One reason that few responses came from the southern secretary was that Bedford was lazy and incompetent, spending as little time as possible in

London attending to business. Newcastle quickly came to the conclusion that Bedford was unfit for office, but Bedford was protected by his friendship with Cumberland. Newcastle mounted a campaign to get rid of Bedford, but the king refused to fire him, so Bedford remained in charge of colonial affairs.[60]

DeLancey controlled New York affairs and continued in his attempts to reduce the royal prerogative and embarrass Clinton. One such opportunity presented itself on 7 June 1750. The incident involved a ship of the Royal Navy, the *Greyhound*, at anchor in New York Bay. A sloop belonging to William Ricketts of New Jersey passed but did not salute the *Greyhound*, as was customary. An officer on the royal ship tried "to bring her to by firing some shot." The sloop continued on its way, and a second shot was fired. A maid, Elizabeth Hibbins, on board the pleasure boat was killed by the shot. The gunner's mate, James Parks, who fired the shot was sent on shore by ship's captain Robert Roddam, who was also Clinton's son-in-law, to give evidence at a coroner's inquest. At DeLancey's order, the mate was immediately arrested on the charge of murder. DeLancey, who was responding to crowd pressure, intended to try Parks before a New York jury. New Yorkers and most other provincials hated the Royal Navy, which systematically impressed New York seamen into its ranks. Sailors, loud, rowdy, and boisterous, were also detested by New Yorkers. Roddam demanded the mate's release, but DeLancey refused to comply, and Parks was tried and convicted of manslaughter in August 1750.[61]

The incident infuriated Clinton, since it was deliberately aimed to embarrass him as royal governor, as an admiral in the Royal Navy, and as the father-in-law of the ship's captain. It also elevated his hope that DeLancey had finally overstepped his authority and provided Clinton with an opportunity to oust him as chief justice. DeLancey's good behavior commission meant he could only be removed from office for cause. According to Clinton's instructions, "all offences committed on board his Majesty's ships are exempted from the common Jurisdiction of this Province." It seemed clear to Clinton and his advisor Colden that DeLancey had acted improperly in trying to "extend his Jurisdiction to places persons or offences exempted from his Jurisdiction." Clinton's efforts to remove DeLancey as chief justice were fruitless.[62]

Continuing resistance from DeLancey led Clinton to take a stand against DeLancey and the assembly. The conclusion of the war meant that Clinton no longer was desperate for money to defend the province. He told the assembly that he would accept only a five-year revenue, "in the same manner it had formerly been done, in the time of my predecessors." The assembly "absolutely refused," and so "the Governt remains without support, and many just services and debts remain unpaid." Clinton dissolved the still defiant assembly in 1749, but finally capitulated in December 1750, accepting one year's support.[63]

The fault was not entirely Clinton's. Despite his repeated calls for support from the home government, the ministry did nothing. Clinton pointed this out to Bedford in December when he noted that "the King must enforce the Authority of his own Commission, or else resolve to give up the Government of this province in to the hands of the Assembly." He may very well have been right when he continued "that it is not in the power of any Governour (on the present footing of affairs) to support his Authority in this province, and in the present state of the Courts of Judicature in it, while the Assembly retains such an influence over all the Officers of Governt." Clinton's capitulation to the assembly may have come both from lack of official support and for personal reasons. Clinton's daughter, Mrs. Roddam, ill since November 1750, died on 21 December. The distraught governor closeted himself away from his acquaintances until 2 January 1751. With Clinton's capitulation to the assembly, the fight was over. The assembly had clearly won. Clinton was from this point merely biding his time until the home government named a successor.[64]

DeLancey's efforts to undermine Clinton were confirmed in the 1750 assembly election. Clinton lacked assembly support because he increasingly lacked popular support. The Livingstons, persecuted by Clinton, had allied with the DeLanceys. In the 1750 assembly elections, Robert Livingston, Jr., third manor lord after the death of his father, and his brothers campaigned for DeLancey candidates. William Livingston, Robert's younger brother, was the chief polemicist of the family. William attacked Governor Clinton in print with great effectiveness. With Livingston support, however temporary it was, DeLancey and the country opposition had little trouble again obtaining control of the 1750 assembly. The alliance between the Livingstons and the DeLanceys continued only until 1751. In that year, the Livingstons again became disenchanted with the DeLanceys when Robert Livingston, Jr., sought James DeLancey's assistance. Some disgruntled tenants on the manor's eastern border refused to pay their rents, rebelled, and decided to obtain deeds for their land from Massachusetts. The tenant controversy sprang from the senior Robert Livingston's clandestine land purchases from the Stockbridge Indians. The Indians claimed that they never sold the land to Livingston and were now selling it to speculators who in turn offered it to farmers. In addition, Massachusetts claimed jurisdiction over much of the land in question. Many manor tenants took the titles offered by Massachusetts, and then refused to pay their rent to Livingston. Robert Livingston immediately sought to dispossess his rebellious tenants through the courts. The result was a border war.[65]

The problems of Robert Livingston, Jr., were increased following the passage of the 1750 parliamentary Iron Act, which threatened the profits from the Ancram Iron Works on the manor. The intent of the act was to limit local privilege by barring competition with English manufacturers. The DeLancey assembly, more from indifference to the Livingstons than from a desire to strengthen imperial interests, did little to assist the Livingstons with either iron or tenants. Their inaction lead William Livingston to observe to his brother Robert that James DeLancey "cares not a Groat for you nor your Manor, nor any man living. That always was my opinion about him; now is so; and ever shall be, world without End." Disgusted with DeLancey, the Livingstons now turned to the only other legitimate source of power in the colony, Governor George Clinton.[66]

On 16 April 1752, Robert Livingston petitioned Clinton for assistance in his border controversy with Massachusetts. Clinton promptly ordered Surveyor General Cadwallader Colden and Attorney General Richard Bradley to submit their opinions on the disputed territory. Despite their dislike of the Livingstons, self-interest about their own uncertain land titles and those of other oligarchs prompted Colden and Bradley to agree that the lands were part of the manor and in New York.[67]

Despite Clinton's subsequent intercession with the governor of Massachusetts, the controversy with Massachusetts continued and tenant uprisings spread to other eastern border manors, including the largest, Renssaelaerswyck. Tenants, disgruntled after decades of exploitation, were eager to accept from Massachusetts title for the lands they farmed. The situation quickly worsened on Livingston Manor, with rioters harrassing, kidnapping, and imprisoning loyal tenants, and even attacking and kidnapping the sheriff of Albany. On one occasion, a hundred rioters came to the manor and then "went to the Iron Works at Ancram," where they kidnapped eight ironworkers. On another occasion, rioters burned over a thousand trees near the iron works. Robert Livingston retaliated by dispossessing rebellious tenants, seizing their crops, and burning their fields, leading disgruntled former tenants to threaten to burn Livingston's "house over his head" and to come with the Stockbridge Indians to murder him.[68]

The land-hungry, acquisitive nature of colonists, evident in the Massachusetts-New York border wars, was part of the reason friction continued between the French and the English. According to the terms of the 1748 Treaty of Aix-la-Chapelle, the French and the English were to agree on national boundaries in North America. Commissioners from both countries met in 1749 to settle these boundaries, but the commissioners were instructed not to compromise their governments' territorial claims in North America. Both countries believed that they had valid claims to the disputed territories in Nova Scotia and the Ohio River Valley, and neither would budge. The situation was made more difficult because English colonists ignored all boundaries and continued to push to the west onto land the French claimed as theirs, with both countries ignoring Iroquois claims. To thwart such westward movement, in 1749 a French expedition moved down the Ohio River burying plates claiming the territory for France.[69]

The boundary commissioners for England were supervised and instructed by the ineffectual Bedford, who as southern secretary remained in charge of colonial affairs. Newcastle continued his efforts to oust Bedford. These efforts proved unsuccessful as long as Bedford was protected by Cumberland. Newcastle, assisted by fate, effected Bedford's ouster following the 1751 death of the heir to the throne, Prince Frederick. In the event of George II's death, the next king would be Frederick's son, Prince George, still a minor in 1751. It seemed likely that Cumberland, George's uncle, would become regent. To forestall this, Newcastle introduced a bill in Parliament naming Augusta, dowager princess of Wales, as regent. Parliament passed the bill, and Cumberland's power declined. Without protection, Bedford was forced to resign as southern secretary on 14 June 1751.[70]

Newcastle's choice to succeed Bedford was Lord Holderness. Holderness, clearly Newcastle's man, was not a particularly strong administrator. Perhaps realizing this, Newcastle began to shift more responsibility for colonial affairs away from the southern secretary to Halifax, president of the Board of Trade. Halifax, like Newcastle, was an imperialist who believed the French should be driven from the North American mainland.[71]

Under Halifax's direction, the Board of Trade in 1752 tried to bring the colonies into the imperial system. The Board, to reduce provincial autonomy and the power of local assemblies, insisted all royal governors obtain permanent revenues, that there be suspending clauses in most acts passed by the legislatures so that acts could be approved by the ministry before they went into effect, and that governors adhere more closely to their instructions. In an attempt to further curtail assembly power, in 1753, Board of Trade member Charles Townshend proposed that royal officials be made financially independent of the assembly. The Townshend plan was not acted upon. Since the Board did not have the power to enforce its directives, its efforts were largely ineffective.[72]

To forestall the continued rise of the New York assembly, Halifax and Holderness acted on a report prepared by the Board of Trade for the Privy Council in 1751. They agreed that Clinton, grown increasingly ineffectual, had to be replaced. The governor was further hampered by poor health and decreasing interest in his New York governorship, which led him to request repeatedly that he be relieved of his post. In 1753, the ministry responded to Clinton's requests and appointed a successor, Sir Danvers Osborn. Osborn had been mentally depressed to the point of attempted suicide since the death of his wife some ten years earlier. He secured the New York appointment because of his connections in the ministry, his dead wife having been the sister of Board of Trade president Halifax. Osborn arrived in New York on 7 October 1753, and was sworn in on 10 October. Minutes before Osborn took the oath of office, Clinton reluctantly handed DeLancey the commission of lieutenant governor. The ceremony completed, Clinton retired to his country estate to wind up his affairs and wait for suitable transportation back to England.[73]

That night, the city celebrated the end of Clinton's regime with illumination, bonfires and "the consumption of Maderia; and every company rung with maledictions against the late commander in chief." The only person unaffected by the revelry was Sir Danvers Osborn, upon whose "Countenance sat a melancholy gloom."[74]

The next day, 11 October, Osborn convened a meeting of his council. In accordance with the Board of Trade's recommendations, Osborn's commission specifically stated that he was to secure permanent support from the New York assembly. William Livingston blamed DeLancey for this instruction, saying it was the Board of Trade's response to the "enormous power" wielded by DeLancey as chief justice and was "purposely calculated to render our future Governors independent of his [DeLancey's] influence over the assembly." Livingston exaggerated DeLancey's influence. In fact, all New York governors since 1683 had been instructed to obtain permanent support. Osborn had been similarly instructed. The governor realized the importance of financial independence, but he also realized the difficulties involved in dealing with the assembly. At the council meeting, with James DeLancey in attendance, Osborn "prayed their sentiments on the probability of obtaining a permanent support, according to his instructions. That the point was unattainable, they all delivered as their unanimous opinion. . . . Upon this, he turned himself about in apparent distress, uttered a deep sigh, and reclining his head against a window, in a desponding accent, said, 'What then am I come hither for?'"[75]

Early in the morning of 12 October 1753, Osborn was discovered dead by his own hand, "strangled in his Handkerchief" in the garden of the house where he was staying. James DeLancey took control of the government, much to the dismay of former Governor Clinton, who "not only heard himself execrated, and saw his enemy advanced and applauded, but was a witness to the ungrate[ful] desertions of some of those he had raised and obliged." Clinton sailed for home, sadder but richer, since his New York post had yielded to him £84,000 in profits. In England, Clinton was elected to Parliament, after paying £500 for the privilege and continued for years to solicit Newcastle for an increase in his naval pension from £1000 to £1200 a year.[76]

New York had not been well served by British administrators. The important and lucrative governorship of New York was all too often given to inept placemen who put their own interests above those of the monarch. Colonists recognized that "Government will never recover any Strength here, till it is in other hands, and in general will be loosing Ground as the Colonys increse, till other people are sent out to fill the most interesting Officers, than such as are fit for nothing at home." The result was a decline in the royal prerogative, which went hand-in-hand with declining respect.[77]

Then, too, Englishmen at home were preoccupied by European affairs. Although Halifax, as president of the Board of Trade, tried to tighten colonial administration, his efforts were largely ineffective because the board lacked the power to compel. He was not assisted by the ministry, whose responses to colonial problems were well meaning but slow, ineffective, and frequently nonexistent. While the ministry was aware of the growing economic importance of the colonies, it had not yet formulated a high-level, well-defined administrative plan, much less had time to implement such a plan. During Clinton's ten-year administration, the royal prerogative, as personified in the governor, had significantly declined, while the power of the assembly had increased. Clinton had been unable to stem the tide by the use of patronage[78] because he did not use his patronage powers wisely. Typical of his stupidity was the granting of a lifetime judicial commission to James DeLancey, thereby ensuring the latter's control of provincial politics. This power enabled DeLancey to advance provincial interests at the expense of metropolitan interests. As James DeLancey took the oath as acting governor, provincials wondered whether he would continue to advance the sway of the assembly now that he represented the royal prerogative.

5

Republicans in Principle, 1753–1757: The Administrations of James DeLancey (1753–1755, 1757–1760) and Sir Charles Hardy (1755–1757)

> Presbyterians by profession, and republicans in principle, being all together in friendship, in principle, in politics, and religion, they formed themselves into a triumvirate, and determined if possible, to pull down Church and State, to raise their own Government and religion upon its ruins, or to throw the whole province into anarchy and confusion.[1]

The factions that took form in New York at mid-eighteenth century were rudimentary political parties, although they lacked the formal structure of modern parties. These factions embraced philosophies that were similar to those of Whigs and Tories in England. By 1753, New York's factions focused on the province's two leading families: the DeLanceys and the Livingstons. The former embodied Tory principles of order imposed from above, while the latter reflected Whig views of popular government, with the people as the source of authority. As observed by Cadwallader Colden, because of "the different Political and Religious principles of the Inhabitants opposite parties have at all times and will exist in this Provce, which at different times have taken their denomination from some distinguished person or family which has appeared at their head."[2]

While much of the struggle between the two families was prompted by self-interest, as each tried to retain and enhance their power base, both the DeLanceys and the Livingstons were deeply committed to the principles they represented. The religious and philosophical ideals that separated the two families also shaped New York provincial politics until the Revolution. These principles later served as the foundation for the political parties that developed in America during the early national period. Perhaps the most persuasive arguments were offered by the Livingston faction whose chief polemicists, William Livingston, John Morin Scott, and William Smith, Jr., were particularly effective in popularizing Whig philosophy. In so doing, the trio defined the necessity of separating church and state and protecting freedom of the press. By 1757, William Livingston was the most persuasive propagandist and also the head of the Livingston faction. As such, Livingston took particular pleasure in attacking the rival faction and its leader, James DeLancey. In the resulting battle, the political philosophy of both the DeLanceys and the Livingstons was developed and popularized, while the constitutional principles that would lead Amerian colonists to independence were further defined.

The struggle for mastery of New York's internal politics by the DeLanceys and Livingstons were played against the backdrop of imperial concerns. New York was caught in the middle as France and England tried to extend their empires. New York's importance was recognized by the British ministry, which backed off from its intent to force the New York assembly to vote a permanent revenue. Colonial administration was in a state of flux. The ministry was aware that changes needed to be made, but unsure how and when to implement such changes.

The Livingstons and DeLanceys, along with all the colony's elite, were determined to resist change as they vied for political power. The rivalry between the DeLanceys and the Livingstons began in the late seventeenth century when the founding fathers of the dynasties, Huguenot refugee Stephen DeLancey and Scottish refugee Robert Livingston, vied for control of the fur trade. The two men differed ideologically, religiously, and economically. The Livingstons fled English imperial oppression while the DeLanceys were driven from their homes by the French crown and found a haven in an English colony. The alliance of the DeLanceys with the crown and of the Livingstons with local interests during the Revolution is perhaps not surprising in light of their families's histories.

Despite past or present allegiances, both families, throughout the colonial period, worked assiduously to reduce the royal prerogative in New York and to advance local privilege. The predominantly landowning Livingstons favored an imperialist philosophy, scorned by the largely mercantile DeLanceys. The DeLanceys carefully cultivated and exploited their high ranking English connections, unlike the imperialminded Livingstons who had no such connections and were not favored by the ministry. Both the favor shown to the DeLanceys and the lack of it exhibited to the Livingstons also goes far to explain why, during the Revolution, the former were loyalists and the latter patriots.

In the colonial period each family gathered into its fold like-minded adherents, usually grouped as landowners and merchants. Stephen DeLancey, Robert Livingston, and their descendants have been seen as the respective heads of these factions in New York. But the DeLanceys, like all major New York merchants, also had extensive landholdings, and the Livingstons were profitably engaged in trade. Members of the DeLancey and Livingston families did not become consistent leaders of their respective factions until mid-eighteenth century. Prior to that date, both families were politically active, but leadership of the factions was shared or usurped by other leading New York families, including the Morrises, the Alexanders, the Philipses, and the Coldens. Nor were the DeLanceys or Livingstons consistent in upholding the principles of the factions that would later bear their respective names. During Leisler's 1689 rebellion, for instance, Robert Livingston, founder of a Whig dynasty, was an ardent Anti-Leislerian, bitterly opposed to the Calvinist (Whig) Jacob Leisler.[3]

The differences between the Livingstons and DeLanceys were further defined by political and military events in the 1750s. For the remainder of the colonial period in New York, political fortunes were determined not so much by conflict between court and country—although this conflict continued to exist—but rather by competition between country factions and the Whig and Tory ideology each represented. The philosophical differences between the two factions emerged more clearly during James DeLancey's tenure as acting governor.

In 1753, as James DeLancey began his gubernatorial term, the Livingstons's primary goal was to regain the influence, power, and prestige they lost during Clinton's administration. To do so they had to weaken and discredit the DeLanceys. In order to function, the Livingstons needed a political base in the assembly, but James DeLancey controlled the assembly. The Livingtons had to reach the voters so that they could get Livingston candidates elected as representatives. They used the press to reach voters, and by so doing, further defined the differences between themselves and the DeLanceys.[4]

James DeLancey was faced with a difficult task after the 1753 suicide of New York governor Sir Danvers Osborn. As lieutenant governor, DeLancey was sworn to follow the letter of Osborn's royal instructions, which were now his instructions. These included an order to obtain a permanent revenue. DeLancey, as the country leader, had for years advised the assembly to resist paying either a long-term or permanent revenue. Only thus could the governor be kept subservient and responsive to the needs of the assembly and the people it represented. As William Livingston wondered, "Could the man, who but a day or two before had intrigued with the members how to elude that very instruction, preserve his gravity, while acting such a tragi-comical farce? . . . As his Majesty's representative, he was obliged to urge their compliance with seeming sincerity and warmth; but as James DeLancey, Esq. their old friend and best adviser, it was his real sentiment, that never ought they to submit."[5]

On the horns of an imperial dilemma, DeLancey on 31 October 1753, asked the assembly to vote a permanent revenue—and the assembly respectfully declined. DeLancey forwarded their objections to the Board of Trade and, obedient to his instructions, refused to accept a one-year revenue, consequently remaining unpaid.[6]

As DeLancey explained to the Board of Trade, when he urged compliance on the assembly, "The principal members frankly told me, I might dissolve them as often as I pleased, as long as they were chosen (which I hear most of them would be again if dissolved on that point) they would never give it up." The following December, as the threat of war with France grew more likely, DeLancey was desperately trying to get the assembly to vote money for military expenses. A new fort was needed on the Hudson above Albany, but the assembly refused to vote construction funds. Consequently, DeLancey personally bore the expense for the construction of the fort, although he had already "laid out since I came to this government fifteen hundred pounds above my own income, and have had no salary, owing to the Assembly's unwillingness to provide for the support of government in the manner prescribed by His Majesty's instructions." Despite DeLancey's dilemma, the assembly continued to insist they would "make no other than an annual provision." [7]

In dealing with the assembly as governor, DeLancey, now the representative of the royal prerogative, faced a quandary. DeLancey resolved it by shedding many of his country principles, just as did other provincial opposition leaders who found themselves in similar situations. As William Smith, Jr., noted, DeLancey's philosophy changed to the extent that he even established prerogative courts, which, he had previously opposed. Smith noted "that ascendency therefore which he had acquired as an independent demagogue, now began to abate, and his conduct, like other Governors, to be suspected, as meditating rather his own and the advancement of the interests of the Crown, than the security or the rights of the people."[8]

DeLancey, as an imperial governor, gave the Livingstons a well-defined target, and they employed the traditional methods used by the New York opposition to make his tenure of office uncomfortable and unproductive. They attacked the lieutenant governor in print and sought to belittle him through the use of satire.

Although used by both court and country factions, satire was most effective as an opposition weapon. Its primary purpose was to reduce the influence of opponents while advancing that of like-minded associates. Satire was a weapon that particularly appealed to American colonists, as it did to country Tories and country Whigs in England. Each believed themselves excluded from power, economically imposed upon, and politically coerced by the imperial government. Colonists in particular saw their position as analogous to that of English Puritans in the 1640s and Whigs in the 1680s. In the eighteenth century, American colonists eagerly grasped the natural rights philosophy that the Puritans and Whigs used in the seventeenth century to advance parliamentary power while rejecting or limiting royal rule and royalty.[9]

It was this Calvinist-based, Puritan-Whig philosophy that informed the thinking of DeLancey's chief opponents, the Livingston faction. With the revolutionary settlement of 1689, Whig philosophy, with its commitment to a limited monarchy and representative government, became the basis of the British government. In America, as in England, Whig philosophy was reenforced by Enlightenment thought. The Enlightenment was late in reaching America, but, by mid-eighteenth century, it exercised a powerful affect on educated colonists who responded enthusiastically to the philosophes' optimism and realism. Like European philosophes, American Whigs were aware that man was all too often ruled by emotion rather than reason. The educated Whig elite believed it their duty to encourage the common man to overcome his nature and achieve perfection through the use of reason. American philosophes acknowledged the achievement of such perfection was only possible through self-discipline and education.[10]

Education was sadly lacking among New York's newly rich merchants, landowners, shopowners, artisans, and farmers who often acquired money faster than they did the social graces. This lack of finesse disgusted the more refined members of the elite, themselves only a generation or two removed from poverty and boorishness. In 1752, to remedy the lack of culture in the newly rich, William Livingston, William Smith, Sr. and Jr., and John Morin Scott, "form'd a Design of publishing weekly Essays . . . upon the plan of The Spectator, for correcting the taste and improving the Minds of our fellow Citizens."[11]

Livington, Scott, and Smith, Jr., all of whom would exert a strong influence on the course of New York politics, had met and become friends in the 1740s when they were serving legal apprenticeships with William Smith, Sr. The younger men, all educated at Yale, were con-

nected with the Livingston family by birth, marriage, or business affil-
iation. All three became attorneys, all three eventually joined the
Presbyterian Church, all three shared a similar Whig political ideology, and all three disliked and distrusted James DeLancey and his faction. Termed the "triumvirate" by contemporaries, the trio remained
friends until Livingston moved to New Jersey in 1772. By that time
Smith and Livingston had grown more conservative, while Scott was
more liberal. Loyalist Thomas Jones noted of them that they were all
"presbyterians by profession, and republicans in principle, being all
together in friendship, in principle, in politics, and religion, they
formed themselves into a triumvirate, and determined if possible, to
pull down Church and State, to raise their own Government and religion upon its ruins, or to throw the whole province into anarchy and
confusion."[12]

Anarchy was not the intent of the leader of the triumvirate, William
Livingston, youngest son of second manor lord, Philip Livingston.
Strongly influenced by his Calvinist upbringing, reinforced by his education at Yale, William Livingston disliked religious or political hysteria or excesses. Trained against his will as an attorney, Livingston
would much rather have pursued a career as an artist. Forbidden to
acquire formal artistic training, Livingston continued to sketch and
draw throughout his life. His creativity also found outlet in his literary work. A superb and effective essayist, he also wrote poetry of a
remarkedly indifferent character, although much admired at the time.
Like most members of the elite, he was strongly influenced by British
opposition writers, particularly Milton, Harrington, Trenchard, and
Gordon.[13]

Livingston was himself deeply religious. Like most eighteenth-century Western intellectuals, he saw no incompatibility between religion
and reason. His commitment to reason led him to be tolerant of all
Protestant sects, although this toleration did not extend to Roman
Catholics or Jews. Like Whigs in England, Livingston believed the
preservation of English liberties was directly tied to the continued
dominance of the Protestant church with its strong Calvinist under-
pinnings. But within that Protestant church, Livingston recognized
there was room for diversity, as he indicated in a 1744 letter to a former classmate, James Sprout. Livingston noted his sorrow on hearing
"you are so divided among yourselves with respect to religion. . . .
Every man has a right to think for himself, as he shall answer for himself, and it is unreasonable for me to be angry with any one for being
of different principles . . . truth is comprised in a small compass . . .
we shall not be so positive and dogmatical, to set up for infallibility,
and anathematize those of contrary opinion."[14]

William Livingston, ca. 1748–52, by John Wollaston, Collection of the Fraunces Tavern Museum, Gift of John A. Devereaux and Walter A. Devereaux. The youngest son of second manor lord Philip, he remained an outstanding polemicist throughout his long life. As governor of New Jersey during and after the American Revolution, Livingston was particularly effective in attacking Tories and rallying public support for the war and the new government.

Livingston's tolerance was apparently not always obvious to his contemporaries. Thomas Jones accurately assessed Livingston as "a sensible, cunning, shrewd fellow . . . satirical and abusive in his writings; violent in his conversation." Jones was perhaps less accurate when he termed Livingston "a bigot in religion; wanton, cruel, and unfeeling in his temper; ungenerous in his sentiments; uncouth in his manners," but few of Livingston's political enemies (or friends) could doubt he was on occasion "impatient of contradiction; and of a savage persecuting spirit."[15]

One of William Livingston's first opportunities to make his opinions known in New York came with the publication of the newspaper the triumvirate called the *Independent Reflector.* The elder Smith withdrew early from the paper, but the younger Smith, Livingston, and Scott proceeded with their plan. The *Independent Reflector* differed from other colonial newspapers in that the entire issue was devoted to a single and timely topic. In the first several issues, Livingston, Smith, and Scott were concerned with such social and political problems as unfair taxation, exorbitant profits, unlicensed physicians, and low standards in the legal profession. They also warned of the dangers of political parties or factions and decried the English practice of transporting convicted felons to the colonies.[16]

It was a religious issue that changed the Addisonian mission of the *Reflector* with the 22 March 1753 issue, while Clinton was still in office. After this date, the essays were more concerned with political and religious issues than with social problems. The immediate cause of the change was the plan to establish an Anglican-backed college in New York, which would be partially supported with public money. The trio feared the influence of a church-controlled college on the province, and opposed the college because it was backed by the DeLancey dominated assembly, although DeLancey himself was not particularly in favor of the college.[17]

The triumvirate recognized the ties between the English government and the Anglican state church, which was its ideological buttress. They rightly viewed the establishment of an Anglican college as an attempt to bolster the royal prerogative in New York. They feared that assembly support of a religiously oriented college was the first step to fully establishing the Church of England in New York, at that time established only in New York's four lower counties.[18]

Between 1746 and 1754, the assembly on five separate occasions passed legislation to raise money for the college through the sale of lottery tickets. Another act was passed to set aside an annual sum of £500 from the excise tax for the support of the college. Voters raised no objection to the use of public money for the projected King's College (later Columbia), until Livingston, Smith, and Scott in the pages of the *Independent Reflector* began to inform them of the potential threat such a venture presented to both their freedom of worship and their pocketbooks.[19]

Livingston renewed his attack in the *Independent Reflector* after Trinity Church offered part of its land as the site for the proposed college. Livingston expressed his concern over what he preceived as the Anglican Church's bid to fully establish that church in New York. Livingston readily acknowledged that a college was badly needed. He and his friends were part of a handful of college graduates in New York County. Livingston shared with the philosophes a belief in the public utility of education, but feared that a college under the control of a religious sect might discriminate among applicants or try to indoctrinate students. Livingston instead wanted a strictly nondenominational college under the control of the legislature. He advanced his plan in the *Reflector*, where he reminded New Yorkers of the importance of religious toleration for Protestant nonconformists. He noted that "Next to the most patriot KING that ever grac'd a Throne, and the wisest LAWS that ever bless'd a People, an equal TOLERATION of Conscience, is justly deem'd the Basis of the public Liberty of this Country. . . . Let us, therefore, strive to have the College founded on an ample, a generous, an universal Plan. Let not the Seat of Literature, the Abode of the Muses, and the Nurse of Science; be transform'd into a Cloister of Bigots, an Habitation of Superstition, a Nursery of ghastly Tyranny, a School of rabbinical Jargon. The Legislature alone should have the Direction of so important an Establishment."[20]

Part of Livingston's concern over King's College sprang from the fact that, if the Church of England was fully established in New York, Anglicans, who were not the majority of the population, would dominate the colony's political and economic life in New York as members of the established church did in England and Ireland, to the cost of nonconformists like himself. Livingston feared that with an established church, nonconformists would be prohibited from attending universities and holding public or military office, just as they were in England and Ireland. Such exclusion would severely diminish the Livingston family's prestige and importance.[21]

Livingston's attacks were partially modeled on Trenchard and Gordon, who, in the 1720s, wrote similar tirades against the established church in the *Independent Whig*. The common religious outlook of the *Independent Reflector* and the *Independent Whig* was noted by Anglican minister Samuel Johnson. In June 1753, Johnson informed DeLancey's former tutor, the archbishop of Canterbury, that "Among other pernicious books the Independent Whig grows much in vogue, and a notable set of Young gentlemen of figure in New York, have of late set up for writers in that way, in a weekly paper called the *Independent Reflector.* Several worthy gentlemen of the Church in that province have of late embarked in a design of erecting a College as a Seminary of the Church, though with a free and generous toleration for other denominations. Upon which these Reflectors have been indefatigable in their paper, and by all possible means both public and private, endeavouring to spirit up the people against us, and to wrest it out of the Church's hands, and make it a sort of free-thinking or latitudinarian Seminary."[22]

It was indeed Livingston's intent to establish the college independently of church control. While stirring up animosity against the college, Livingston also used the pages of the *Reflector* to indoctrinate New Yorkers in Whig political philosophy. In an essay on the "Origins of Civil Government," he called for a wise ruler, stating that "no one has a Right to govern, but he that is wise." In later issues he voiced his belief that the English system of a mixed government, that is, democracy, aristocracy, and monarchy, was immeasureably superior to any other political system yet devised. He also attacked the Tory doctrine of passive obedience. Throughout his life, Livingston was an activist who advocated the Calvinist belief that the people retained the right to remove a bad ruler because the monarch's authority was "originally derived from the People." Only thus could liberty and happiness, the true ends of government, be preserved. An evil or corrupt ruler "becomes the dreadful Instrument of universal Evil." Government, he continued, comes from the "free Consent of Mankind." Informed people, aware of their duties as well as their privileges, have a right to oppose any evil ruler who threatens or injures "our Persons, Liberty or Property."[23]

Livingston believed both political and religious freedom were necessary to preserve a subject's happiness. To protect these freedoms, Livingston favored a complete separation of church and state, as he made clear in a two-part essay published on 2 and 9 August 1753, "The Absurdity of the civil Magistrate's interfering in Matters of Religion." Civil power, he said, "hath no Jurisdiction over the Sentiments or Opinions of the Subject," unless those opinions lead to "Actions prejudicial to the Community," and even "then it is not the Opinion, but the Action that is the Object of Punishment." Livingston continued that nothing is more "destructive of the natural Rights of Mankind, than the Interposition of the secular Arm in Matters purely religious."[24]

Among the liberties of particular concern to Livingston, and one that he addressed in the pages of the *Independent Reflector*, was that of the press, which disseminated essential information. Freedom of the press was directly linked to religious freedom since the press was the means by which dissenting religious views were disseminated among the people. The accepted eighteenth-century belief was that a nation could only endure and prosper if it was politically and religiously homogeneous. Hence the advocacy of any dissenting religion was deemed dangerous to the state.[25]

Political dissent was seen as equally dangerous as religious dissent by the state. Libertarians, undeterred by the state's desire to preserve the status quo, believed it was necessary to criticize a bad government in the press, but treasonous to criticize a good one. This can be seen from the essay the Triumvirate contributed to the *Independent Reflector* in 30 August 1753, "Of the Use, Abuse and Liberty of the Press." In this piece, they noted that a printer was obliged to publish "what is not prejudicial to the general Good." Divergent opinions could be published as long as they were "conducive of general Utility." A printer should not publish "any Thing injurious to his Country." Printing this material was "criminal,—It is high Treason against the State. The Usual Alarm rung in such Cases, the common Cry of an Attack upon the LIBERTY OF THE PRESS, is groundless and trifling. The Press neither has, nor can have such a Liberty, and whenever it is assumed, the Printer should be punished."[26]

Despite their conservative interpretation of freedom of the press, the triumvirate continued to attack Lieutenant Governor DeLancey. They believed that their criticism of the DeLancey faction was justified because they saw DeLancey and his family as evil and inept. Thus, to attack the chief justice and his followers—or any corrupt governor—was in the best interests of the country and clearly not "injurious." Hence it was not deserving of punishment.[27]

In 1753, most of the Livingstons's criticism of government centered on a political issue that was religious in origin. DeLancey did not particularly favor the college, but, as a member of the Church of England, he had no choice but to offer it his support. The college issue proved an Achilles heel for DeLancey in that it defined and gave cohesiveness to a broad anti-anglican opposition in the predominantly nonconformist colony. Livingston and other noncomformists were well aware that linking the lieutenant governor with the college controversy was a good way to discredit, embarrass, and weaken DeLancey.[28]

The *Reflector* was effective in creating interest in the college controversy. The public listened and moved from apathy to open and vociferous concern until the college issue became the chief topic of conversation in New York. The impact of the *Reflector* continued until November 1753, when, only a month after taking office, James DeLancey applied pressure on the *Reflector's* printer, James Parker.

who was also the offical government printer. In November of 1753, Parker, fearing not only the loss of government business, but the possibility of being prosecuted for seditious libel, suspended publication of the *Reflector*. Undaunted (and undiscovered, since all essays were published anonymously), Livingston, Scott, and Smith continued their attacks on the college in a series of public letters, petitions, addresses, and public meetings. Livingston reissued all fifty-two of the *Reflector* essays in a single volume. In the preface he stated that the college affair was "one of the most important matters that ever fell under the consideration of our Legislature." Livingston believed that the basic essential right of representative government was at stake "should the government of the College be surrendered to any tribe of bigots, God knows how long they [the legislature] will retain their rights and immunities."[29]

On 16 May 1754, the college trustees presented a draft charter to the full board with a petition to the governor for incorporation in accordance with the terms of Trinity's offer. Livingston was infuriated and in a futile gesture submitted to the board "Twenty Unanswerable Reasons" why the college should not be incorporated. In this report Livingston refuted the Anglican interpretation that the 1693 Ministry Act established the Church of England in New York. Livingston and other noncomformists claimed the act did nothing more than specify that only Protestant ministers be named in New York's four lower counties. Livingston also pointed out that using state funds for religion was equivalent to defrauding the public. The great majority of New Yorkers did not belong to the Church of England, but all would be required to pay for the support of the college. Livingston later presented this report to the Assembly where it raised "a great ferment in the House" and caused that body to delay consideration of the funding issue.[30]

In June 1754, DeLancey and Livingston put aside the college issue temporarily when the Albany Congress was called. This congress would again bring the two to loggerheads. The issue was the French threat in Canada, with the Livingstons urging, and the DeLanceys opposing, a full-scale effort to drive out the French. Such action was necessary for Britain's preservation, since Livingston feared France's "design" was "to subject all Europe to her despotic sway."[31]

William Livingston and his brother-in-law, William Alexander, James Alexander's son, combined public and family business by serving as assembly-appointed commissioners to settle the New York-Massachusetts border dispute. As commissioners, they were in Albany at the time the Congress was opened on 18 June 1754, by New York lieutenant governor James DeLancey, with twenty-three representatives from New York, New Jersey, Massachusetts, Connecticut, Rhode

Island, Maryland, and Pennsylvania. The congress was called "as well to treat with the Six Nations, as to concert a scheme for a general union of the British colonies."[32]

Such a union was desirable for military defense because the ongoing war between France and England had broken out again in the Ohio Valley. The cause of the conflict in that area was a dispute over dominion. Despite claims of French ownership, Virginia granted eight hundred thousand acres west of Virginia and North Carolina to the Loyal Company. A royal charter was issued to the Ohio Company for an additional five hundred thousand acres on the upper Ohio River.[33]

In 1753, the governor of Canada, Marquis Duquesne de Menneville, ordered the building of a fort at the fork of French Creek and the Allegheny River. Virginia Lieutenant Governor Robert Dinwiddie sent George Washington to the Ohio Valley with a party of militia to lodge a protest with the French for building on land claimed by Virginia. A world war began after Washington "assassinated" a French ambassador and then admitted doing so when he surrendered to the French on 3 July 1754.[34]

Witnessing Washington's disastrous capitulation, the Ohio Valley Indians were reluctant to ally with the English. The Iroquois controlled many of the tribes in the Ohio Valley and were themselves an effective fighting force. The Six Nations, although proclaiming a policy of neutrality in the long struggle between France and England, generally allied with the English. Their continued allegiance was doubtful since the Iroquois were angered by English movement west onto territory they believed under their control, the unethical practices of white fur traders, and fraudulent land deals. Their continued goodwill was crucial to English survival in the New World. Hence the Albany Convention was of major importance to the fate of the England's North American colonies.[35]

During the Congress, the Native Americans expressed their outrage at past injustices. One that most rankled was Philip Livingston's purchase of the Canajoharie tract, which the Indians correctly claimed was sold by three drunken Mohawks. Nor was the token payment for the tract ever made.[36]

William Livingston and his brother–in–law, William Alexander, as heirs of Philip Livingston, were asked to attend the meeting to appease the Indians over the Canajoharie Patent. When they learned of the Indian anger over the Canajoharie tract, they "informed the Board, that their Father was one among other Patentees of the land mentioned, that they were interested 1/8 each of them in their Father's Right; the circumstances of this title they had made no enquiry into, but were ready to make any resignation, which either justice or the publick service required." None of the other partners or their heirs made similar offers, so the gesture was meaningless, but along with other promises and numerous presents, it temporarily mollified the Iroquois.[37]

Also considered at the Albany Convention was a plan of union to provide for the mutual protection of the colonies against the French. The plan, offered by Benjamin Franklin with amendments by Thomas Hutchinson, was heartily favored by William Livingston, who reported that it was "approved at the time by every member of the Congress, except Mr. DeLancey," who, despite his new commitment to imperial interests, continued to favor a policy of coexistence with the French. To Livingston, such a union was vital to the survival of England's colonies. He believed that "without a general constitution for warlike operations, we can neither plan nor execute. We have a common interest, and must have a common council: *one head* and *one purse.*"[38]

Despite DeLancey's lack of enthusiam, the Congress on 10 July 1754, approved the plan. If the king and the individual colonies agreed, all the colonies, with the exception of Georgia and Nova Scotia, were to be united under one president general to be named and paid by the Crown. Sharing responsibility with the president general would be a council, elected by each provincial assembly. The council was to have legislative power, subject to the approval of the president general and the crown. The president and council were to have authority over western land and Indian relations. The plan, twenty years ahead of its time, was rejected by every colonial assembly, including New York's and rejected by the ministry as well.[39]

The ministry's objection to a colonial union could have been foreseen. Such an idea had already been proposed and discarded. Newcastle was now prime minister, named first lord of the treasury following the March 1754 death of his brother, Henry Pelham. After the news of Washington's disastrous defeat at Fort Necessity reached London, Newcastle was determined that "the colonies must not be abandon'd." Realizing that English colonial manpower far outnumbered that of the French in the New World, the ministry at first urged the colonies to defend themselves. The lack of unity among the colonies was the greatest drawback to self-defense. To overcome this, a colonial union was discussed by the ministry, but Newcastle and other ministers feared the "ill consequences to be apprehended from uniting too closely the northern colonies with each other; an independency upon this country being to be apprehended from such a union." The union plans were set aside, and so, when word of the Albany Plan reached London in October 1754, the ministry's reaction was unfavorable.[40]

New York's assembly, under DeLancey's direction, also disapproved of the plan, much to the Livingstons's disgust. William Livingston was further outraged when King's College opened in the vestry room of Trinity Church. Despite its opening, Livingston believed that DeLancey would not sign the charter for the college. DeLancey, Livingston said, was "a thorough politician, [who] cares no further about the granting or rejecting the petition, than as the one or the other doth best promote his political interest." New York's voters hated the college. Livingston had succeeded in rousing franchised and unfranchised alike, and all were vociferous in their complaints. Always responsive to New York's voting population, DeLancey was aware that "several members in our present session of Assembly are come with petitions from their constituents to them, against granting any further fund for the college till its constitution and government be settled by an act of legislation."[41]

Livingston was mistaken in believing DeLancey would not sign the charter. On 31 October 1754, Lieutenant Governor DeLancey succumbed to Anglican pressure and approved the charter, leading Livingston to observe that DeLancey "appears to be as great a master of the art of tergiversation as the most consumate politician. It is no longer ago than last Thursday night that I conversed with him on the topic," Livingston continued, "and though he then talked like a man who had a double part to act, yet it appeared to me that he intended I should understand him as being resolved not to grant the petition."[42]

Despite the signed charter, many New Yorkers believed that financial support from the assembly could be forestalled. It was to achieve this end and to further the plan of colonial union that Livingston penned the first of a series of essays beginning on 25 November 1754, called the "Watch Tower," which appeared in the *New York Mercury* for a year. This column would "be a kind of medium between the Reflector and the Spectators." It was to be chiefly concerned with politics, with its purpose "to open the eyes of this province respecting many measures, the concealment of which is the only thing that keeps them from being defeated." Livingston also believed that, even though DeLancey had signed the charter for King's College, there was still hope a nondenominational college could be established. A bill for that purpose was submitted to the assembly by Livingston's brother, manor lord Robert Livingston.[43]

Despite Livingston's polemics, the assembly in November 1756, voted funds for King's College. The assembly acted partly because the new governor, Sir Charles Hardy, who arrived in New York on 2 September 1755, favored the college and moreover allied with DeLancey. Although Livingston considered it a defeat, it was at least a partial victory because the assembly decided that only "one-half of these moneys be given to the College, and the other half to the Corporation of the City of New York for a Pest-house."[44]

While Livingston fought the Anglican Church, the assembly continued its fight against the royal prerogative. Hardy, like Osborn before him, was also instructed by the home government to get a permanent revenue. He told the assembly that they must "consider of a proper Law to be passed, for settling a permanent Revenue upon a solid Foundation." The assembly responded "we have no permanent Funds on which to establish such a Revenue." They declined to consider further "a Measure so directly opposite to the Sentiments of almost every Individual of the Colony." Faced with the assembly's refusal and aware of the political turmoil in New York, compounded by the pressures of the war with French Canada, the Board of Trade in 1756 capitulated and abandoned its campaign to discipline the New York assembly. The board recommended to the King-in-Council that the New York revenue not be made an issue. Hardy was pleased to inform the assembly that the king had given him permission "to assent to such temporary Bills as the Assembly shall from Time to Time frame and pass for the Support of Government" in New York. Such support meant that he and Lieutenant Governor DeLancey were paid their long overdue salaries.[45]

The ministry's concession to the New York assembly was not extended to other colonies where the French threat was not as severe. In 1757, when faced with a defiant and contentious assembly in Jamaica, the House of Commons, acting at the urging of the Board of Trade, censured that body and resolved "that the Colonys have no Constitution, but that the mode of Government in each of them depends upon the good pleasure of the King, as expressed in his Commission, and Instructions to this Governor." The threat to the constitutional liberties of all colonies was clear. The Jamaica assembly (and by implication all other provincial assemblies) had no inherent right to exist.[46]

New York's existence was also threatened by the French. The defense of the colony was the chief concern of its governor, if not of its chief justice. On being relieved of his gubernatorial duties at Hardy's arrival, DeLancey resumed his position of chief justice even though he did not have a new commission. Resuming this office, "the main prop of his power," meant that DeLancey's influence in New York was virtually undiminished. Through his influence on the assembly, DeLancey was able to obstruct adequate financial aid for the French and Indian War. DeLancey's stance separated further his family from the Livingstons, who continued to favor an aggressive war effort to drive the French from the continent. Familial as well as imperial interests would be best served for the Livingstons by the expulsion of the French. The Livingstons wanted to make New York, rather than Montreal, the center of the North American fur trade.

Standing to benefit was William Livingston's brother, Peter Van Brugh Livingston, who had invested heavily in a trading company that hoped to secure a monopoly on the fur trade in western New York. Members of the Livingston family were also personally friendly with Massachusetts Governor William Shirley, whose plan to conduct the French and Indian War differed from that of the DeLancey favorite, William Johnson.[47]

Shirley's friendship with the Livingstons would have been sufficient to cause James DeLancey to hate him. DeLancey was already antagnostic to Shirley because of the latter's erstwhile support of Governor Clinton. DeLancey's enmity was increased when Shirley hired Peter Van Brugh Livingston and Lewis Morris as his military purchasing agents instead of Oliver DeLancey. Shirley also chose William Livingston's friend and brother-in-law, William Alexander, as his secretary. After securing the necessary supplies from Livingston and Morris, Shirley proceeded to enlist troops for his foray against Oswego and Niagara. To raise public support for these campaigns, William Livingston wrote anti-French essays in a newspaper, *The Instructor*, which he published from March to May 1755.[48]

Defense of the colonies was also prominent in the minds of the prime minister. Newcastle's plan was to confine the war to that continent and avoid a European war. The duke at first favored a small British military presence in North America, but quickly realized that his early expectation that the Americans would defend themselves was unrealistic. British troops would have to be sent in large numbers because Americans would not fight under British officers. Britons recognized that "the Americans have an insuperable aversion to enlisting in regular Corps under Officers they do not know, as has been experienced in almost every attempt that was ever made from the Carthagena expedition down to this year."[49]

British military response to the French, whether in America or Europe, lagged because of ministerial changes. On taking office as prime minister, Newcastle, a peer, needed a leader in Commons. Two men were suitable: Henry Fox, who was secretary at war, and William Pitt, paymaster. Newcastle did not favor either, but finally appointed Fox as secretary of state. Pitt, irritated at being slighted, began to attack the duke's conduct of the war. Pitt particularly criticized Newcastle's decision to concentrate the war in North America since Newcastle's primary purpose in attempting to avoid a European war was to forestall an attack on George II's principality of Hanover. Pitt's stand against the expensive protection of the king's principality was a reflection of popular opinion. Britons resented paying taxes for Hanover's defense.[50]

William Pitt, first earl of Chatham, n.d., after Richard Brompton, National Portrait Gallery, London. A strong parliamentarian, Pitt was an effective leader during the French and Indian War. Although a supporter of colonial privilege, Chatham had no sympathy for the defiant New York assembly in 1767.

Despite Pitt's criticism, Newcastle proceeded with his plan to rid the Ohio Valley of French imperialism. Fox, a hawk, favored sending a large military force to America. In this, Fox agreed with the duke of Cumberland, who was now captain general of British forces. At cabinet meetings, Cumberland and Fox prevailed over Newcastle's insistence on sending a small force. Cumberland named another crony as commander of the American expedition: his junior officer in suppressing the '45 Jacobite rebellion, Major General Edward Braddock.[51]

Following his arrival in Virginia, Braddock set out for Fort Duquesne with 1,400 soldiers from Irish regiments. He was accompanied by Colonel George Washington, at the head of 450 colonial troops. In early June 1755, Braddock was at Fort Cumberland and ordered a road cut from there to the Monongahela River and Fort Duquesne. On 10 June, the army began its exceedingly slow progress, in some cases only three miles a day, toward Fort Duquesne. On 9 July 1755 Braddock and part of his army were suddenly and without warning attacked by the French and their Indian allies. The panic-stricken soldiers were slaughtered in the Battle of the Wilderness. Washington had several horses shot from under him, but was unharmed. Braddock refused to let his men abandon line formation, the only type of fighting for which they had been trained. The general was badly wounded during the attack. The English retreated, "leaving behind them all the artillery, provisions, ammunition, baggage, military chest, together with the general's cabinet, containing his instructions and other papers of consequence." They carried their wounded general with them. Braddock died four days later and was buried in an unmarked grave. But the war chest with some £25,000, the arms and ammunition, and the cannon were all seized by the French and later used against the English.[52]

William Shirley was appointed to succeed Braddock as commander–in–chief, but the only American victory won that year was that fought by William Johnson at Lake George on 8 September 1755. By January 1756, the war had spread to Europe with the formation of a new pact between England and Prussia who now fought against Austria and France. In May 1756, Pitt had further cause to attack Newcastle when the French took Minorca after British Admiral John Byng called off a naval engagement with the French. Discontent rose further in England when 8,000 Hessian mercenaries were introduced in England. The mercenaries were needed because the large bodies of troops sent to America had left England virtually defenseless against the French attack that Newcastle believed inevitable. The English hated the presence of foreign soldiers and showed it by staging violent demonstrations. The demonstratons convinced the ministry that they were in more danger from irate Englishmen than from foreign invasion, and in December 1756 the Hessians were ordered back to Germany.[53]

Newcastle, as head of the ministry, was the target for most of the criticism for England's failures. The duke complained bitterly that "Mr. Pitt laid Everything that was blamed upon me." Pitt went so far as to accuse Newcastle of deliberately losing Minorca "as a Design in order to justifie a bad Peace." Pitt was not alone in criticizing the duke. Criticism of Newcastle and the ministry, written by the country opposition, appeared in the press, sparking additional "Riots & Tumults . . . all over the Kingdom." Soon, "Every Daily Paper" was "full of the most Infamous & Seditious Lies, & Attacks upon the Proceedings of Parliament," Newcastle complained. The duke urged the Lord Chancellor "to prosecute those Daily Papers and Libels," since "the not doing it must Shew Fear in the Government & will be interpreted to be a Consciousness of Guilt."[54]

Typical of the press criticism was an anonymous letter signed Britannicus, which appeared in a London newspaper. The author demanded an enquiry "into the Conduct of Those who have been entrusted with the Management of publick Affairs" and noted that "our Rights, Lives, and Liberties, [are] now brought into a very precarious Situation by such unconstitutional Measures as introducing a Foreign Army, and neglecting our own Militia." The author went on to demand an investigation "into the Cause of our losing Minorca in so shameful a Manner, and in obtaining Justice on all Those who shall be found guilty of so foul a Crime."[55]

The public wanted a scapegoat, and Newcastle was willing to supply one, particularly after his carriage was attacked by an angry mob. Byng was brought back to England to face charges of cowardice. Realizing that only the death penalty would satisfy the angry populace, the ministry decided to court martial, rather than impeach Byng, since a person could not be "capitally convicted on an Impeachment, and . . . no lesser Punishment will Satisfie The minds of the People."[56]

Defeats in Europe and rioting in England made victory in America essential. The ministry took steps to achieve that end. To reward and encourage provincial military leaders, in February 1756, William Johnson was awarded a baronetcy and the order of the garter for his Lake George victory, given £5,000, and commissioned superintendent of Indian affairs. The rewarding of the DeLancey favorite Johnson was not lost on the Livingstons. Their own family had been stripped of offices and denied official contact with the Indians because of James DeLancey's influence on George Clinton. Now a DeLancey ally was knighted and granted a potentially profitable post that the Livingstons believed should have been theirs. In addition, the ministry heeded DeLancey's criticism of William Shirley and replaced him as commander–in-chief with John Campbell, earl of Loudoun. Loudoun, who like Braddock had served under Cumberland in the '45 Jacobite rebellion, was a man of little military reputation. In fact he was notorious for losing most of his men in battle. He arrived in New York on 22 July 1756, two months after England formally declared war on France. Loudoun brought with him a small pet dog, on whom, according to Livingston, he lavished an undue amount of care and attention. This led Livingston to question whether a *"general, who is extremely attentive to a lap-dog, [can] ever Conquer Canada?"* The answer, sadly for England, was in the negative.[57]

Livingston believed that Britain's losses in America and elsewhere were due to declining morals among Britons. British "Corruption, Venality, Luxury, profaneness, Immorality, Debauchery, and Voluptuousness" lay at the root of their military failure. Lack of "public virtue" in England was likely to bring "a thorough Purgation" of America by God, now that "public Avarice stalks triumphant . . . [with] the whole Constitution degenerated into the mere Cabal of a few Grandees."[58]

Examples of British neglect were close at hand for Livingston, with Loudoun preferring the relative comforts of New York City to the dangers of the frontier. While Loudoun idled away his time in the summer of 1756, forts Oswego and George in New York were taken by French troops under the command of General Louis Joseph, marquis de Montcalm. The fur trading Livingston family was affected by the French victory at Fort Oswego, when the French diverted the fur trade from New York. William Livingston observed that the loss of Oswego meant that "our fur trade, which has long been the principal object of the national attention, and the support of our frontier city of Albany, is at an end." Even worse for Livingston and other imperialists was the possible loss of territory, for "the French can now . . . secure the inland country, and confine us to the very brinks of the ocean." Moreover, the English defeats had swayed many Iroquois to the French. As Livingston noted, "The six nations are more wavering than ever; and should they no longer think it expedient to preserve their neutrality, the whole continent must inevitably become a field of blood."[59]

Loudoun, who had allied with DeLancey, reported the losses to Newcastle and placed full blame on William Shirley. The news of the American defeats caused Pitt to renew his attacks on Newcastle and Fox, in Commons. In England, public sentiment against the ministry remained high, leading Fox in October 1756, to resign his post as secretary, complaining that Newcastle "did not give Him Power enough in The House of Commons." The absence of a leader in Commons left Newcastle unprotected against Pitt's continued and increasingly virulent attacks. Newcastle, unwilling to face Pitt's criticism, resigned his post on 11 November 1756. The head of the ministry was now William Pitt. Newcastle would gladly have come back into the ministry, but Pitt refused to serve with the duke.[60]

Newcastle's post of first lord of the treasury went to the duke of Devonshire, who was technically the prime minister. Pitt was secretary of state, but in practice headed the administration and formed policy. Pitt's tenure was brief because he lost the support of Commons. On becoming head of the ministry, Pitt, a country politician, backed court policies, much as had DeLancey in New York. Pitt thus lost the support of the country politicians in Commons. He also lost popularity by urging clemency for Admiral Byng. The general feeling in the country was that Byng should be punished and he was hanged in March 1757. Pitt also lost the support of George II and the duke of Cumberland. At Cumberland's urging, the king discharged Pitt in April 1757.[61]

Political expediency and personal ambition dictated that Pitt and Newcastle, bitter enemies, would be reconciled. In June 1757, they agreed to take office together, despite Pitt's earlier claim that he "absolutely refused to come into the Administration" while Newcastle "had a Share in it." Newcastle resumed his post as first lord of the treasury with Pitt as northern secretary of state and prime minister. The two men brought together the formerly warring factions of court and country. Pitt regained the support of country members of Parliament, while Newcastle had the continued loyalty of the old court Whigs.[62]

It was Pitt who took over the primary direction of the war both in Europe and North America. His command was made possible after Cumberland's military ineptitude forced him to resign. Sent by his father to protect Hanover, the duke instead, on 8 September 1757, surrendered to the French without firing a shot, leaving Hanover for the enemy. He returned to England secretly to face the furious king and resigned as captain general of British forces.[63]

Cumberland's resignation and the alliance of court and country factions under Newcastle and Pitt brought a political stability to England that was not possible in New York. In fact, discord increased in June 1757 when James DeLancey again became acting governor after Charles Hardy returned to active duty in the Royal Navy. Continuing attacks by Loudoun and the DeLanceys led to the recall of William Shirley to England to face charges of neglect. Shirley was accompanied by William Alexander. Alexander's intent was to assist Shirley in his defense and to secure for himself the title of earl of Stirling. On board ship, Alexander carried with him William Livingston's history of the French and Indian War, *Review of the Military Operations in North America*, dated 20 September 1756. The essay, published anonymously in London in 1757, was a brilliant, but heavily biased, account of the war to that point. The essay also surveyed recent New York history.[64]

In the *Review*, Livingston was highly critical of Lieutenant Governor DeLancey, whom he termed that "monopolizer of power." Livingston accused DeLancey of deception, dishonesty, and even, in the case of Sir Danvers Osborn, murder by implying that James DeLancey deliberately made negative comments to the unstable Osborn about the impossibility of obtaining a permanent revenue. These comments had the desired effect of driving the despairing Osborn to suicide and cleared the way for DeLancey to assume command of the province. DeLancey, Livingston said, was responsible for the unrest in the province, and "by blowing up the coals of contention, did the province more injury, than he will be ever able to repair." DeLancey's behavior, Livingston charged, was influenced solely by self–interest.[65]

Livingston also questioned DeLancey's political alliances. Recalling DeLancey's break with Clinton, Livingston said, "He will only stand by a governor while at his devotion, and standing fair with the people." Livingston also charged that DeLancey showed no loyalty to his own adherents. But Livingston had to acknowledge the breadth of DeLancey's popular appeal, although he ascribed it to evil means. DeLancey, Livingston said, ruled "By hints, by threats and blandishments, by emissaries, by dark insinuations and private cabals, he is able to render any measure hateful or popular; to put down, or raise up, whom, when, and what he pleases."[66]

While highly critical of DeLancey, Livingston's *Review* was lavish in its praise of Governor Shirley. Indeed, Livingston's defense of Shirley's military conduct may have been instrumental in reducing the criticism directed at Shirley in London and averting an outcome similar to that faced by Admiral Byng. Shirley regained the favor of the duke of Newcastle and secured the governorship of Bermuda.[67]

The *Review* raised a sensation when published in London and was widely read there. It made an even greater sensation when the first copies found their way to New York in the summer of 1757. The books were immediately seized and destroyed by DeLancey's agents. DeLancey's efforts at confiscation probably enhanced the appeal of and interest in Livingston's polemic. Enough copies escaped detection to circulate widely among interested New Yorkers. Livingston, fearing prosecution for seditious libel, cautiously acknowledged authorship to only one person, his close friend Noah Welles, but did

First Baron Jeffrey Amherst, ca. 1780, by Thomas Gainsborough, National Portrait Gallery, London. An effective, if ruthless, commander, Amherst is best remembered in America not only for his victory over the French, but also for his inhumane suppression of defiant Indians during Pontiac's Rebellion.

not publicly admit to writing the essay until several years later. As he told Welles, he well knew the publication was "uncontestably Lybellous" and hence, he, the author, did "not choose to appear, unless he should happen to find his Ears extremely incommoddious." Livingston's reference was to the Star Chamber prosecution of Puritan William Prynne who wrote *Histriomastix*, a criticism of the royal court of Charles I. Prynne was fined £5,000, pilloried, had his ears cut off, and was imprisoned for life in the Tower of London.[68]

Livingston was undoubtedly pleased to retain his ears and help Shirley to salvage his career. This, however, had not been his primary intention in writing the *Review*, which was above all an imperialist plea for British dominance in North America through the destruction of the French in Canada. This end became a real possibility with William Pitt in charge of the war effort. Pitt's appointment was welcomed by New Yorkers, including William Livingston, who exclaimed, "What a surprising alteration in affairs is one honest minister capable of producing." The alteration was quickly apparent in North America when Pitt recalled Loudoun and successively named Major General James Abercromby and Major General Jeffrey Amherst as commanders-in-chief.[69]

By 1757, William Livingston's use of the press in fighting the DeLanceys had indeed proved effective for his faction. With satire, Livingston had blocked full assembly support for King's College and in the process exposed James DeLancey's political and personal weaknesses. The college issue and the French and Indian War also permitted Livingston to define and delineate the philosophical differences between his party and that of the DeLanceys. In so doing, Livingston expressed and popularized the idea of the separation of church and state and the necessity to maintain a free press to check potential tyranny.

Such a definition of essential freedoms led elite New Yorkers to resist what they deemed tyrannical efforts by the home government to control the assembly. The war with France caused Halifax and the Board of Trade to temporarily abandon plans to bring the assembly into line. Military necessity dictated that once again New York would be left to its own devices. The elite, whether members of the Livingston or DeLancey factions, took advantage of the ministry's wartime distraction to further refine their political expertise. With an imperial battle raging for the control of North America, the ministry realized its efforts to impose metropolitan authority on the colony would have to wait for peace.

6

Property Reputation and Extensive Connections, 1758–1765: The Administrations of Cadwallader Colden (1760–1761, 1763–1765) and Robert Monckton (1761–1763)

The Livingston Family during the last War had the chief Influence in the Assembly and their Power founded in Property Reputation and extensive Connections and stood firm till the Year 1765.[1]

By 1758, in an age of very personal politics, there were two distinct political factions in New York that took their names from the province's two leading families. Differing political philosophies, based on religious principles, effectively divided New Yorkers into separate camps through the eighteenth century. Both Livingstons and DeLanceys shifted in and out of these ideological groupings, just as they did out of court and country factions. By midcentury, the Livingstons were committed to presbyterian (i.e., Whig) ideology, while the DeLanceys were just as deeply committed to episcopal (i.e., Tory) principles.

By the late 1750s, William Livingston was acknowledged by his contemporaries as "the leader of the Livingston party in New-York." Thoroughly committed to presbyterian-Whig principles, Livingston's philosophy was evident in his writings. Through the press, he attacked chief justice and lieutenant governor James DeLancey and his faction. Livingston's literary efforts were well received by New Yorkers of all classes. The DeLanceys were weakened, and the Livingstons began a decade-long dominance of New York politics, influencing enough

New York voters so that they swept assembly elections in 1758 and 1761. As William Smith, Jr., aptly observed, "The Livingston Family during the last War [the French and Indian War] had the chief Influence in the Assembly and their Power founded in Property Reputation and extensive Connections and stood firm till the Year 1765."[2]

To achieve his family's dominance, William Livington used the press to reach the lower and middling sort. He was quite successful in obtaining their acquiescence and support because he swayed the lower and middling sort with "popular arguments" that stressed natural rights and representative government. Livingston believed these classes should participate in the political process but in a subordinate position. Eventually and ironically, Whig rhetoric led the lower classes to demand, and then to exercise, a more active political role.[3]

The lower and middling sort were particularly responsive to the republican rhetoric Livingston used to attack the DeLanceys. Livingston's attacks on the DeLanceys and a succession of governors who allied with the DeLanceys, along with the rhetoric of other opposition writers, heightened the long-standing climate of dissent within the colony. This unstable and volatile climate was further exacerbated by the contentiousness of the assembly. That body, self-imbued with republican-commonwealth principles, had grown politically sophisticated during the course of the eighteenth century. The assembly, which usually served as the seat of the opposition party, continuously challenged royal authority through its control over finances. Its efforts to undermine the authority of royal governors were often successful, as privilege and prerogative clashed. This brought a redistribution of power within the colony as governors lost control of some key functions to the increasingly experienced assemblies. The office of the executive, occupied by a series of inept placemen, who were under constant attack by opposition leaders and forced into numerous compromises with the assembly, suffered a loss of prestige, although, theoretically at least, not a loss of power.

Both governors and lieutenant governors made determined attempts to regain lost influence. As had always been the case, governors needed more than intelligence and determination to govern well; they also needed a forceful and conciliatory personality. Any governor who lacked these attributes left the door open for the further erosion of executive power. Colonial oligarchs, themselves grown politically astute, continued to seek out the favor of still powerful royal governors to form court factions but, much like James DeLancey, increasingly used their own knowledge of local affairs or their contacts with British officials to further local interests at the expense of the royal prerogative.[4]

Britain's interests prospered by 1758. The string of disastrous defeats that Britain had suffered during the early days of the French and Indian War ended on 26 July 1758. On that date, and for the second time in little more than a decade, five hundred colonial soldiers and two hundred English regulars led by Major General Jeffrey Amherst and Brigadier General James Wolfe captured Louisbourg. Wolfe went on to defeat the French at Quebec on 12 and 13 September 1759. There, during a battle on the Plains of Abraham, he and the French general Montcalm were both killed.[5]

The DeLanceys's consistent refusal to take a strong prowar stance ultimately affected their hegemony in the assembly. In 1758, that body was dissolved, and new elections brought the first tangible signs of a backlash against the DeLanceys. The backlash was prompted by the popular discontent stirred by William Livingston in the 1750s over James DeLancey's failure to fully support the war effort and by the controversy over the King's College charter. New York voters, particularly the large percentage who did not belong to the Church of England, proved responsive to Livingston's rhetoric. Fear that the Church of England would be fully established and that they would have to pay for its support led middling and lower class voters to elect Livingston candidates. Fifteen new members were chosen in this election, four of whom were named Livingston—including William Livingston, who represented the manor. Thus began the Livingstons's decade-long dominance of New York politics under the leadership of William Livingston. Livingston served only two years in the assembly, but, while there, promoted war measures and in 1759 served on a committee with his brother Philip to plan frontier defenses.[6]

Although by 1758 the Livingstons had achieved an assembly majority, James DeLancey as lieutenant governor retained his influence over politics. This influence ended only with DeLancey's sudden death on 30 July 1760. DeLancey was succeeded as head of government by the senior councilman, Cadwallader Colden, an old enemy of both the DeLanceys and the Livingstons. Even after James DeLancey's death, his family retained a good measure of influence. During Colden's tenure, soon confirmed by his commission as lieutenant governor, James DeLancey's son, James, Jr., educated at Eton and Cambridge, and other members or allies of the DeLancey family dominated the council, while the Livingstons dominated the assembly. Both families despised Colden, who was now sworn to protect the royal prerogative from assaults by local privilege. Colden found this difficult to do because, unlike most previous governors, he found himself without a court party.[7]

Colden, although lieutenant governor intermittently until 1776, never fully controlled the province. His personality was at fault. As he acknowledged to James Alexander, to be successful, a governor had to join "with the more general interests of the country," that is both merchants and landowners, upper and lower classes. This union eluded Colden, as it had Clinton before him. During Colden's terms, rather than the governor and the opposition vying for control of assembly elections, it was usually the two opposition country factions of the Livingstons and DeLanceys who fought for supremacy, with the governor exercising little influence over the courses of the elections. The result for Colden were troubled and rudderless administrations.[8]

The animosity directed at Colden by the Livingstons and the DeLanceys was reciprocated by Colden, who particularly detested the lawyers in both families. As Colden noted, New York's attorneys were troublemakers who were "insolent & petulant, & at the same time as well skilled in all the chicanerie of the Law, as perhaps are to be found any where else." Trained in the law, attorneys naturally gravitated to politics. Lawyers, according to Colden, "proposed nothing less than to obtain the direction of all the measures of Government, by making themselves absolutely necessary to every Governor in assisting him while he complied with their measures & by distressing him when he did otherwise." To enhance their own power, "every method was taken to agrandise the power of the Assembly . . . & to lessen the influence of the Governor." Attorneys, Colden concluded, well realized "their power is greatly strengthened by inlarging the powers of the popular side of government & by depreciating the powers of the Crown."[9]

Colden particularly resented the influence that James DeLancey, who held a good behavior, or lifelong, commission, had wielded as chief justice, with "more Power than a Governor." Colden was determined to reduce this influence in future chief justices and informed the Board of Trade that, in line with his instructions, he would appoint the next chief justice and all other judges to serve at the king's pleasure, that is, subject to dismissal. Colden extended this policy to all the colony's judges following the 26 October 1760, death of George II, when all royal officials, including judges, resigned with the expectation they would be reappointed. Colden reappointed the judges, but at pleasure. Consequently, many refused their diminished commissions, and the courts remained closed.[10]

New York lawyers were appalled by Colden's stance on tenure since it threatened provincial autonomy and challenged judges's independence from the executive. The DeLanceys and the Livingstons were temporarily united in their opposition to Colden. They based their opposition on English precedent. The issue over judicial tenure had been fought and won by Whigs in England where judges had been independent of the crown since the 1688 Glorious Revolution and the 1701 Act of Settlement. Provincials, whether Whigs or Tories, agreed that all judges should be free from crown control. Both Livingstons and DeLanceys resisted any reassertion of the royal prerogative that would reduce colonial privileges.[11]

The continued reduction of these privileges was very much the intent of George III's ministers. The king's ascension brought the end of the Newcastle-Pitt ministry since George III disliked any ministers who had served his grandfather. The new king's favorite was the earl of Bute, on whom he showered offices and posts. Bute disagreed with Newcastle's and Pitt's conduct of the ongoing war. Newcastle had wanted to limit military action to Germany, while Pitt had wanted to expand the war effort so that Great Britain could achieve all of its aims. Bute favored peace. His opportunity to undermine Newcastle and Pitt came after he was named secretary of state by the king and began to usurp Newcastle's control of patronage. Bute next openly challenged Pitt's war policy. Pitt resigned in October 1761, and Newcastle was forced from office in May 1762 with Bute becoming first minister. The change in ministry also brought an end to the political stability that had characterized British politics since 1757. In the 1760s, inexperienced ministries quickly fell to be replaced by equally inexperienced politicians. The results for colonial administration were devastating.[12]

The New York assembly was also dissolved following the death of George II. Elections for a new assembly were held in March 1761. William Livingston's legislative career ended when he gave up his assembly seat to his nephew, although he retained his leadership of the family faction. The Livingstons acquired even more representatives than they had in the 1758 elections. With a strong majority in the house, William Livingston, along with William Smith, Jr., and John Morin Scott, continued as public spokesman for the Livingston family, using the press to both inform voters and mold public opinion.[13]

When the assembly met in May of 1761, it promptly passed an act, drafted by William Smith, Jr., that provided that supreme court judges should hold lifelong commissions during good behavior rather than at pleasure. The act was approved by the DeLancey Council but not by Cadwallader Colden, who sent it on to the Board of Trade with the observation that "there is no fixed Sallary to the judges. It is from year to year on the pleasure of the assembly & while they are thus dependent on the people for their subsistence this Bill may be highly prejudicial to the just rights of the Crown." Colden later noted that he "told several of the Members that if they would make proper provision

George III, ca. 1767, by the Studio of A. Ramsay, National Portrait Gallery, London. Vilified by historians for losing the American colonies, George III was a victim of inexperienced ministers. The king's attempts to assert the royal prerogative in the colonies were ill-timed.

for the Judges Sallaries, to have the same continuance with their Commissions, it would be a great inducement to give my assent." In other words, lifelong tenure should carry with it lifelong support, and judges should be as independent of the assembly as the assembly wanted them to be independent of the crown.[14]

The judicial issue came up again at the next sitting of the Livingston assembly, and another bill was passed to grant lifelong tenure to judges. The bill was again approved by the DeLancey council. The legislature again refused to consider Colden's compromise offer to grant a perpetual salary in exchange for a perpetual commission.[15]

In an effort to end the impasse, Colden sought to appease the dominant Livingston faction by offering the chief justiceship to one of their number, William Smith, Sr., but Smith refused to accept the post. In fact, no suitable New York attorney could be found who was willing to risk the scorn of his colleagues by accepting the appointment. The Bostonian, Benjamin Prat, was named by the Board of Trade and accepted the post with many misgivings.[16]

Prat arrived in New York in October 1761 to find he was socially and professionally ostracized by local lawyers, who well realized that local privilege suffered with this crown appointment. Even worse, the Livingston assembly refused to vote Prat or any other judge a salary. Most New York judges refused to serve with diminished commissions, hence the courts were closed, and "many prisoners had been long confined, at New York, without a trial, by reason of scruples of the Puisne Judges, & that all those Judges had absolutely determined to resign unless their commissions were renewed *During Good Behavior.*" Long-term imprisonment of their peers raised animosity among rank-and-file New Yorkers, who became highly receptive to antiadministration, antiprerogative propaganda published by both Livingstons and DeLanceys. The assembly kept the pressure up on the governor by indicating they would pay Prat less than DeLancey had received—and that sum only if his commission was tenured. Prat despaired of ever receiving money from the assembly and asked the Board of Trade if he could take his salary from New York's quit rents. The Board so recommended to the King-in-Council.[17]

Prat recognized that the issue with the assembly was not just over salary or tenure, but rather that he was an outsider, not a native New Yorker, and one who had been appointed arbitrarily by the Crown to flaunt prerogative power. As he told Board of Trade secretary Thomas Pownall, "at Bottom the Point in View is to compel the Crown to appoint one of themselves Ch: Justice." He was correct in his observation. New York's large landowners were disturbed by the tenure of judges issue because it threatened their security. Not only did limited tenure reduce the prestige of the office, but patronage powers had been usurped from royal governors and assumed directly by the British government. If landowners had no influence on governors in the appointment of judges and if the Board of Trade continued to appoint foreigners to the office, New York's elite could not be sure of obtaining favorable decisions as they had in the past when one of their own sat on the bench. The Livingstons hated the influence a James DeLancey wielded from the bench, but it was still preferable to having an outsider as chief justice.[18]

William Livingston and other members of the elite identified the culprit in the tenure of judges dispute as the lieutenant governor, even though the order for a limited commission and Prat's appointment came from London. Hence Livingston and other opposition writers began an anti-Colden propaganda campaign aimed at the general public. Most prominent among these writers was Livingston, who started a newspaper, *The American Chronicle*, with which to attack the lieutenant governor. Most of Livingston's anonymous essays appeared in a column called "From the Lion's Mouth." Typical of their flavor was the tirade that appeared in the *Chronicle's* first issue on 20 March 1762, calling attention to a nameless ruler (obviously Colden) who was "intoxicated with the Grandeur of his Elevation—proud, self-conceited, and all-sufficient—impatient of Advice, ignorant of the Constitution . . . crafty and rapacious—without Honor—void of Truth." New Yorkers had little difficulty in identifying the target as Colden; Colden had little difficulty in guessing that the author was Livingston.[19]

Livingston's attacks increased Colden's stubborness and hatred. The governor and Livingston, Smith, and Scott were ideologically opposed on most issues, with the exceptions that all were imperialists who favored territorial expansion and that all but Scott distrusted democracy, which they equated with anarchy. Colden particularly hated the Whiggish republican principles of Livingston, Scott, and Smith, whom he believed had been unduly influenced by their youthful exposure to New England Calvinist thought while at Yale. On 4 April 1762, he told the Board of Trade that "for some years past, three Popular Lawyers, educated in Connecticut, who have strongly imbibed the Independent principles of that Country, have zealously endeavoured to propagate their principles both in Religious and civil matters & for that end make use of every artifice they can invent to calumniate the administration in every Exercise of the Prerogative."[20]

In the past, Colden had done more than his share of challenging the royal prerogative. Although by the 1760s Colden embraced episcopal or Tory philosophy in imperial politics, he earlier had been an ardent Whig. As a young man, Colden exhibited his Whiggism as an opponent of the autocratic administrations of Montgomery and Cosby. Despite his youthful defiance, Colden's Whiggish principles evaporated when his status changed, although much of his later conservatism was probably the product of advanced age. Like James DeLancey and Lewis Morris, once Cadwallader Colden was lieutenant governor, he had no choice but to set aside his commonwealth principles. He was not alone. English-born Whigs reacted similarly when appointed colonial governors.[21]

The change in attitude was demanded by the nature of colonial administration, recognized as being arbitrary. Although colonists respected British government in the abstract, virtually none liked British colonial administration, which they equated with tyranny. Colden had entertained similar Whiggish sentiments toward imperial administration in his youth, but, as lieutenant governor, he had no choice but to conform to political realities. He no longer believed, as did the three young lawyers, that all authority was derived from the people. Such philosophy was not applicable in or compatible with provincial administration.

Despite misgivings about royal rule, the Livingstons were realists who recognized the source of power. Hence the faction quickly allied with Robert Monckton, the new imperial governor, after his October 1761 arrival. Perhaps at the urging of the Livingston faction, now the court party, Monckton demanded that Colden pay him half of the salary and perquisites he had received as lieutenant governor from the time of Monckton's appointment to his actual arrival in the colony. The demand was similar to that made by Cosby to Van Dam. A disgruntled Colden refused, as had Van Dam.[22]

The alliance of the Livingstons to the executive gives some indication of the extensive power wielded by the governor. For a member of the New York elite, an alliance with the chief executive was still the most direct route to favor. The executive's authority was further reinforced when the home government backed Colden's stance on good behavior commissions, although the assembly continued to refuse to pay Benjamin Prat's salary. As Prat observed, the fundamental issue was "that the Crown should not Send them a Chief Justice nor the govr commission any ... *During his Majestys Pleasure*." In May 1762, a discouraged Prat beat a hasty retreat back to Boston, where he mercifully died before he had to return to New York. But the royal prerogative, backed by an effective provincial court party, triumphed in this contest. Monckton, soon after his arrival, named Daniel Horsmanden as chief justice, and William Smith, Sr., David Jones, and Robert R. Livingston as lesser judges on the supreme court. All accepted their posts during pleasure. The appointment of locals, not "foreigners", as judges gave provincials some comfort and perhaps even a partial victory in their struggle against the royal prerogative.[23]

The Livingstons, like the DeLanceys, were quite willing to support the royal prerogative if it benefitted their immediate interests. Now allied with the governor as the court party, the Livingston faction accepted the fact of diminished judicial commissions without question. Monckton was the beneficiary. With the willing assistance of the dominant Livingston party in the assembly, the governor enjoyed a relatively tranquil administration. The triumvirate contributed to the governor's peace of mind by suspending their attacks on New York officials during Monckton's tenure. They resumed their brutal propaganda only after June 1763 when Monckton returned to England. Colden again governed New York, and the Livingstons became an active opposition party.[24]

In that same year, Bute resigned from office and was replaced as prime minister by George Grenville. English hegemony in North America followed the signing of the Treaty of Paris on 10 February 1763. By the terms of the treaty England gained Nova Scotia, Cape Breton, and Canada and all territory east of the Mississippi River except New Orleans. Great Britain dominated North America. The goals of provincial imperialists such as the Livingstons had been fully realized.

The end of the war and the defeat of the French also brought the end of Iroquois influence in North America. Without a French enemy in Canada, the Six Nations were no longer strategically important. With peace, English population movement to the Ohio Valley and beyond accelerated onto land previously claimed by the French and still claimed by the Iroquois. The Seneca, the westernmost Iroquois tribe, and other Ohio Valley tribes, opposed this westward movement in a frontier war named for the Ottawa chief, Pontiac. Colonial legislatures, including the Livingston-dominated assembly in New York, contributed neither men nor money for imperial defense. Great Britain bore the expense of putting down the rebellion. With colonial indifference and the continued possibility of frontier war, the British reluctantly came to the conclusion that it was necessary to keep a large body of regular troops in America. The Americans did not agree, and the long-standing fear of standing armies was revived. With the French gone from Canada, it seemed logical to Americans that the British soldiers were there not only to prevent frontier wars but also, and perhaps primarily, to keep colonists in their place. Local privilege, it seemed, would be reduced by armed might.[25]

Grenville, saddled with an enormous war debt of £132,716,000, continuing Indian warfare on the American frontier, and provincial

John Stuart, third earl of Bute, 1773, by Sir Joshua Reynolds, National Portrait Gallery, London. Bute, who served as a father figure to the young George III, was the first in a series of inept ministers who implemented policies that ultimately drove the North American colonies to independence.

assemblies that refused to raise troops or money for their own defense, initiated an investigation into colonial affairs.[26] At Grenville's request, a bureaucrat in the office of the southern secretary of state prepared an elaborate plan for the reorganization of the colonial system. To reduce the continual challenges to the royal prerogative the author concluded, as had Robert Hunter several decades before, that "The interposition of Parliament is absolutely necessary . . . because no other Authority than that of the British Parliament will be regarded by the Colonys, or be able to awe them into acquiescence."[27]

The author also acknowledged that royal governors, although they "be Kings Representatives," had "neither his Power, nor Regalia." They were further weakened, and hence weakened the royal prerogative, because they were "dependent on the good-will of the assemblys for their subsistence." The assembly's inevitable response to a point of contention with the governor was "to curtail or withhold their Salary." Consequently "the point in contest has perhaps been given up by the Governor" whenever a dispute arose. The author recommended that all civil officers be made independent of the assembly by paying their salaries from quit rents or from parliamentary imposed taxes payable to the Treasury. Grenville considered, but ultimately rejected, this plan to establish a civil list.[28]

The writer also suggested that a suspending clause for a twelve- to eighteen-month period be included in certain bills passed by colonial legislatures. The bureaucrat also noted the need for unified control of Indian affairs and the fur trade. He observed that the present system, whereby each colony had different and often contradictory Indian policies, led to discord and warfare.[29]

The author believed it was necessary to keep British troops in America because of the continued danger of attack by the French and Spanish and also because of "an Internal Enemy," that is the Indians, who gave colonists the "apprehension of being Massacred." While Grenville rejected the idea of directly taxing colonists to pay royal officials, he and most other Britons agreed that a military presence was necessary and that provincials should pay for protection. Grenville believed that at least part of the estimated cost of £224,904 for sustaining some ten to twenty thousand troops in America should "be obtained from ye Colonies . . . by a single act of Parliament."[30]

Grenville, in 1763, took steps to achieve the goals set forth by the bureaucrat. The first step was a royal proclamation that forbade settlement west of the crest of the Appalachians, a measure that could concentrate English colonists on the eastern seaboard and leave Indians and the fur trade in peace. Grenville also took control of the fur trade and Indian affairs away from the individual colonial assemblies.

All Indian affairs would in the future be handled by crown-appointed officials, thereby effectively reducing provincial autonomy and the role of local legislatures.[31]

The royal proclamation raised alarm in colonies with extensive western land claims, but had no immediate effect in New York, where the colony was distracted by a local, legal issue, which again pitted prerogative and privilege. The immediate cause of the renewed conflict between the Livingstons and Colden was an interpretation of law and involved a case in which William Livingston, John Morin Scott, and William Smith, Jr., participated as attorneys. Contention sprang from a suit filed by Thomas Forsey for assault and battery against Waddel Cunningham in the summer of 1763. Scott represented Forsey, and William Livingston, William Smith, Jr., and James Duane represented Cunningham. In his civil suit, Forsey was awarded damages of £1500. Cunningham understandably objected to the award and asked his attorneys to file for an appeal. Contrary to precedent, Cunningham insisted that the facts of the case be reviewed by the appellate. British practice—and the practice in New York—dictated that civil suits could be heard by the appeals court, which consisted of the governor and council, only in cases of error. Smith, Livingston, and Duane explained this to their client and, when he persisted, refused to continue to represent him. Cunningham, with new attorneys, filed the appeal.[32]

Colden, as chief appellate judge, wanted to hear the Cunningham appeal. Before agreeing to hear the case, he first asked the advice of Chief Justice Daniel Horsmanden, Attorney General John Tabor Kempe, and his own council. The latter body, which sat as a court, advised the lieutenant governor that the "Appeal could not be recieved." Colden stormed at them in "the most evident Partiality & Rage, and fell upon the Council and the Judges charging them with indecency, Want of Respect to the Kings Authority and with unwarantable Freedoms." The Supreme Court and attorney general concurred with the council, but Colden insisted on hearing the appeal. He based his decision on an omission. In 1753, Osborn's instructions stated clearly that he was forbidden from hearing appeals in cases of error. This phrase was omitted from Colden's instructions, and he interpreted this as permission to do so.[33]

Colden's decision to review the facts of the case led the Livingstons and the DeLanceys to charge Colden with attempting to dispense with trial by jury. William Livingston led the attack. He based his argument on the fact that jury decisions that could be overturned at the whim of a higher court were meaningless. Livingston's charge against Colden was repeated publicly by DeLancey ally, Chief Justice Horsmanden, who turned over to the triumvirate the speech he made in a

19 November 1764, council meeting against granting the appeal. William Livingston paid for the publication of the speech in pamphlet form, while John Morin Scott wrote what Colden termed "an inflammatory preface." On hearing of its publication, Colden sent his son to get a copy from the printer, but learned that "all the copies are delivered to John Morin Scott." Scott, at the lieutenant governor's request, gave Colden six copies the next day. Colden was outraged that Horsmanden had personally given his copy of the speech to the triumvirate for publication. The speech, as well as other papers relating to the case, was published in the *New York Gazette* beginning 3 January 1765 embarrassing Colden and weakening the royal prerogative.[34]

The majority of New York's population had little interest in whether or not Cunningham paid the fine or whether Colden's interpretation of the law was right. Livingston realized that, to gain the support of the middling and lower sorts against Colden, he must convince them that the lieutenant governor's stance threatened them directly. He accomplished this by emphasizing the danger Colden's position posed to the right of trial by jury. Livingston was so successful in raising indignation and bringing the case to the attention of the public that the appeal became momentarily the chief subject of conversation among indignant New Yorkers. In fact, the lower classes showed some signs of taking the protest into their own hands. The possibility of undirected crowd action alarmed William Smith, Jr., who commented to the absent Monckton, "I do not remember any Subject that has so much ingaged the public Attention—People in general think their all at Stake—I wish their Heat may not transport them into Improper Steps."[35]

In an effort to calm public outrage and settle the appeal controversy, Colden asked the King-in-Council to rule on the case. To sustain interest in New York while the case was considered in London, William Livingston, on 28 February 1765, began a new series of essays by "The Sentinel" in the *New York Gazette*. Livingston was the primary author although undoubtedly Scott and Smith also made contributions. In the essays, William Livingston called the Cunningham appeal "the most momentous affair that ever engaged our attention." Livingston warned that the legal system Colden wanted to introduce would endanger trial by jury. "From such a system, the *Star Chamber* would be a redemption," he concluded.[36]

Colden realized that Livingston's Sentinel essays were published with the "design to prejudice me with the people personally." The paper, Colden noted, was "filled with the vilest and most abusive invectives which malice could invent, in order to render the Lieut Gov odious to the people." He rightly suspected "that these scurrilous abu sive and malicious papers were wrote by two or three distinguished Lawyers in the City." The triumvirate's intent, said Colden, was to fill "with Treason the minds of the People . . . to sow dissension and create animosities between Great Britain and the Colonies." Despite the provocation, Colden decided he would not respond to the charges in the "licencious abusive weekly printed paper."[37]

Livingston's motivation in attacking Colden was based on his concern to preserve the legal system, but this was only partly the reason for his rhetoric. While the possible surrender of the basic right of trial by jury was a valid concern for all New Yorkers, Livingston, his family, and other landowners were equally intent on preserving a system that favored them by permitting landlords to exploit their tenants. The colony was run by the large landowners, and the system was designed to perpetuate and preserve their wealth and status. Large landowners, as Colden reported, comprised the topmost rank of New York society. The second rank were people like William Livingston. Usually younger sons or married to landowners' daughters, they often gravitated to the law. The interests of lawyers were practically indistinguishable from those of landlords, Colden noted, since "the Gentlemen of the Law, both the Judges and the principal Practitioners at the Bar are either, Owners, Heirs or strongly connected in family Interest with the Proprietors."[38]

The extent of the control exercised by the landowners and their extensive families was as evident in politics as it was in the judiciary. Landowner strength was particularly reflected in the composition of the assembly, where one-third of the seats were controlled by the great landowners. During the course of the eighteenth century, at least fifty-two out of seventy seats were held by men related to the manor lords. Three of the great manors, including Livingston, elected their own representatives, this privilege assured "in their Grants, . . . so that the Proprietors are become hereditary Members of that House." The landlords' dominant role ensured they had "sufficient influence to be perpetually elected for those Counties." As Colden noted, "The General Assembly then of this Province, Consists of the owners of these extravagant Grants, the Merchants of New York, the principal of them strongly connected with the owners of these great Tracts by Family Interest."[39]

It was this political and judicial control, or the excessive local privilege it represented, that Colden tried to shake in *Forsey v. Cunningham*, meeting bitter opposition from Livingston, Smith, Scott, and other attorneys. Colden charged that, because of close familial relationships between landlords and lawyers, the rank and file of New Yorkers had no chance of securing redress or even of receiving a sympathetic hearing in a court of law. The elite did not control the appellate, particularly those cases referred to the King-in-Council. Hence there was no similar assurance of a favorable verdict in a higher court. In cases where the lower and middling sort filed an appeal, prerogative power might show mercy to those convicted and sentenced by the elite. Such was the case in New York following the kangaroo court trials of blacks in 1712 when Governor Hunter recommended mercy for several of those convicted. Hunter's recommendations were confirmed by the Crown, whose actions contrasted sharply with the hysterical and vindictive justice dispensed by New York oligarchs. For these reasons, Colden said, the elite feared appeals because "They know what must be the consequence in suits depending between them and other the Kings Tenants, or the consequence of Information of Intrusion, which may be justly brought against them etc. in case the merits of the Cause be brought before the King & Council."[40]

The prolandlord, proelite stance of Livingston, Scott, and Smith placed them in direct opposition to their own professed liberal and ethical beliefs. Landlords, including William Livingston's grandfather, father, and brother, acquired Indian land illegally and exploited their tenants and farm laborers. Livingston was sensitive to wrongdoing by others and in print repeatedly attacked malfeasance in office. His self-appointed role, Livingston said, was that of public watchdog, continually on the alert for "public Vice . . . [and] the Actions of Rogues, especially dignified Rogues. . . . Prostitution in Office, shall be the Mark of keen and everlasting Resentment . . . public Mismanagement he will attack at all Hazards." Livingston also recognized social inequities and often championed the cause of the poor, the friendless, and the underprivileged. While sympathetic of the powerless and critical of corruption, particularly if practiced by a DeLancey, Livingston was blind to exploitation or wrongdoing by members of his own family.[41]

Such tunnel vision was shared by the DeLanceys. Virtually the only issue on which the DeLanceys and Livingstons agreed without dissension was that they wanted the system that gave them wealth and status to endure. Control of the courts ensured this dominion. Colden was partially correct in stating that the real issue in *Forsey v. Cunningham* was that landlords and large merchants did not want favorable jury decisions regarding their land or tenants or other interests overturned by higher courts. Lower-class New Yorkers may not have understood the legal nuances of Livingston's argument, but they did understand Livingston's claim that Colden threatened their basic right to trial by jury. Livingston's arguments convinced them the governor was a threat to that right. Consequently strong feeling among New York's lower classes arose against the lieutenant governor.[42]

The elite wanted Colden replaced. Livingston and other oligarchs realized their best chance to achieve this end was to keep popular sentiment high against Colden. Their expectation was that, once word of unrest reached England, Colden would be removed from office. The elite were even more convinced of the necessity of replacing the lieutenant governor when Colden appeared determined to conform with the Board of Trade's 13 July 1764, order to inform the Board "of the true State of the Grants which have been made of Lands within the Province." The order represented another attempt by the ministry to tighten colonial administration. The Board wanted specific information on land grants and quit rents dating "from the first Establishment of the Colony, specifying the names of the Grantees, the time when each Grant was made, the Quantity of Acres, and the Quit Rent."[43]

An investigation of quit rents was a disturbing prospect. New Yorkers were notoriously slow in paying their relatively modest rent of 2s. 6d. per one hundred developed acres and, by 1768, were £19,000 in arrears. But the threat of an investigation of grants was truly appalling. The elite in New York and other colonies had already seen the fruits of previous investigations. In William Livingston's case, Sir William Johnson's insistence that the Canajoharie Patent was invalid forced Livingston and other heirs in 1761 to sell their shares to George (Ury) Klock, perhaps the most unscrupulous of New York's unscrupulous land dealers. William Livington was aware that the land was obtained illegally from the Mohawks by his father, but insisted that the Canajoharie Patent was valid. So convinced was he of the legitimacy of the patent that Livingston served as Klock's counsel in 1763 when Klock was prosecuted for ejecting settlers with Indian titles from the Canajoharie tract. The case was thrown out of court.[44]

Despite his actions on Klock's behalf, Livingston deplored the land-grabbing methods of Europeans and was sympathetic to Native Americans. In 1785, for instance, he spoke against "depriving them [Indians] by fraud of, or expelling them by force from those lands which the almighty had given them by prior occupancy." He opposed "the spirit of settling other people's lands without paying for them." Despite this conviction, Livingston steadfastly believed that the Canajoharie Patent was legal and his past ownership of it ethical. William Livingston believed this despite the fact that the Canajoharie tract included the tribe's village and planting ground and was bought from drunken Mohawks who did not have the authority to sell. Livingston never forgave Johnson for questioning its validity. As late as 1787, Livingston told his son William, Jr., that he should not have any dealings with Johnson's son since "Sir William Johnson by means of his connection with the Delancey family was ever an enemy to mine; & has wronged me particularly out of a fine tract of Land in the Mohawk country," that is, the Canajoharie Patent. Titles to the rest of Livingston's property were equally as questionable as the Canajoharie. Neither he nor any other New York landowner could afford to have land grants investigated and risk invalidation.[45]

Philip Livingston's unscrupulous behavior in obtaining the Canajoharie Patent was by no means unusual. Elites realized that local privilege could be most successfully attacked by the loss of property. Hence they would brook no threat to their holdings. Their intent was to increase these holdings at any cost. All large landowners in New York, including that champion of Indian rights, Sir William Johnson, were equally guilty of deception and dishonesty in their Indian land dealings. While Johnson protested the Livingstons's illegal title to Canajoharie, Johnson himself secured a royal patent of ninety-two thousand acres for Canajoharie with the conivance of Cadwallader Colden. In 1765, Colden told Johnson that he could get around the law limiting patents to two thousand acres by patenting the Canajoharie land under fictitious names. Colden decried such unethical behavior on the part of landowners with whom he was not allied. He also did "solemnly declare" to the Board of Trade "that I am in no shape interested in any purchase of lands from the Indians, or in any license to purchase, or in any grant of Lands in any share or part, either great or small, or by any person in trust for me, at any time since the administration of Government has been in my hands." He did not need to invest in land because he was making a fortune as lieutenant governor by charging the exorbitant fee of $31.25 for every thousand acres of patented land. Despite their own sins, all elite New Yorkers deplored their enemies' unethical behavior even though all were equally unethical when their personal interests were at stake. Hence Johnson, although taking thousands of acres of Indian land for himself, saw no incongruity in charging the Livingstons with unethical behavior because of their theft of Indian land. With shady dealings characterizing virtually all land transactions in the colony, no member of the elite could afford a detailed investigation into his affairs. Exposure could undermine their political influence and potential wealth, and local privilege would suffer.[46]

The political influence of the elite could also be undermined if they lost the support of the lower classes. Aware of this, each faction sought to win the lower classes to its cause. The bulk of New York's voters were of the middling sort, many of them tenant farmers, freemen, and small merchants, who "have suddenly rose from the lowest Rank of the People to considerable fortunes and chiefly in the last war, by illicit Trade." Colden noted of the middling sort, "they are as to condition of life in no manner superior to the common Farmers in England; and the Mechanics such only as are necessary in domestic Life. This last Rank," Colden continued, "comprehends the bulk of the People and in them consists the strength of the Province. They are the most usefull and the most moral, but alwise made the Dupes of the former [the landowners and the lawyers], and often are ignorantly made their Tools for the worst purposes." Colden believed this potentially influential group consisted of "Men easily deluded, and led away with popular arguments of Liberty and Priviledges."[47]

Livingstons, DeLanceys, and governors courted the middling sort. Without the support of this class, no faction in New York could hope to achieve office. Governors and opposition needed the voting support of the middling sort for the assembly candidates they backed. Only by achieving a proadministration majority in the assembly could governors be assured of a successful and tranquil administration.[48]

Even those New Yorkers who did not vote were important to the elite and to royal governors as the eighteenth century progressed. The unfranchised increasingly took to the streets to protest unpopular measures or governors. Opposition oligarchs, such as William Livingston's cousin, Robert R. Livingston, not only incited, but often personally led, urban mobs. The crowds usually remained manageable and, in the manner of preindustrial crowds, agitated only until some concession was made by the elite, and then went home. Rural dwellers also rioted, as William's brother Robert, the third manor lord, knew all too well from past tenant riots on the manor. Hence, the middling and lower sorts of New York society, whether urban or rural, whether franchised or not, wielded considerable, if indirect, political influence in the province.[49]

The elite's propaganda campaign made the lower classes particularly vocal in criticizing Lieutenant Governor Colden, the head of the province and the visible representative of royal rule. The middling and lower sorts blamed Colden and the Crown for the economic slump that followed the French and Indian War. During the war, the economy boomed, leading many New Yorkers of middling origin to make fortunes. This led others to believe they too could be successful, but in this period of rising expectations, gains were not equal. Most remained poor, but now resented their inferior status. When the depression that followed the war closed most avenues of advancement, the lower classes blamed the governor for their degraded condition, and the royal prerogative suffered.[50]

If the lower classes blamed the governor for their poverty, the elite blamed him for enforcing the 1764 Sugar Act and the 1765 Stamp Act, both parliamentary imposed taxes, passed at the behest of George

Grenville. The Revenue or Sugar Act not only imposed new taxes on imported goods, but also cut off the illegal trade of the elite with the French West Indies. To enforce the act, the jurisdiction of vice-admiralty courts was expanded. New Yorkers were indignant at both the favor shown to British West Indian interests and the increased use of admiralty courts, which sat without juries. The Sugar Act was particularly devastating to the Livingstons since it forced the closing of the family's New York sugar refinery that had previously profited because the Livingstons had bought cheaper French sugar. The resultant monetary loss led the family to support vigorous measures to protest the bill.[51]

Among the measures undertaken to protest the act was an 11 September 1764 petition to the home government by the Livingston assembly, which was written by William's brother Philip. In the petition the assembly stressed the importance of the colony's trade with the French West Indies. It also emphasized the colonists's belief that they should be taxed only with their consent. In a separate letter to Colden, the assembly expressed the hope that "your Honour will heartily join with us in an Endeavour to secure that great Badge of English Liberty, of being taxed only with our own Consent; to which we conceive all His Majesty's Subjects, at Home and abroad, equally intitled."[52]

Colden, in forwarding the address to the Board of Trade, commented that New York's manor lords paid no tax on their undeveloped property, while small farmers were taxed for virtually every acre they owned. The reason for the assembly's petition was that the manor lords had heard from their English correspondents that Parliament had a "design to Tax all Lands equally." The unwelcome prospect of carrying their fair share of the tax burden caused the large landowners to protest any new tax.[53]

Economic considerations also prompted the oligarchs' initial objection to the Stamp Act, since they were the principal users of legal documents, licenses, and other taxed papers. The act was passed by the Grenville ministry despite the objections of colonials to the Sugar Act and was meant to assert parliamentary authority over the colonies. Particularly irritating to the ministry was the 11 September 1764 address of the New York assembly. The Board of Trade observed that in the address, "the Acts and resolutions of the British Parliament were treated with indecent disrespect, and principles of a dangerous nature and tendency adopted and avowed."[54]

No objection was foreseen by the ministry to the Stamp Act since similar taxes had long been in force in England. Stamp taxes had even been periodically proposed for the colonies. But at least one governor, George Clinton, had warned the ministry that colonists would not accept such a tax. In 1744, Clinton, on hearing there was a plan afoot to raise money by placing a parliamentary "duty upon stamp papers and parchment in all the British and American Colonys," forecast resistance. As Clinton told Newcastle, "the People in North America are quite strangers to any duty, but such a scheim to take place without their knowledge it might prove a dangerous consequence to His Majesty's interest." Clinton's prediction was to prove true.[55]

The money raised from stamp duties was to remain in America where it would pay one-third the cost of the military establishment. Parliament during this same period also passed the American Mutiny Act, which provided for the billeting of British soldiers in empty houses and barns. The colonies were to contribute to the troops's support by providing them with such necessities as vinegar, salt, firewood, candles, cooking utensils, beer, and cider.[56]

There was no immediate protest to the Mutiny Act in New York, but the Stamp Act drew immediate response. In fact, protest simply continued. The elite, for most of the colonial period, encouraged the rabble to take part in politics by voicing their discontent through mob action. The effectiveness of elite propaganda in rousing the lower orders was shown when Livingston made the *Forsey v. Cunningham* appeal the most talked about issue in New York's colonial history. Public fury toward imperial government raised by that case and other issues melded in 1765 with growing opposition to the Stamp Act and other revenue raising measures passed by Parliament. As Governor Henry Moore observed, the *Forsey v. Cunningham* appeal had "laid the foundation in a great measure of many of the succeeding disorders here."[57]

Colonists believed they had solid constitutional grounds to resist the Stamp Act since it threatened trial by jury, as had *Forsey v. Cunningham* and the Sugar Act. The Stamp Act also expanded the jurisdiction of juryless vice-admiralty courts. The act implied that ecclesiastical courts would be established in America, since it stated that stamp taxes could be collected on documents used in such courts. Since ecclesiastical courts could only be erected with a resident bishop, nonconformists, such as William Livingston, were apprehensive that religious toleration would cease in England's colonies. Colonists's animosity was further raised by the passage of a Currency Act, which threatened the economic well-being of the colonies by demanding fees for the stamps be paid in specie.[58]

Conviction also played a part in the resistance of William Livingston and other oligarchs to the act. Livingston, Scott, and Smith believed that people should only be taxed by their elected representatives. Hence, the Stamp Act was unconstitutional. The triumvirate promptly took action drafting assembly representations to Parliament and petitions to the king. In these petitions, they claimed that exemption from involuntary taxation was a basic English right. The Livingston assembly appointed a committee of correspondence to keep in touch with sympathetic colleagues in England and New England.[59]

In addition to assembly protests, large-scale agitation was needed to challenge the Stamp Act with sufficient rigor so that the clamor could not be ignored by authorities at home. Only the colony's lower orders were numerous and volatile enough to mount such opposition. The problem of the elite was how to secure this support since the lower classes were not initially affected by the Stamp Act. The oligarchs instructed the masses about the Stamp Act's long-range implications, just as they had with the *Forsey v. Cunningham* appeal and with just as much effect. The oligarchs convinced the people that accepting the Stamp Act would lead to further oppression on the part of the ministry. They pointed out that the act would establish a precedent by which the British government could impose any tax it pleased on the colonies. The lower and middle classes were particularly responsive to such propaganda since they, as consumers on tight budgets, not the wealthy landowners, bore the brunt of taxation in New York. A financial policy such as that contemplated by the ministry, the elite explained, would bring financial hardship to every colonist and would also reduce provincial liberties.[60]

The oligarchs delivered the full force of their attack against the Stamp Act in "the Public Papers," which, as commander-in-chief General Thomas Gage observed, were "cramm'd with Treason." As a result of the propaganda, Gage said, "the Minds of the People [are] disturbed, excited and encouraged to revolt against the Government[,] to subvert the Constitution, & trample on the Laws. Every Lye that malice can invent is propagated as Truths by these Enemys of their Country to sow Dissension and create Animosities between Great Britain and the Colonys."[61]

Most propagandists attacked the Stamp Act indirectly on constitutional grounds. William Livingston pointed out that "It is a standing Maxim of *English Liberty*, 'that no Man shall be taxed, but with his own Consent.' When the Legislature decree a Tax, as they represent the Community, such Tax ought to be considered as the voluntary Gift of the People." In another essay he referred to the British constitution as "a rock, repeatedly defended against lawless encroachments by oceans of blood . . . is such a constitution . . . now to be altered or abolished, by—the dash of a pen?"[62]

The urban middling and lower sort in New York responded to elite propaganda by staging numerous demonstrations against the Stamp Act throughout the summer and fall of 1765. Most members of the Livingston family remained confident that the mobs were manageable and could be halted whenever necessary. Colden, perhaps more sensitive to the situation, feared the effects of "the inflammatory Papers . . . exciting the People to oppose the execution of the Act of Parliament for laying a Stamp Duty in the Colonies." The lieutenant governor well realized that the mobs, grown increasingly unruly, were looking for "an opportunity to begin a riot."[63]

Such riots occurred in Massachusetts, where on 26 August 1765, Boston mobs had terrorized the city and destroyed the home of Chief Justice Thomas Hutchinson; the mobs had forced the resignationof the stamp distributors there. New York's appointed stamp collector, James McEwers, quickly followed suit. The news from Boston was enough to make most of New York's elite revise their opinion as to the manageability of urban mobs, particularly when the *New York Gazette* reported the Boston riots with the comment that it was a "Noble Example" which should "be unanimously follow'd by all the Colonies." The spectre raised by these actions in the eyes of the Livingstons and other oligarchs was that of democracy and mob rule. The prospect of rule by the majority, instead of rule by the elite, was sufficient to cause William Livingston to cling to the old order and the stability represented by the British Empire.[64]

William Livingston published his last Sentinel column on 29 August 1765, or just about the time news of the Boston riots reached New York. Livingston distrusted rash emotional behavior, such as had occurred in Boston. He believed that, once begun, "such Tumults and Convulsions" would continue until the old regime was overthrown, as it had been in England during the civil wars. Only after having undergone such a violent outcome could society hope to "restore . . . its Original Peace and Tranquility." Livingston in 1765 feared such cataclysmic events. As he wrote in 1768 under the pseudonym of "The American Whig," "I could not look on the late tumults and commotions occasioned by the unhappy Stamp Act, without the most tender concern, knowing the consequences ever to be dreaded, of a rupture between the mother country and these plantations, which is an event never to be desired by those who are true friends to either."[65]

The lieutenant governor also feared turmoil in New York. To his dismay, Colden found that he had no means to control unruly mobs because the city's defenses had been allowed to deteriorate after the French and Indian War. At Colden's request General Thomas Gage sent one hundred troops to New York with "some Field Pieces and Howitzers, together with a sufficient quantity of ammunition and other stores." The fort was readied, with the guns turned from the harbor to face the city. This time, city residents realized, soldiers and weapons were not meant to hold off the French enemy but rather to subdue New Yorkers.[66]

The summer of 1765 was also memorable in England where it brought an end to the Grenville ministry. Succeeding Grenville was the earl of Rockingham, chosen as first minister by Cumberland, with Henry Seymour Conway as southern secretary. Cumberland, an imperialist who had long recommended a hard line in colonial administration, was in fact the head of government. Crown policy as to the Stamp Act would likely remain unchanged as long as Cumberland was in charge, but the duke died suddenly on 31 October 1765.[67]

By October 1765 the climate in New York City was unstable, created in large measure by the leaders of the Livingston faction, William Livingston, William Smith, Jr., and John Morin Scott. Their motives in raising the sentiments of New Yorkers to a fever pitch were mixed. On the one hand, as republicans, they believed in the benefits of an educated and aware citizenry. They felt that, as members of the educated elite, it was their duty and responsibility to lead New York's lower sort. They also believed in the republican principles of representative government they advocated. They were convinced that their opposition to tyrannical imperial policy was necessary to preserve basic and essential liberties. They believed that the power of provincial government, which represented the people, should expand, while the power of imperial government, which did not represent them, should decline. On the other hand, their motives were self-serving, as Cadwallader Colden correctly pointed out. The elite, by "inlarging the powers of the popular side of government & by depreciating the powers of the Crown," were in reality strengthening their own power.[68]

By 1765, the power of the Livingston Family was considerable. The Livingstons, through their control of the assembly and their alliance with royal governor Robert Monckton, dominated New York politics. William Livingston was the spokesman for an oligarchical interest, the real authority of which continued to lay in economic power and familial alliances. This interest retained control of New York society and politics. That control faced a challenge from the increasingly knowledgeable and politically astute lower and middling sort who had been informed of their rights as Englishmen by New York opposition writers. That control was also threatened by the royal prerogative, which sought, increasingly in the 1760s, to limit local privilege by attacks on their property.

The elite were in a bind—and one partially of their own making. Opposition writers had courted the middling and lower sort through a massive and persistent propaganda campaign that stressed Whig philosophy. In the late 1750s, Whig-republican propaganda won the Livingstons the support of the majority of New York's lower orders, and that support was used effectively to thwart the royal prerogative and to topple the DeLancey family from their premier position in New York. In 1765, the Livingstons needed the continued support of the lower orders to retain their privileged places and to fight off attacks on their position by the ministry. But as the Stamp Act protests escalated, the crowds, imbued with Whig beliefs, showed disturbing signs of thinking and acting for themselves. The elites' position was now threatened from above and below. In the fall of 1765, many members of the elite realized that their program to heighten public awareness about the threat of British tyranny had raised a popular force that might be difficult to control.

7

The Spirit of Mobbing, 1765–1770: The Administrations of Sir Henry Moore (1765–1769) and Cadwallader Colden (1769–1770)

> The great, as well as the little Vulgar, are liable to catch the Spirit of Mobbing; and cluster together to perpetrate a Riot, without knowing the Reason that set them in Motion.[1]

The Livingstons quickly realized in 1765 that their efforts to propagandize and politicize the lower orders of society led to rising democratic tendencies. The elite's fear of democracy, anarchy, and mob rule were confirmed by urban riots in 1765 and rural tenant uprisings in 1766. These disturbances made New York's elite wary of popular agitation, leading the politically dominant Livingstons to stop their courtship of the lower orders. This neglect by the Livingstons presented an opportunity for the DeLanceys to regain their influence, and they began to cater to the rank and file. In return, lower-class voters offered the DeLanceys their support at the polls. In the 1769 assembly election, this support caused the Livingstons to lose control of that body. The DeLancey ascendancy left the Livingstons with a difficult choice. They could ignore the lower and middling sort and continue to remain on the political sidelines. An alternative was to compromise their principles by courting the democratic Sons of Liberty, leaders of the more radical members of the middling and lower sort. By doing so, the Livingstons might regain their political influence. Despite their fear of popular rule, the Livingstons chose the latter.[2]

The Livingstons's fear of democracy was deep-seated. Most of the family were committed to Whig republican principles. As republicans, they feared and distrusted democracy, which they equated with mob rule and anarchy. William Livingston particularly distrusted the unconsidered actions of the mob and realized the dangers in stirring up the lower classes. As he noted, "the great, as well as the little Vulgar, are liable to catch the Spirit of Mobbing; and cluster together to perpetrate a Riot, without knowing the Reason that set them in Motion."[3]

Livingston and most other members of the elite believed that the lower orders of society had to be contained. Only if the lower classes recognized and accepted their limited political role could a good government on the English model be attained. Livingston was convinced that the best government was "a Compound of Monarchy, Aristocracy and Democracy, such as is the English Constitution," with no single element predominant and each balancing the other. Livingston and other members of New York's elite excused their attempt to suppress rising democratic tendencies after 1765 by claiming it was done to retain that balance.[4]

The elite had been able to control public protest prior to 1765 and had every reason to believe they could retain that control when they roused the lower and middling sort to oppose the Stamp Act. As in other colonies, the first formal protests came from the assembly. When this proved ineffective, an intercolonial conference was called in New York City at the behest of Massachusetts. Representatives from New York, Connecticut, Delaware, Maryland, Massachusetts, New Jersey, Pennsylvania, Rhode Island, and South Carolina met in New York City from 7 to 25 October 1765. They debated, as General Gage reported, "the Independency of the Provinces on the Legislature of Great Britain." Congress in its petition reiterated the belief that taxes could only be imposed by elected representatives and further pointed out that, because stamps had to be paid in specie, stamp taxes would impose an insupportable burden on colonists.[5]

Congress's relative moderation irritated both franchised and unfranchised members of the lower classes in New York City, who staged anti-Stamp Act demonstrations in the fall of 1765. The rank and file, irritated by Cadwallader Colden's introduction of manpower and weapons to Fort George, announced its determination to prevent the use of stamps by such tactics as nailing up handwritten signs around town. One such sign read, "the first Man that either distributes or makes use of Stampt Paper let him take Care of his House, Person, and Effects. We dare. VOX POPULI."[6]

Popular protests escalated after the 23 October 1765 arrival of the vessels carrying the stamps. New York City mobs demanded that the stamps be delivered to them or they would destroy the ships carrying them. Colden ordered the stamps unloaded and stored in Fort George for safekeeping. On 31 October, the day before the Stamp Act was to go into effect, Colden asked Royal Navy Captain Archibald Kennedy to place the stamps on board his ship *Coventry* for safekeeping. Kennedy refused, fearing for the safety of his property in the city. The stamps remained in the fort. That same day, colonial opposition stiffened when the merchants in New York City agreed to nonimportation of British goods until the Stamp Act was repealed.[7]

Spurred by mercantile resolve and in turn spurring mercantile resolve, the lower classes in New York, without guidance from the elite, set forth their agenda on how to resist the royal prerogative. To make their point effective to the British ministry, several people appeared on the streets dressed in mourning for the death of liberty. On the night of 31 October a mob "went through the Streets crying "liberty,'" while breaking lamps and windows and threatening those who supported the Stamp Act. The next day, November first, an anonymous letter was delivered to Governor Colden, warning him not to order the British troops to fire on New York's citizenry. To "perpetrate any such murderous Act," would bring Colden's "grey hairs with sorrow to the grave." The letter linked New York's cause to that of Scotland, another English province. It warned Colden "you'll die a martir to your own villainy, and be hanged, like Porteis upon a Sign Post, as a memento to all wicked Governors." The reference was to Captain John Porteous, who, in 1736, was in command of the Edinburgh city guard when his troops fired into an unruly crowd. Several demonstrators were killed or wounded. Porteous, convicted of murder, was given a royal stay of execution, but was seized by the mob and hanged.[8]

Having delivered the warning to Colden, the rabble, two thousand strong, embarked on a nightlong orgy of destruction. They marched on the fort, where commanding officer Major Thomas James, realizing he was badly outnumbered, ordered his men not to fire. James believed he could have "killed 900 of them," but was aware that the provincials could raise "in New York and the Jerseys 50,000 Fighting Men," while he had only "151 men & officers" in the fort. Having failed to provoke a confrontation with the soldiers, the mob took to the streets.[9]

The crowd chose its targets with care. They included Lieutenant Governor Colden, who had ordered the fort reinforced, and Major James, who had promised the crowd that he would ram the stamps down New Yorkers's throats. In retaliation, New Yorkers now threatened to bury James alive for his words and deeds and for protecting the stamps. In addition, both governor and commander represented imperial rule in New York. They not only served imperial interests, but both further offended the crowd by flaunting their wealth and living ostentatiously during a period of severe economic depression.[10]

The mob was led by "a great number of Boys [who] carried lighted torches" and a scaffold with two images, one the devil and the other the lieutenant governor. The crowd of about two thousand consisted largely of youngsters and "Men who had been privateers & disbanded soldiers," that is, those about to enter the job market and the adult unemployed. The ranks of urban rioters were reinforced by "many who have come in from the Neighboring Country and provinces." Colden, who wisely took refuge with his family on a British man-of-war in New York harbor, later reported that, "as they went from the gate they broke open my coach house, took my charriot out of it & carryed it round the town with the immages, & returned to the Fort Gate, from when they carryed them to an open place, where they had erected a Jibbett, within 100 yards of the Fort Gate & there hung up the Immages." Colden's effigy carried a drum, a reference to his presumed role in the 1715 Jacobite rebellion. After the effigies had been "hanging some time," Colden reported, "they were burnt in a fire . . . togethr with my charriott, a single horse chair and two sledges,.. which they took out of my Coach house." After destroying that obvious symbol of wealth and privilege, the governor's chariot, the crowd descended on Major James's luxurious and finely furnished house in Ranelagh Gardens. There, according to a contemporary observer, they broke every window, "beat to pieces all the doors, sashes, window-frames and partitions in the house, leaving it a mere shell," tore down every shutter, and "distroyed 9 1/4 casks of Wine & . . . all his plate, Furniture[,] apparel[,] Books[,] to the value of £1500." A New York newspaper, sympathetic to the rioters, sought to downplay the chaos. It reported that the destruction of James's house "was conducted with such Decorum, that not the least Accident happened."[11]

Claims of decorum aside, the crowds had clearly gotten out of control, despite attempts by the elite to direct and moderate their actions. Two of William Livingston's relatives, his nephew by marriage, James Duane, and his cousin, Supreme Court judge Robert R. Livingston, had walked the city's streets during the riots trying unsuccessfully to disband the mobs. A small minority of the elite, such as John Morin Scott, welcomed agitation because they believed that it would lead to independence. Most oligarchs, however, were more conservative.[12]

The rioters, who soon termed themselves *Sons of Liberty*, were led not by the elite, as they had been in former demonstrations, but by such men as "King" Isaac Sears and John Lamb, who were of humble origins. The lower- to middling-class character of the leadership was noted by William Dunlap, who commented that the New York riots "were led by men, as is always the case, from the ranks of people and many of them without property [that is, unfranchised]."[13]

Of all the observers, none was more shaken by the events than the lieutenant governor. Colden's distress and fear were so obvious that Major James, who left for England immediately after the riots to report on events to the ministry, urged the governor to accompany him to safety, but Colden refused. Colden had no doubt as to who was responsible for the outrages and the wanton destruction of property. Colden asserted "that the Lawyers of this Place are the Authors, Promoters and Leaders of" the Stamp Act riots. Colden was correct in assigning blame for urban unrest and disorder to the triumvirate and their colleagues. The elite had encouraged defiance of British rule through exhortation and their own example as they continued to challenge the prerogative. But Colden was wrong in believing the elite had led the mobs. Most oligarchs, except for a handful, like Scott, were as disturbed and threatened by events as was the lieutenant governor.[14]

The riots were effective in that Colden, still on board the man-of-war, promised on 4 November 1765, that he would not distribute the stamps, which remained in the fort. This promise was not deemed sufficient by the people, who demanded and received custody of the stamps on 5 November. As Colden noted, the mob had been so irate and insistent, that "at last I consented to deliver up the stamped paper to the Mayor and Corporation of the City. . . . After which the Mob entirely dispersed, and the City remained in perfect tranquility." The next day, Colden finally decided it was safe to return to New York.[15]

The independent actions of the crowd further alarmed the oligarchs. Robert R. Livingston feared "the destruction of all Law Order and Government," while William Smith, Jr., was appalled at the prospect of enduring a "most melancholy State of Anarchy under the Government of a Mob." It was more than a prospect. As Colden admitted to secretary Conway, the people rejected all royal authority. In this most successful, if temporary, defiance of royal rule, both privilege and prerogative were weakened because it had been accomplished by the lower classes. Elite leaders were powerless, for the time being, and Colden ruefully acknowledged he could not offer royal officials any protection because "the Power of Governt was too weak." He was able to restore a semblance of order only by the complete "suspension of those powers" of government. Legal government ended in New York on 31 October and resumed only after the 13 November arrival of the new governor, Sir Henry Moore. Secretary Conway was outraged at Colden's lack of leadership and distressed that Colden had "suspend[ed] the Power of Government, till the arrival of the Governor."

Colden, chagrined by his rebuke from Conway, offered as an excuse his status as a lame-duck governor, claiming that Moore's imminent arrival left him unable to command obedience. He ascribed his extreme agitation to fear for his property, because his "whole fortune was exposed to the Mob."[16]

Colden remained so shaken by recent events that the new governor, Moore, reported that on his unexpected arrival he was appalled to find the fort gates locked and was forced to make his entry at the wicket. Inside the fort, Moore, who had little sympathy for his predecessor, found a frightened Colden. At Moore's insistence, the fort gates were thrown open and the people of New York invited inside to witness the publishing of the governor's commission. Despite the peaceful ceremony, Colden was so intimidated by the crowds that he refused to walk with Moore from the fort to the city hall, a distance of only a few blocks. Governor Moore proceeded without the lieutenant governor and was rewarded to see that "the Gloom which hung over them in the Morning was totally dispers'd in a few hours, and the evening concluded with Bonfires and Illuminations throughout the whole City."[17]

To ensure that calm remained in New York, Moore, who eventually allied with the Livingstons, first used concessions. To placate New Yorkers, the offending fort was disarmed of "every thing which Major James introduced of artillery, artillery stores and Gun Powder removed out of it." Moore also asserted royal authority.[18]

Moore could not force New Yorkers to use stamps, but he could stop all business if New Yorkers persisted in their defiance of the Stamp Act. Hence he "absolutely refused the holding of any Courts of Administration or Chancery which together with the Courts of Common Law are now shut up." The port as well as the courts were closed since Moore determined that "no vessel will be suffered to go out of the Harbour" without stamps. Both port and courts remained closed from November 1765 to May 1766.[19]

Except for those people awaiting trial, New York City's lower classes were relatively unaffected by the closing of the courts. They were, however, affected by the closing of the port. This action was a calculated risk on Moore's part since it decreased trade and hence increased unemployment and discontent. No ships were permitted to sail without stamps. Hence seamen and dockyard workers remained unemployed, and their ranks were constantly swelled by seamen on incoming ships. These ships were permitted to dock without stamped paper, but were not permitted to leave if they lacked stamps. Consequently, a constantly increasing number of idle seamen added to the number of the city's unemployed. The resultant economic distress led the lower classes to demand that the ports be reopened without stamps. Such an open act of defiance was feared by the elite who reasserted their authority over the middling and lower sort.[20]

The elite moved decisively on 25 November when the Sons had the temerity to call a meeting of New York City's voters to draw up instructions for the city's assemblymen. At the meeting, the radical Sons demanded the assembly openly defy Parliament; they wanted the representatives to "pass an Act to annull the Stamp Act, and afterwards to force the Governor and Council to confirm it." The oligarchs, fearing the consequences of such an extreme position, quickly gained control of the meeting and "quashed these Attempts of the inferior Burghers." The elite then persuaded the voters to adopt moderate resolutions that simply reiterated the oft voiced sentiment that the Stamp Act was illegal. The next day, a committee, headed by William Livingston, John Morin Scott, and William Smith, Jr., presented these instructions to a relieved assembly. In fact, as Smith later observed, "the Ardor of the Populace . . . outstripped the Zeal of the assembly."[21]

The Sons, understandably offended by this high-handed treatment from the elite, sent their own anonymous petition to the House of Representatives. The new self-assurance of the lower classes, as well as their sense of injury, was apparent in the petition. It demanded that the assembly deduct from Colden's salary the money needed for repairs on the fort and further demanded that certain recently passed acts be repealed. The message, signed "FREEDOM," further admonished the representatives that they should "be not so Conceited as to Say or think that other People know nothing about Government[,] you have made these Laws & say they are Right but they are Rong & take away Liberty, Oppressions of your make Gentlemen[,] make us *Sons of Liberty* think you are not for the public Liberty."[22]

The document disturbed New York's elite. The lower classes had shown signs of no longer accepting their inferior status and of identifying the elite as their immediate oppressors. The problem was partially of the elite's own making. Oligarchs had politicized the masses by calling attention to attempts by the British government to deprive colonists of their liberties and rights as British subjects. At the urging of the elite, New York's middling and lower sort had taken up the cause against the British government. This was particularly evident after the passage of the Stamp Act, when the "Plan of the People of Property has been to raise the lower class to prevent the Execution of the Law." The lower class responded, and the elite not only "encouraged" the mob, but also "many perhaps joined them." The attitude of the elite to popular demonstrations changed in November 1765, when the "Inferior Sort" began to engage in "Proceedings which might be deemed Treasonable or Rebellious." When that occurred, "Persons and Propertys being then in Danger, they [the elite] have endeavored to restrain them."[23]

Prompted partially by conviction and partially by economic distress, the lower orders, whose determination to act independently was reinforced by contact with Sons's organizations in other cities, now staged demonstrations on their own initiative. They also gave orders to their betters in the House of Representatives. Far more frightening to the elite, the lower classes showed evidence of their growing awareness that their homegrown rulers were depriving them of their rights and limiting their freedom as much, if not more, than were their imperial rulers. Moreover, radical elements among the mobs had illustrated their capacity and willingness to attack the property, if not as yet the persons, of the elite. The frightened Livingston assembly tried to reassert local elite privilege and promptly labeled the message from the Sons as "lybellous, Scandalous and Seditious." A reward was offered to find the author so that he could be charged and brought to trial.[24]

The assembly then turned its attention to forms of protest more acceptable to them against the Stamp Act. Long-standing constitutional principles formulated by the elite were incorporated in an assembly address to the ministry dated 18 December 1765. In the address, the assemblymen voiced their concern that Parliamentary acts "granting Stamp, and other Duties to his Majesty, restricting the Trade of this Colony" would lead to the "Abolition of that Constitution under which they have so long and happily enjoyed the rights and Liberties of Englishmen." The assemblymen reminded the ministry that "Colonists did not forfeit these essential Rights by their Emigration" from England. The Parliamentary act set a dangerous precedent, since it "deprives them [colonists] of the essential Right of being the *sole* Disposers of their own Property." This led colonists to fear that "the People of *Great-Britain*" believed they were "vested with absolute Power to dispose of all their [the colonists'] Property." The duties placed by the acts were "very grievious and burthensome" and were "impossible to be paid."[25]

Despite tensions caused by class conflict, increasing unemployment, and a stagnant economy, New Yorkers of all classes continued to refuse stamps. The *New York Gazette* on 9 January 1766 loudly proclaimed that it spoke with "The united Voice of all His Majesty's *free* and *loyal* Subjects in AMERICA—LIBERTY and PROPERTY, and NO STAMPS." Defiance meant still additional worsening of economic conditions. This led the Sons to further violent measures and, on 16 January 1766, mobs under their direction seized and destroyed the stamps. The lower class continued to reject appeals by the elite for moderation, leading

Cadwallader Colden, now in retirement, to wonder "whether the Men who excited this seditious spirit in the People have it in their power to suppress it." Governor Moore was also alarmed by the continued belligerency in the province. Moore responded to heightened emotions by "making a private Application to Genl. Gage for some military Assistance," since there were only 160 men in the fort.[26]

The stamps and colonists's resistance to them were cause for concern in London. News of New York events reached London when Major James arrived there on 9 December and gave a full report of the riots to Henry Conway. Conway and Rockingham were deeply disturbed by the agitation in New York and other provinces, which demanded immediate action to reassert the royal prerogative. Two courses were open to the ministry—conciliation or force. Grenville, during whose ministry the tax had been passed, now urged force be used to implement the Stamp Act. Rockingham was more inclined to repeal the Stamp Act. To effect this, Rockingham turned to Pitt, who in Commons came out strongly for repeal and denied Parliament's right to tax the colonies.[27]

The Rockingham ministry agreed that repeal was the right course, but could not agree with Pitt that Parliament had no right to impose taxes on the colonies. The ministry's decision to seek repeal may also have been swayed by the petitions of British merchants, whose trade declined from £537,614 in 1764 to £404,644 in 1765. The decline in trade was probably due to a general economic depression, which affected Great Britain as well as the colonies, rather than nonimportation, the effect of which would not have been felt early in 1766. The ministry, by stressing the Stamp Act's potentially negative effect on Britain's economy, persuaded Parliament to repeal the act in March 1766. At the same time, Parliament reaffirmed its right to assert its authority over the colonies with the passage of the Declaratory Act.[28]

The Declaratory Act was similar in intent to the 1719 act of the same name designed to confirm Parliament's right to legislate for Ireland. The intent of the more recent act was to attack local privilege in the American colonies by curbing the power of provincial assemblies that claimed they alone had "the sole, exclusive Right of imposing Duties and Taxes upon his Majestys Subjects in the said Colonies and Plantations." The act stated that such claims were "against Law," reiterating the fact that the colonies were "Subordinate unto, and Dependent upon the Imperial Crown and Parliament of Great Britain." The King–in–Parliament had "full Power & Authority to make Laws and Statutes of sufficient Force and validity to Bind the Colonies and People of America, Subjects to the Crown of Great Britain." The act further declared null and void any provincial act that denied this authority.[29]

Until news of Parliament's actions regarding the Declaratory Act and the repeal of the Stamp Act reached New York, the Sons remained active, enforcing nonimportation, threatening Cadwallader Colden, attacking and provoking British sailors and soldiers, "venting threats and Insulting the Crown & Officers under it." Contributing to the unrest in New York was the continuing controversy that surrounded the Cunningham appeal. On 26 July 1765, the King-in-Council instructed Colden and his council to hear the appeal. In complying with the directive, Colden was severely criticized by New York attorneys for abetting *"dangerous machinations . . . destructive of the peace and security of the subject."* The Livingston assembly continued its deliberations on the case. On 14 December 1765 the House's Grand Committee for Courts of Justices examined witnesses and "sundry papers" relating to the attempt "to introduce Appeals *from the Verdict of a Jury.*" The assembly resolved that "Trial by Jury, is the Right of the Subject, not only by Common Law, by Statute Law, and the Laws of this Colony, but essential to the Safety of their Lives, Liberty, and Property." The assembly further resolved, "That the conduct of the said Lieutenant Governor Colden, has filled the Minds of His Majesty's Subjects in this Colony with Jealousies and Distrust, to the great Prejudice of the public Service."[30]

Still unknown at that time to Colden and other New Yorkers was the observation of the Board of Trade to the king that in their opinion "confining such Appeals to cases of error only, was upon the principles of law a rule so absolute of itself and so well established by the usage and constitution of this Kingdom, that it was thought unnecessary to point it out by express words in the Instructions." In February 1766 a letter arrived in New York that England's attorney and solictor generals agreed with the Board's recommendation. They pointed out that hearing appeals only in cases of error was a practice firmly established not only in English law but also in "the Custom and usage of the Province, ever since its Settlement." By the time the decision was received in New York, colonists had lost interest in the case, and the fine had been paid. Colden had not forgotten the cause and was outraged by the decision, which embarrassed him. Colden's erroneous stand regarding appeals served in the long run to diminish respect for the royal prerogative he represented.[31]

Declining respect, along with the inability of England to enforce revenue measures such as the Stamp Act, further weakened imperial authority. The British government, facing determined and widespread opposition from colonists, was powerless to compel obedience in those colonies where population was increasing but the military presence remained constant. Noting this disparity in New York prior to the Stamp Act agitation, Colden and other imperial officials observed that an inadequate military presence was worse than none and requested that New York's troops be increased to a battalion. These officials claimed that stamps were accepted without complaint in colonies where there was sufficient armed force to back up the act, despite the fact that assemblies in many of these provinces were every bit as zealous as was the New York assembly in asserting their powers—and often more experienced as well. Hence, compliance came easily in "Quebec, Halifax, Pensacola, Jamaica Barbadoes Antigua and the Granadas. The singular advantage of troops and fleets to enforce his Majesty's orders are here plainly demonstrated."[32]

The implication of contemporary imperial observers was that force would defeat privilege and compel mainland Americans to accept Parliament's authority. In fact, this was impossible. These officials failed to consider that conditions in the North American colonies and the West Indies were dramatically different. There simply was no population in a position to rebel in the West Indies. Mainland colonies in the north had a large, militant, contentious, informed, and armed middle- and lower-class white population. In the West Indian provinces, black slaves, unarmed and powerless, constituted the overwhelming majority of the population. The islands had a miniscule middle class and a largely absent upper class, since most planters preferred to live in England. Conditions also differed between Britain's North American colonies and Canada, recently won from the French. Canada, small in population, lacked a tradition of representative government and thus had no constitutional basis for rebellion. This constitutional basis was deeply entrenched in New York. Government there and in other colonies rested on the consent of the governed and lasted until that consent was withdrawn.[33]

Constitutional principles formed the basis of the elite's objections to parliamentary money acts. These acts convinced many colonists that the ministry intended to reduce American liberties. The resultant agitation and its sequels brought the first signs of a rupture among Americans. Typical was the triumvirate, although all retained their republican Whig principles. John Morin Scott, who identified with mob leaders, rejected parliamentary authority over the colonies, favored a break with Great Britain, and encouraged rising democratic tendencies. William Livingston, more conservative, believed that Parliament had a right to legislate for the colonies and that a break with England would be disastrous. Livingston also feared mob rule, as did William Smith, Jr. By 1765, Smith, more conservative than Scott or Livingston, had started to ally his interests with those of royal governors, who represented to Smith stability and order. His commitment to royal rule was further strengthened in 1767 when Governor Moore named Smith to the governor's council, as Moore moved closer to the Livingston faction.[34]

Livingston's and Smith's fears of anarchy and disorder were confirmed in the spring of 1766 when rioting broke out on the manors. Contemporaries believed the rural riots had been directly inspired by urban riots. Moore observed in April 1766 that "the disorders which began at first in the Towns have by degrees spread themselves into the Country, and inflicted the people with Notions that at this time every thing which had the appearance of resisting Government might be undertaken with impunity."[35]

Inspired by urban Stamp Act disturbances, rural tenants with longstanding grievances began to riot. At issue was the ownership of land in Dutchess, Westchester, and Albany counties. Tenants wanted their own land. Their cause seemed hopeful because landlords' titles were often in dispute. Tenants simply denied the authenticity of the manor lord's claim and refused to pay rents. Rioting resulted when landlords used the courts to evict their defiant tenants. In May 1766, shortly after the Stamp Act riots, Westchester tenant farmers put dispossessed tenants back on the farms. Their leaders were seized and jailed in New York City. This caused some five hundred farmers to march on the city to obtain the release of their jailed leaders, or, failing that, to set "the City on Fire in several different Places." The tenants expected help in their quest from the urban Sons of Liberty, but the Sons proved remarkably unsympathetic to the rural rioters, leading one contemporary to observe the Sons were "of opinion no one is entitled to Riot but themselves." The Sons apparently feared the rural influx as much as did the horrified oligarchs. At Moore's order, the farmers were dispersed before they entered New York City by a combined force of militia and regular army troops.[36]

Rural rioting continued and was particularly severe on Livingston Manor, where, in June 1766, five hundred irate tenants rose against Robert Livingston. Two hundred of them marched on the manor house with the intent of murdering the manor lord and burning his house unless he signed new leases that would excuse tenants from paying rent and taxes. Moore ordered armed soldiers sent to the manor from Albany and a battle ensued. The farmers, armed only with sticks and pitchforks, were turned back by an armed force commanded by Robert's son, Walter.[37]

The plight of the beseiged landlords was recognized as being of their own making. As General Gage commented, "They certainly deserve any Losses they may sustain, for it is the work of their own Hands. Th[e]y first Sowed the Seeds of Sedition amongst the People and taught them to rise in Opposition to the Laws, what now happens is a Consequence that might be easily foreseen after the Tumults about the Stamp Act."[38]

The elite believed that rural rioters were trying to seize and redistribute land with the intent of removing all societal distinctions. The actions of their tenants appeared to landowners similar to those of Levellers during the English Civil Wars. The landlords' fear of losing their land and lives caused them to turn to the royal prerogative for assistance. The elite requested British troops in June after seventeen hundred Levellers gathered at Poughkeepsie. The British responded by sending troops from the 28th Regiment to disperse the rioters. The use of troops to put down civilians horrified tenants, particularly when the soldiers began to loot and pillage. One observer commented, " 'Tis beyond the Power of Language to paint in lively Images the Horror! the Surprise and Astonishment of this poor distressed people on that occasion. To see their Habitations some demolished, some robbed and pillag'd and others of them envellop'd in Flames of Fire."[39]

Despite the terror caused by troops and the jailing of several leaders, some of whom were tried for treason, the rioting continued through the summer of 1766. At the forefront in leading efforts to suppress, prosecute, and judge the rioters were William Livingston, John Morin Scott, and William Smith, Jr., the very same men who had inspired urban unrest with their criticism of the imperial government. Livingston represented landowners who instituted dispossession proceedings against non-rent-paying tenants, appearing before the New York supreme court on at least fifty different occasions. Scott and Smith sat as judges on the court that tried rebels. The court rejected recommending pardon or reprieve or even sympathy to the condemned. At the August 1766 treason trial of rebel leader William Prendergast, Smith opposed Chief Justice Daniel Horsmanden's recommendation that the blow of the sentence to be hanged, drawn, and quartered, be softened with a "tender Speech." Smith believed that "Terror in the Sentence was most consistent with Commiseration to the Crowd & the great Number of Criminals." The royal prerogative, on the other hand, and in sharp contrast to the elite, came to the assistance of the rebels when Moore's wife put up bail for several of those arrested.[40]

Prendergast, whose sentence was later reversed by order of the Crown, was aware of the opposition his judges had lately mounted against the British government, as they sought to protect local privilege. He noted the hypocrisy of the court that convicted him when he commented "that if opposition to the Government was deemed Rebellion, no member of that Court was entitled to set upon his Tryal." Cadwallader Colden also commented acidly on "the difference of Sentiment and Zeal in this case and in others where the authority of

Parliament was contemned, and the Kings authority was continually insulted, for several months together, by most dangerous Riots, without the least attempt to suppress any of them, but rather with public applause."[41]

Oligarchs had reason to fear rural rioting. The urban Stamp Act riots were directed at Parliament and only indirectly, almost as an afterthought, at the elite. The farmers' uprisings were aimed directly at the elite—hence the landowners' swift efforts to contain, suppress, and punish their rebellious tenants.

The oligarchs had in fact made determined efforts to contain the urban rioting as well, but only after it had gotten out of hand. Their efforts came too late to stem the tide of rising aspirations among the urban and rural lower orders. Nor were the oligarchs able to put a halt to either rural or urban rioting even after the repeal of the Stamp Act. William Livingston and other members of the Livingston family were appalled by the terror they had created, and the Livingstons temporarily ceased their courtship of the masses.[42]

Despite the Livingstons's silence, the continued belligerence of the urban mobs fortified the resolve of the Livingston assembly, which in June 1766 refused to vote money for the support of British soldiers in New York under the provisions of the Mutiny or Quartering Act, even though other colonies had complied. The assemblymen's refusal came despite the fact that British soldiers were putting down rebellious tenants on the manors of their families. The assembly's stand was in response to voter distrust of and hatred for the soldiers, who represented imperial rule and reflected the British fear of standing armies. Americans hated British soldiers, and that hatred was fully reciprocated. To Americans, the soldiers were a continual reminder of the potential use of force, a potential that was realized in the Hudson River Valley. When the soldiers in New York City made a point of irritating New Yorkers by cutting down that symbol of colonial defiance, the Liberty Tree, civilians retaliated by attempting to bar soldiers from city bars and markets.[43]

The New York legislature refused to vote funds for British soldiers in response to popular pressure from the lower and middling sort. Their defiance led the ministry to reassert royal authority. The prime minister was William Pitt, now earl of Chatham, who regained power in July 1766 after Rockingham resigned. Pitt's acceptance of the peerage weakened his ministry because he could no longer control Commons. Conway was promoted to northern secretary, and the earl of Shelburne was named southern secretary. Under Chatham, the power of the Board of Trade, whose president was the earl of Hillsborough, was reduced. Shelburne controlled all colonial patronage, and all cor-

respondence from the colonies was addressed to him with only copies
going to the Board of Trade.[44]

Chatham may have been pro-American, as his opposition to the
Stamp Act showed, but he also believed that colonies should be subordinate to the mother country. He might well have echoed Thucydides
when the Corcyraean colonists complained to the Corinthians that
"they were not sent out in the first place . . . to be ill treated." The
Corinthians responded "that we did not found colonies in order to be
insulted by them, but rather to retain our leadership and to be treated
with proper respect."[45]

To most Britons, New Yorkers behaved disrespectfully when they
challenged the sovereignty of the British Parliament, the bulwark of
British liberties since the 1688 Glorious Revolution. To Britons at
home, Parliament represented the people, with its role that of restricting any royal inclinations to tyranny. All Britons recognized that their
liberties were guaranteed by the 1689 revolutionary settlement. Both
Britons at home and in America defended what they considered traditional British liberties based on the revolutionary settlement. Neither
could understand the other's position because they failed to consider
that different experiences since 1689 led to different interpretations of
constitutional freedoms. Britons at home saw Parliament as the guar-
antor of freedom. Colonists believed that Parliament was acting in a
fashion similar to that of the Stuart monarchs, whose inclinations to
absolutism were rejected by the English. This view of Parliament's
role was completely alien to Britons at home, who saw the House of
Commons as supreme and worthy of respect and obedience.[46]

Neither Chatham nor most Britons would tolerate such colonial disrespect as that exhibited by the New York assembly. Colonists might
claim their charters protected them from parliamentary control, but
even if New York had a written charter, it would not protect them from
Parliamentary interference. Britons at home believed provincial charters guaranteed only local privileges and did not supersede Parliamentary authority. The ministry's resolve to discipline the New York
assembly was strengthened when defiance of the Mutiny Act was followed by a petition from some 240 New York merchants, received in
London in January 1767. The merchants had the temerity to complain
about trade restrictions. The two incidents convinced Secretary Shelburne that New Yorkers were possessed by "a spirit of infatuation."
He predicted to Chatham that "their disobedience to the Mutiny Act
will justly create a great ferment here." He found "the petition of the
merchants of New York" to be "highly improper; in point of time, most
absurd; in the extent of their pretensions, most excessive; and in the
reasoning, most grossly fallacious and offensive." Shelburn wondered

"what demon of discord blows the coals in that devoted province." The consequences of such defiance was sure to "draw upon their heads national resentment . . . and ruin."[47]

Shelburn advocated the use of military force in New York, but Chatham was dissuaded by fear that if New York resisted, France and Spain would come to the aid of the colony. Even if the military were not used, some show of "vigour" was needed "to support the authority of Parliament and the coercive power of this country." Shelburne suggested to Chatham that Parliament pass an act that would make it high treason to ignore a Parliamentary act. He also advocated replacing Governor Henry Moore with "some one of a military character," who would have the discretion "to act with force and gentleness as circumstances might make necessary," suggesting either John Burgoyne or past New York governor Robert Monckton. Shelburne also urged that ,as punishment for New Yorkers' defiance, soldiers be billeted in private homes. Similar retribution had been inflicted on lowland Scots in 1678 when Charles II order the quartering of the "Highland Host" in the homes of lowland peasants. The Highlanders, notorious for their propensity to pillage, stole £200,000 worth of goods before returning to the hills. Shelburne believed that such action was warranted in New York because of the colony's "peculiar ingratitude" since the repeal of the Stamp Act. It was constitutionally permissable, since New York was a conquered province and did not have a charter.[48]

The defiance of the New York assembly was deemed so serious that Chatham and Shelburn believed that it must be handled by Parliament. That body considered the problem and agreed that New York had to be forced to comply as a matter of principle and as an example to other colonies. A Restraining Bill, which revoked the legislative powers of the New York assembly after 1 October 1767 was passed by Parliament in June 1767 and approved by the King-in-Council the next month. Governor Moore did not enforce the Parliamentary act, but only because the Livingston assembly, on 6 June 1767, fearing the ministry more than the mobility, capitulated by voting £3,000 for the Quartering Act. The Sons were outraged at the capitulation and branded the Livingstons as traitors and cowards.[49]

In another effort to centralize imperial authority, southern secretary Shelburne, on 11 December 1766, requested from New York's governor an estimate on the cost of running the government, apparently with the intent of apportioning revenues to pay the military establishment. Shelburne also requested that Moore send him "a full and clear Account of the manner of imposing Quit Rents and of levying them, as also the mode of granting Lands in your Colony; specifying the amounts of the arrears of Quit Rents." Moore responded that the payment of quit rents was almost £19,000 in arrears, but that he adhered to Crown restrictions on land grants. Moore supplied the required figures, explaining there was no "settled Revenue here, if we except the Quit Rents," with all salaries depending "entirely on the Breath of the Assembly, who grant it but from year to year." To New Yorkers, this renewed interest on the part of the ministry in land grants and income raised fears of future interference in New York's internal affairs.[50]

Further evidence of such interference in colonial affairs by the Chatham ministry came with the 1767 Townshend Acts, another attempt to raise revenue in the colonies. The acts represented a significant break from past practices because the revenue was to be used to pay the civil establishment, not the military, as with past revenue acts. Charles Townshend, as a member of the Board of Trade in 1753–54, had advocated that provincial assemblies be relieved of the responsibility of paying the salaries of royal officials. This idea did not originate with Townshend but, in fact, had been suggested by numerous provincial officials, including Robert Hunter and George Clinton, as a means to bolster the royal prerogative by removing governors from the financial control of assemblies. As chancellor of the exchequer in 1767, Townshend proposed the acts, which placed a tax on British manufactured goods and on tea imported into the colonies. The revenue raised was to be used to pay royal colonial officials. The expectation of the ministry was that, in addition to providing money for the civil establishment, the acts would stop some, if not most, of the illegal traffic in tea. By the terms of the Townshend Acts, customs officials could enforce regulations by the use of writs of assistance, which gave officials broad powers to search for contraband. Such means were deemed necessary because of widespread smuggling in the colonies, with the revenue lost in America from smuggling tea alone estimated at £750,000 a year.[51]

The Townshend Acts, approved in June 1767, would have a limited effect as far as immediately moving governors from the control of assemblies. Only six of the thirteen colonies that would eventually rebel had governors who depended exclusively on their assemblies for salaries, New York being among them. Even in New York, the impact would not be felt immediately. New York's attorney general was to be paid with Townshend revenue in 1768, but the governor would not be paid from this tax until 1770.[52]

By 1768, Chatham was seriously ill and only in active control of government during increasingly rare lucid moments. The ministry placed colonial affairs under the direction of the earl of Hillsborough, who had resigned as Board of Trade president in December 1767.

Hillsborough was then named as the first secretary of state for the American Department when the duties of the southern secretary were split. Chatham, finally permitted by the king to resign his office in October of 1768, was replaced as prime minister by the duke of Grafton, who held office only fifteen months.[53]

Political instability was equally evident in New York as animosity between factions and social classes continued. The Sons of Liberty turned on the Livingstons for not standing firm against Parliament in the matter of the Mutiny Act. The radical, urban Sons were not alone in despising the Livingstons. Tenant farmers were appalled at the Livingstons' brutality in suppressing the tenant uprisings. New York's merchants were disgusted with the Livingstons because they recognized them as the instigators of the lower-class riots that had terrified respectable city residents. Then, too, the Livingston faction was in the ascendancy, and so reaped the blame when New York's economy soured following the French and Indian War. The Livingston party, associated in the public mind with attorneys, also suffered when New Yorkers of the middling sort, many of whom were in debt, grew to resent the influence of lawyers, who were rightly believed to favor the interests of the creditor class. Hence lawyers were particularly hated in periods of economic depression. In the March 1768 assembly election, called by Moore in accordance with New York's Septennial Act, attorneys associated with the Livingston family did not get elected. Even John Morin Scott, "One of the most popular among them, attempted to be elected for the city of New York, by the interest and influence of the body of the Law and of the Presbyterians and Independants, who are very numerous but faild. The general cry of the People both in the Town and Country was *No Lawyer in the Assembly*." The result of this animosity toward the Livingstons in 1768 was that their decade-long control of the assembly was weakened.[54]

While the Livingstons still held a majority in the 1768 assembly, the DeLanceys, headed by James DeLancey, Jr., and his uncle, Oliver DeLancey, made significant advances. The DeLanceys's gains were primarily due to their alliance with the Sons of Liberty and the support of the Sons at the polls. The urban and rural disenchantment with the Livingstons, together with the fact that "the DeLanceys join'd the Multitude and supported them in the general Cry of Liberty," enabled the DeLancey faction to place thirteen new members in the assembly out of a total of twenty-seven representatives. The DeLanceys newly acquired strength was enforced by their control of the four influential New York City representatives, "who generally," according to Colden, "have the direction of the House of Assembly." The DeLancey alliance with the Sons paid off handsomely since three of the four urban assemblymen were pro-DeLancey. Livingston candidates running in those counties that had been rocked by tenant agitation were also repudiated. Robert R. Livingston, running in the landlord county of Dutchess, quickly realized the turn of events and gave up before half the votes were cast.[55]

The DeLanceys's political gains, as seen by William Livingston, was also a religious victory for the Anglicans over the Presbyterians and other nonconformists. The DeLanceys won partially because of politicking efforts by Anglican ministers to prevent the nonconformist Livingstons from gaining too much power. Nonconformists feared that with the support of a predominantly Anglican assembly, the Church of England would take steps to deprive nonconformists of religious toleration, thereby excluding them from political office. The Anglican DeLanceys would be secured in political power, while dissenters would be just as permanently excluded. To many nonconformists, a first step to this would be the installation of a Church of England bishop in New York.[56]

The threat was not an idle one. A Test Act had been passed in Ireland in 1704, barring all Roman Catholics and nonconformists from voting or holding public office. The possibility of a similar occurence in other of England's provinces was serious enough for William Livingston to end his almost three-year literary silence. In a renewed effort to awaken the lower and middling classes to the threat posed by the Church of England, Livingston began a series of essays on 14 March 1768. Using the pseudonym "American Whig," Livingston was determined to "shew them on the other side of the water that even the Apprehension of a Bishop's being sent, has raised a Flame here. . . . Tis Noise and Clamour that is at present our best Policy."[57]

Livingston realized the obvious fact that the Church of England in New York, as in other colonies with a large non-English population, was an instrument of Anglicization. But the Anglican church in America lacked significant authority and influence because there was not a resident bishop, with the colonies falling under the dominion of the bishop of London. Periodic but futile attempts had been made to appoint a resident North American bishop.[58]

The episcopal or diocesan controversy was renewed in 1767 when Anglican New Jersey minister Thomas Bradbury Chandler advanced a plan for a colonial diocese. Livingston objected, fearing that the appointment of a bishop would lessen religious freedom in New York, thereby weakening local privilege while strengthening the royal prerogative. The long-term result might be the loss of political influence by dissenters such as William Livingston and perhaps their exclusion from all civil and military posts. To avoid this, Livingston had long advocated the separation of church and state, not only to protect the state from the church but, more importantly, to protect the church from the state. As he noted, of the "many Instances of the Abuse of government, there is none more immediately destructive of the natural Rights of Mankind, than the interposition of the secular Arm in Matters purely religious." On the other hand, Livingston believed that a state backed by an established church was the "most fatal engine ever invented by satan for promoting human wretchedness."[59]

Livingston continued his anti-episcopal campaign in an open letter to John Ewer, bishop of Landaff. The letter was actually written in response to an attack on Americans made by the bishop, who decried the fact that there was opposition among Americans to a resident bishop. Landaff saw this as evidence of betrayal and ingratitude on the part of colonists. He pointed to the care and attention England lavished on the colonies and referred to colonists who objected to an episcopacy as "Infidels and Barbarians." In response, Livingston noted that England did little for the colonies. In fact, said Livingston, "many of the colonies were not only settled without her protection, but by reason of her persecution and intolerance. The emigrants fled from her into the wilds of America, to find an asylum from those usurpations over the consciences of men which she so wantonly exercised, after having forsaken houses and lands, and the most tender connexions." Among the religious emigres of the seventeenth century were William Livingston's great-grandfather, John Livingstone, and his grandfather, Robert Livingston. John Livingstone, a Presbyterian minister, was banished from Scotland by Charles II in 1664 and fled to Holland with part of his family, including his son, Robert. Robert Livingston lived briefly in Holland and then in 1673 emigrated to America, settling first in Massachusetts and then, in 1674, in New York, where he founded the Livingston dynasty. As William Livingston commented to the Reverend Samuel Cooper, "As this country is good enough for me, and I have no notion of removing to Scotland, whence my ancestors were banished by this set of men, I cannot without terror reflect on a bishop's setting his foot on this continent." The controversy was effective in convincing nonconformist New Yorkers that efforts to impose Anglicanism on them must be resisted.[60]

The DeLanceys, afraid of alienating voters, took little public part in the religious controversy. They needed popular support to stay in office. Hence, in their role as an effective country opposition party, they continued to "Head the Mob to disturb his [Governor Moore's] Administration." Their campaign to court the lower classes caused the DeLanceys to heed popular demands for the assembly to protest the Townshend Acts, which were depleting the colony's source of specie. The mob also wanted the assembly to respond to the Massachusetts

Circular Letter, sent to the other twelve mainland colonies in February 1768. The letter called for cooperation among the colonies against Great Britain. The ministry unwittingly provided the DeLanceys with the means to unseat the Livingstons when Hillsborough ordered provincial assemblies not to consider the letter or risk immediate dissolution. The Livingston assembly was secure in power as long as it did not respond to the Massachusetts letter. The intent of the DeLanceys was to force the Livingston assembly to do just that.[61]

Soon after the assembly session began, the DeLanceys incited New York's lower classes to take to the streets. The lower classes, hit hard by unemployment, were eager to vent their discontent. The marchers, "that licentious Rabble" led by "the Sons of Liberty, had formed a design soon after, the meeting of the Assembly to disturb the tranquility of the City by carrying the effigies of certain persons thro' the Town in procession, and afterwards, burning them publicly." The demonstrators, Moore said, were "of the lowest people." The rabble leaders circulated for signatures a petition with "a sett of Instructions to the Citty Members," urging consideration of the Massachusetts letter.[62]

The Livingstons were aware of the DeLanceys's intent. To forestall popular displeasure, the assembly was forced to act by sending petitions to king and Parliament to voice their objections to the Townshend Acts. The petitions were written by William Livingston and William Smith, Jr., the most effective writers in New York. As Smith reported, he and William Livingston initially refused "any Aid till our Friends were actually added to the Committees & that procured the Order on Friday last for that Purpose." After the Livingston faction insured that assemblymen still loyal to them were included on the committees Smith and Livingston "Consented." "I drew a new Draft," said Smith "& instead of a Memorial turned it into a Petition—W Livingston drew that to the King."[63]

These resolutions advanced traditional Whig arguments of the contractual nature of government and the threat the Townshend Acts presented to traditional English liberties. They acknowledged that subjects owed allegiance to the sovereign who in return provided "Protection and Defence of his Constitutional Rights and Privileges." The petition argued that New Yorkers enjoyed all traditional English liberties and rights. They pointed out that since 1683 there had "been a regular Legislature in" New York. They believed they "had gained by uninterrupted Usage, by the Concessions of the Crown and the British Parliament such a civil Constitution as would remain secure and permanent." They asserted that Parliamentary-imposed taxes were "utterly subversive of their constitutional Rights," since they disposed of New Yorkers' property "without their Consent." Taxes should be imposed only "by their own Representatives." The petitions also condemned the Parliamentary Restraining or Suspending Act as "still more dangerous and alarming," since the act, if implemented, would bar assemblymen from any say "in a Matter so important to their Constituents as the Disposition of their Property."[64]

Popular pressure had forced the Livingston assembly to respond to the Massachusetts Circular Letter with "violent Resolves," leading "Henry Moore to dismiss them after a Session of a few Weeks." The assembly was dissolved on 31 December 1768. As Moore reported to Hillsborough, "my duty would not permit me to pass over unregarded the extraordinary resolves the house of Assembly had entered on their Journals." The assembly was led by "a small faction . . . [who] found means to intimidate the rest of the members." [65]

Moore called an election in January 1769. Squaring off against each other were the DeLanceys, the opposition or country party, and the Livingstons, now the court party, "favoured by the Govr." The fear that the Livingston faction would be defeated caused leaders of the Livingston party to propose to James DeLancey, Jr., that the two parties join to nominate a single ticket in the elections. Their bid for political unity was rejected by the DeLanceys, who retained control of the assembly by garnering nine hundred of the fifteen hundred votes cast. Only one Livingston was elected in this age of oral voting, and that was Philip Livingston for the Manor, a representative unacceptable to the DeLanceys. To get rid of Philip, the DeLancey assembly revived an almost forgotten and seldom applied 1699 law that provided assemblymen must reside in the area they represented. Philip Livingston, a chronic thorn in the DeLanceys's collective side, and an ally of Moore's, did not live on the manor and was expelled from the assembly.[66]

Also expelled was Livingston ally Lewis Morris who was elected from Westchester but did not live there. The DeLanceys suggested to the Livingstons that Peter R. Livingston would be acceptable to them as the manor's delegate. The Livingstons instead put up Supreme Court judge, Robert R. Livingston, who was promptly elected. The DeLanceys just as promptly passed a law barring supreme court judges from serving as representatives. Robert R. Livingston ran again and again and was elected each time, and each time the assembly refused to permit him to sit. Judge Livingston finally gave up in 1774.[67]

Contemporaries recognized that the DeLanceys had achieved dominance in provincial politics because of their hold on the lower classes, much as had the Livingstons the previous decade. On 3 June 1769 Governor Moore, referring to the DeLancey sweep of the four assembly seats in New York City, noted the influence of the DeLanceys's lower-class supporters. Moore termed them a "licentious set of Men, who call themselves Sons of Liberty, and who have had very great influence on the Elections of Members for this City."[68]

Moore's concerns about New York's politics died with him on 11 September 1769, bringing Cadwallader Colden out of a four-year retirement to again head the province until a new governor was appointed. Colden disliked both factions, but his greatest animosity was reserved for the Livingstons. Consequently, one of Colden's first acts as governor was to eject as many Livingstons and Livingston allies as possible from government posts. An early target was Philip Livingston, Jr., who had served Moore as private secretary. Before Moore's death, he had appointed Livingston as surrogate and register of the prerogative court. Livingston wanted to continue in those posts. On bringing Colden news of Moore's death, Colden informed him "that I should not be continued in my Department." Colden was adamant, despite Livingston's pleas, and appointed his ally Goldsbrow Banyar in Livingston's place.[69]

The DeLanceys continued to dominate the assembly, placing the Livingstons at a distinct political disadvantage. Influencing neither governor nor legislature, the Livingstons remained on the periphery of power in New York. By necessity, they turned more and more to the lower classes to garner support for the next assembly election.

Colden returned to New York City to face a problem all too familiar for him. Colden was unable to seize personal control of either the council or the assembly, both of which were controlled by the DeLanceys. Nor could he hope for any assistance from the Livingstons, who despised the lieutenant governor as much as did the DeLanceys. Consequently, Colden, by now an old man, decided not to fight. As Smith observed, Colden had "a Council and an Assembly in the Hands of a Family [the DeLanceys] who were his Antient Enemies and being utterly Friendless & helpless could have no Hopes from a Dissolution & therefore suddenly resolved to resign his Government intirely into their Hands."[70]

Despite Smith's claim, Colden's accommodation with the DeLancey assembly represented a mutually beneficial agreement more than it did a surrender. Colden wanted to be paid his gubernatorial salary, and he wanted another bill passed for the continued support of British troops in New York in line with the Mutiny Act. The DeLancey assembly had to address the serious shortage of cash in the colony by authorizing an immediate issue of money. The absence of both specie and paper money caused a severe decline in prices. Many people were imprisoned for debt, while others were forced to sell "their Estates for one Half of their Value; the trading Part of the Colony are unable to make Remittances; the British Merchants and Manufacturers are prevented from receiving their just Debts, and the General, and other public Officers of the Army, are obliged to negotiate their Bills of Exchange considerably below the usual Par."[71]

A currency bill was needed that would go into effect immediately. Despite his instructions not to approve money bills without suspending clauses, Colden signed the currency bill. The assembly in return voted to pay Colden's salary and to raise £2,000 to supply British troops based in New York City. This measure, passed 21 November 1769, was bitterly opposed by both the radical Sons of Liberty, led by Sears and Lamb, and the more moderate branch of the Sons, led by Alexander McDougall. The Sons now turned on the DeLanceys, as they had previously turned on the Livingstons. The criticism of the DeLanceys led the Livingstons to ally with McDougall when the family, in 1769, seeking to regain its influence, resumed its efforts to court the Sons and, through them, the lower classes. In order to ingratiate themselves with the Sons, the Livingstons realized they needed to ally with a popular leader. They found the perfect foil in Alexander McDougall, who, by 1768, had emerged as a leader of the more moderate faction of the Sons. A self-made man, McDougall, the son of a dairy farmer, had prospered as a privateer and then, with his new-found wealth, acquired respectability as a merchant and landowner. A Presbyterian who was thoroughly committed to Robert R. Livingston, the Livingston family, and the republican cause, McDougall had recruited sailors to swell Stamp Act mobs. He was eager to serve the Livingston cause.[72]

The furor raised by the DeLancey assembly's appropriation caused the radical and moderate Sons to put their differences aside. The now united Sons protested the passage of the assembly measure with a new series of riots. McDougall, on 16 December 1769, published an anonymous handbill, "To the Betrayed Inhabitants of the City and Colony of New-York." In the handbill McDougall criticized the DeLancey assembly for voting funds for British soldiers and urged that a public meeting be held to formulate plans for opposing the measure. The meeting, held on 18 December, was attended by some fourteen hundred New Yorkers and was conducted by Sons of Liberty leader John Lamb. The crowd decisively condemned the DeLancey assembly's action. So did William Livingston, who published a letter in the New York Gazette reminding colonists not only of the cost, but also of the inherent danger a standing army presented to a free society.[73]

The opposition propaganda outraged the DeLanceys and Lieutenant Governor Colden, who well knew that William Livingston, Scott, and

Alexander McDougall, n.d., Museum of the City of New York. The Scottish-born McDougall began life humbly as the son of a dairyman. After amassing a fortune during the French and Indian War, McDougall became politically active as a devotee of the Livingston family. His career continued during the Revolution, rising to major general. He also served in the Continental Congress and the New York Senate.

Smith were again instigating the lower classes to mischief. His suspicions were confirmed on 19 January 1770, when Scott was seen taking an active role in the two-day Battle of Golden Hill. Scott encouraged the melee along by "working on the passions of the populace, and exciting riots." The battle was presumably fought between New Yorkers and British soldiers over the erection of a liberty pole. Tensions had increased "between the Towns people and Soldiers, which produced several affrays, and daily, by means of wicked incendiaries, grew more serious[.] At last some Towns people began to arm, and the Soldiers rushed from their Barracks to support their fellow Soldiers."[74]

The real issue was not liberty poles, but rather the presence of royal soldiers in New York, there to keep civilians in line. The issue was also economic, since off-duty soldiers worked in the city for lower wages than did New Yorkers. Colden blamed the triumvirate for the disturbance. He claimed they incited the populace "to raise an indignation against the Assembly (then sitting) for granting money to the Soldiers, who were represented as ready to cut the throats of the Citizens." Colden left little doubt as to who was leading these people of "inferior rank" in the riots. They were people like Yale-educated William Livingston, John Morin Scott, and William Smith, Jr. They and their cohorts were "independents from New England, or educated there, and of Republican principles."[75]

The DeLancey assembly, mindful of their prestige, voted the McDougall pamphlet an "infamous and scandalous Libel." Colden agreed to prosecute the author and publisher of "To The Betrayed Inhabitants." McDougall was identified as the publisher and charged with seditious libel. The McDougall case paralleled in many respects the sedition trial of parliamentary representative John Wilkes, who, in 1763, had published an essay critical of the king. The Livingstons were as quick to point out these similarities as had been Lewis Morris to link Governor Cosby's actions with those of Robert Walpole.[76]

The colonial public was well aware of the Wilkes case. In 1763, all three New York newspapers reprinted Wilkes's offensive essay. The work, in which Wilkes criticized George III, had originally appeared in number 45 of *The North Briton*. New Yorkers were offended by the king's abuse of the law when he ordered the use of a general warrant to search Wilkes's home. They further voiced their concern over the king's attack on the fundamental rights of freedom of the press and speech.[77]

The New York press also reported Wilkes's flight from England, his return, and, in 1768, his fine and imprisonment, and the subsequent rioting in London in protest to the king's persecution of Wilkes. The populace seized on these incidents as yet additional examples of

British tyranny. Hence, New York crowds were sensitized to the issues represented by Wilkes and quick to associate these same issues with McDougall. The cases were not exactly parallel since Wilkes criticized the executive, while McDougall criticized the legislature. The main similarities were that both cases involved a challenge to established authority—one royal, one provincial—and both represented a threat to freedom of the press. In case New Yorkers missed the association with Wilkes, the Livingstons took pains to emphasize the similarities. As Colden observed, McDougall was wealthy and "could easily have found the Bail required of him, but he choose to go to Jail, and lyes there immitating Mr. Wilkes in every thing he can." In jail, much to the delight of the Sons of Liberty and the Livingstons—and the embarrassment of the DeLanceys and the lieutenant governor—McDougall became a martyr, identified as the American Wilkes. Since Wilkes criticized the king in number 45 of the *North Briton*, McDougall and his supporters seized on that same number to identify their cause with that of Wilkes. Forty-five pounds of beef from a forty-five months-old steer were sent to the prisoner by Thomas Smith, while Peter R. Livingston sent him forty-five bottles of wine. Visitors came in groups of forty-five, including forty-five virgins, who, it was said, were each forty-five years old. The DeLanceys insisted that only twenty-eight of the women were virgins.[78]

To prove to the Sons the sincerity of their new commitment to the radical members of the lower and middling sort, Livingston, Smith, and Scott took pains to be seen with McDougall, visiting him in prison, marching in processions, and publishing letters and essays defending his actions. They also took an active role in McDougall's legal defense, with Scott and Livingston serving as his attorneys. In April 1770, Livingston, in a vain effort to prevent the grand jury from indicting, introduced as evidence other anonymous essays circulated in New York that were all critical of government. These included Livingston's own 1757 *Review of the Military Operations*. Despite the revelation, the grand jury, loaded with DeLancey partisans, on 25 April, found a true bill. McDougall pled not guilty to the charge.[79]

Crowd support for McDougall and sentiments against British imperialism were raised further on 12 March 1770, when news of the Boston Massacre was published in the *New York Mercury*. John Morin Scott garnered additional support for the Livingstons when he again attacked the DeLancey assembly for granting money to arm British troops. As he pointed out, "real and independent Sons of Liberty" opposed funding soldiers "to Butcher their fellow Subjects, as was lately the Case in the horrid Massacre at Boston."[80]

The lower classes were further disenchanted with the DeLanceys because of the assembly's handling of the McDougall case. The Crown's case against McDougall was dropped because of the death of a witness, and he was released after eighty-one days in prison. In December of 1770, McDougall was rejailed for contempt of the assembly and brought before that body. The DeLancey assembly, led by John DeNoyelles, was more concerned with preserving its prestige than with furthering freedom of expression. When McDougall refused to answer DeNoyelle's questions, he was terrorized with threats of being pressed to death. The assembly members, hardly champions of personal liberties, voted that McDougall "does deny the Authority of this House, and is therefore guilty of a high contempt." He was ordered to "be taken into Custody by the Serjeant at Arms" and thrown in the common jail. McDougall was finally released in April of 1771.[81]

Assisted by such outrages as McDougall's persecution and the Boston Massacre, the Livingstons's efforts to court the Sons proved successful. The Sons were loyal to the upper-class Livingstons, but since no assembly elections were called in New York between 1769 and 1775, the DeLanceys retained control of New York's assembly.

By 1770, the political influence of the lower classes was obvious to and feared by the elite. Sentiments raised by the Livingstons and other propagandists caused widespread rioting in 1765 and 1766 that went well beyond what the oligarchs considered acceptable limits. In New York, rural riots were usually spontaneous, but urban rioters customarily took their cue from the elite. This changed in 1765 when urban mobs acted spontaneously and rejected all direction from the upper class. These disturbances convinced the Livingstons that by opposing the British government, New York's elite raised popular sentiments that endangered their own lives and property. Fears created by these riots reinforced William Livingston's distrust of mob rule and democracy and caused him to stop courting the lower classes.

The Sons of Liberty had displayed both their political muscle and their political savvy. The change to activism began with the Stamp Act riots and the turmoil that succeeded them. At that time, the lower classes began to act and think for themselves. Oddly enough it never seemed to occur to New York's Sons of Liberty to propose one of their own class for public office. The elite and the elite alone dominated New York politics for the remainder of the colonial period. The DeLanceys and the Livingstons continued "in violent opposition to each other—one is careful to preserve their popularity in order to secure their seats in the Assembly, and the other takes every method to gain popularity in hopes of a Dissolution of the Assembly on the arrival of a new Govr."[82]

Despite—or because of—the perennial struggles for power between political factions, the middling and lower sort were gaining a knowledge of their own political importance. Increasingly it was the lower classes who were responsible for setting the tone and leading the resistance to Great Britain. This fact was recognized by contemporaries who noted that it was the "middle rank of people" to whom the "colony and the common cause is indebted for the bold stand made for liberty in this province, and not to the first rate inhabitants." The increasing independence of the lower class led the "first rate" inhabitants to be wary of them. In turn, the lower class grew increasingly alienated from the elite, whom they recognized as their exploiters. The elite's acknowledgement of the assumption of leadership by the lower order was apparent in 1769 when the Livingstons made an alliance with the Sons of Liberty.[83]

On an imperial level, New York's continuing defiance caused the ministry to adopt an increasingly hard line in colonial administration. As the decade of the 1760s advanced, Britons' early irritation with all Americans escalated. Initially irritated with colonists, particularly New Yorkers, who continued to trade with the French in Canada during the Seven Years' War and who refused to raise soldiers or money to protect themselves, annoyance among Britons increased as the colonists rejected Parliamentary authority. It was inconceivable to Britons at home that American colonists could question legitimate authority, particularly the authority of Parliament. The colonists had clearly forgotten that they existed only to serve the mother country. The colonists, for their part, were equally convinced that if they did not resist encroachments on their liberties, constitutional privileges would be stripped from them one by one. As the struggle between prerogative and privilege escalated, the increasing political participation of the lower and middling sorts added another, thoroughly unpredictable, factor to the equasion.

Despite distractions presented by class strife, New York's elite were determined to resist the crown's continued efforts to reduce the colony to submission. The persistence of these attitudes lends credence to Edmund Burke's observation that "The Americans have made a discovery, or think they have made one, that we mean to oppress them: we have made a discovery, or think we have made one, that they intend to rise in rebellion against us. . . . We know not how to advance; they know not how to retreat."[84]

8

To Restore Union and Harmony, 1770–1776: The Administrations of Lord Dunmore (1770–1771), William Tryon (1771–1780, on leave 7 April 1774 to 25 June 1775), and Cadwallader Colden (1774–1775)

Fully trusting that this honorable House will listen with Attention to our Complaints, and Redress our Grievances, by adopting such Measures, as shall be found most conducive to the general Welfare of the whole Empire, and most likely to Restore Union and Harmony among all the different Branches.[1]

The gilded equestrian statue of George III ordered by New York from England was delivered in the summer of 1770 and erected "in a square near the Fort and fronting the principal street of the City." New Yorkers's loyalty to the king was demonstrated on this occasion by numerous toasts, the playing of martial music, and the "discharge of 32 pieces of Cannon while the Spectators expressed their joy, by loud acclamations, and the . . . ceremony concluded with great chearfulness and good humour."[2] The statue remained in place for six years, until Governor William Tryon reported that the "King's statue has been demolished, as well as the King's Arms in the City Hall, the established churches shut up, & every Vistage of Royalty, as far as has been in the power of the Rebels, done away."[3]

The rejection of royal rule symbolized by the destruction of King George's statue came because of a string of misconceptions on the part of Americans and Britons. New Yorkers were convinced that the intent of the British government was to reduce colonists to slavery. Their fears of tyranny were apparently confirmed in 1774 when Parliament altered the charter of the Massachusetts Bay Company, creating fears that all colonial charters would be changed. New York was particularly at risk since, lacking a written charter, its rights were based solely on tradition and custom. As the contest between prerogative and privilege reached its final stages, the elite was alarmed by Parliament's continued efforts to impose taxes on the colonies. Anxiety increased among provincials about the safety of their property, the foundation of all English liberties and freedoms. The British, for their part, remained convinced that Americans were engaged in a plot to shake off British control. These fears, and continued social tension, produced a highly volatile climate in New York in both rural and urban areas.[4]

No plot to rebel existed on the part of Americans. In fact, the provincial upper class until 1776 remained largely opposed to separation and committed to the status quo. The lower class, having the most to gain from any alteration in the political and social orders, tended to favor change in both areas. By 1770, it was apparent to most elite New Yorkers that the lower and middling sort wanted greater political participation. Increasing demands for a more democratic form of government appalled all but the most ardent republicans. The elite believed they alone were best qualified to lead. Efforts by the elite to maintain the old order increased class divisions and resentment. More and more, lower-class anger was aimed at the provincial elite as well as the British ministry.

The elite-dominated assembly was the most obvious target for lower class agitators who wanted more political power. While that body grew politically adept in its struggle with the Crown for autonomy, it made few concessions to cries for autonomy from the lower class. As the provincial period progressed, lower- and middle-class leaders, aware of their growing influence, came to resent the exclusive power wielded by the elite in the assembly. The New York assembly, and all other provincial assemblies, was also under attack by the British ministry. This attack sprang from the assembly's success in reducing the royal prerogative, now represented by Governor John Murray, earl of Dunmore, who arrived in New York on 18 October 1770. Imperial authorities, responding at last to complaints and suggestions of numerous governors, successfully worked to reduce the now overblown power of the assembly.

Continuing friction between metropolitan and provincial forces and between elite conservatives and lower-class radicals heightened the climate of discontent that ultimately produced rebellion. When revolution became inevitable, those members of the elite who chose not to ally with Great Britain moved quickly to seize control of the revolutionary machinery that had been set up by lower-class radicals; when revolution occurred, the elite wanted to be in control to effect a revolution in the classic sense of the word. They wanted first, to recreate in America a new and better England than existed in Europe and, second, to return society to the way it had been in some idealized past, with themselves still in control. Only by leading and moderating the rabble could the elite hope to retain their privileged places in society.

Unrest was endemic in New York during the 1770s in both urban and rural areas, although rural dissension had little to do with imperial rule. Typical of this rural dissension were the riots that broke out on New York's northeastern border in the late 1760s and 1770s, brought about in part by the action of manor lords during the 1766 land riots. After the ruthless suppression of the Hudson Valley riots in the summer of 1766, tenants on the manors realized they had no chance of owning the property they tilled. They could either resign themselves to remaining tenants or move. Many chose the latter alternative, but there were few places for them to go, with the settled provinces of New England and the Middle Atlantic to the northeast and south and the Iroquois to the west. The only area open to settlement was to the north in the Green Mountains. Similarly, New Englanders who were facing land shortages wanted to move west, but they could not settle in land below Albany that was controlled by New York's manor lords. The land above and to the west of Albany was still under the control of the Iroquois. Hence New Englanders too looked to the Green Mountains. Both displaced Yankees and displaced Yorkers became New Hampshire grantees.[5]

This area had been in dispute since 1749 when New Hampshire Governor Benning Wentworth wrote to New York Governor George Clinton to ask precisely where New York's northeastern boundary lay. Clinton responded that New York's border was the west side of the Connecticut River, as indicated by the duke of York's 1664 patent. Wentworth claimed the duke's patent was obsolete and set New York's boundary only twenty miles east of the Hudson. Hence Wentworth contended the Green Mountains were part of New Hampshire. Even before Wentworth's initial letter to Clinton, he had granted land for a six-mile-square town to be called Bennington, which was located thirty-five miles west of the official Connecticut River boundary. Wentworth informed Clinton that he would appeal to the home government for a ruling on the border issue. New Hampshire grants in the Green Mountains continued so that by 1764 there were well over a hundred townships created on the west side of the Connecticut River in the area that would eventually become the state of Vermont. That year the King-in-Council ruled that the west bank of the Connecticut was the boundary between New York and New Hampshire.[6]

In line with the royal order confirming New York's border at the Connecticut River, Cadwallader Colden as lieutenant governor began granting land in the Green Mountains to New Yorkers. Among the grantees were William Livingston, William Smith, Jr., and John Morin Scott. Despite Colden's deep antipathy toward the triumvirate, he approved land patents for all three in the disputed territory. In New York, personal animosities were put aside when land was at issue and profits were to be made. Colden stood to profit handsomely from land grant fees. Among the patents issued by Colden was a 1766 patent for William Livingston, William Smith, Jr., and Whitehead Hicks, who represented twenty-seven other patentees, for thirty thousand acres in the Green Mountains.[7]

Opposition to New York owners and tenants arose because, in many cases, the land granted by New York had already been granted by New Hampshire. Cadwallader Colden demanded those New Hampshire grantees already in possession of disputed land obtain legal New York titles for fees of $31.25 per every thousand acre grant. Most New Hampshire grantees could not afford these fees. They were also reluctant to pay New York's higher quit rent of 2s. 6p. per one hundred acres as opposed to New Hampshire's rent of 1s. per one hundred acres.[8]

The New Hampshire grantees refused to pay what they considered to be exorbitant and unnecessary fees to New York. They solicited the Society for the Propagation of the Gospel to help in their appeal to the Board of Trade against New York. The result was a 1767 royal proclamation that ordered New York governors to "make no new Grants of these Lands and that you do not molest any person in the quiet possession of His Grant." The order pointed out that expecting New Hampshire grantees to pay what amounted to "the immense sum of thirty three thousand pounds in Fees . . . for no other reason than its being found necessary to settle the Line of boundary between the Colonies in question is so unjustifiable that his Majesty is not only determined to have the strictest enquiry made into the Circumstances of the charge, but expects the clearest and fullest answer to every part of it."[9]

The order had little effect on New York's governors. In all, over two million acres were granted by New York governors Colden, Moore, Dunmore, and Tryon, and all but 180,620 acres were granted in defiance of the 1767 royal proclamation. Colden alone granted almost a million acres for a personal profit to him of $30,171.18 in fees, a small indication of the profits to be earned by New York's governors and of the greed of these governors who defied—and thus diminished—the royal prerogative to benefit themselves. Along the way, they bolstered local privilege.[10]

The money to be made from land patents and other fees explains why New York governors continued to grant land in the disputed northeastern area, much to the outrage of the New Hampshire grantees. They responded to Yorker incursion by driving off New York surveyors, burning houses, destroying crops, and pulling down fences. They went so far as to close New York courts and take court officials to Massachusetts. In defense of their actions they claimed to have inside information that "His Majty intends to recall his Royal order" and put the disputed territory "within the Jurisdiction of the Provce of New Hampshire." The rioters, who soon called themselves the Green Mountain Boys, organized into military units to resist dominance by New York landlords.[11]

On the imperial level, except for the contention over land-granting practices, there was relatively little open defiance in New York in 1770. That year, the New York assembly appointed Irish-born member of Parliament Edmund Burke as its London agent. Soon after Burke's appointment, the Board of Trade questioned the propriety of the assembly hiring a colonial agent without the approval of the governor and council. The Board believed the appointment and direction of an agent should be shared by the governor, council, and assembly, as was the practice prior to George Clinton's administration. The Board informed Burke they would in the future insist that this power be wielded jointly. Burke warned the New York assembly that if they accepted the Board's decision, he would resign his post since he wanted his "Employment as a matter wholly detached from Administration."[12]

The ministry's intent was to downgrade assembly power and upgrade imperial influence. In line with that, the colonies were urged to end nonimportation, which continued in New York under the direction of the Livingstons, now strongly allied with the Sons of Liberty. The Sons, to keep public interest high, occasionally staged processions such as that "to expose a Boston Importer, who happened to come to this place." The Sons found themselves almost without a cause when Parliament in April 1770 voted to end the Townshend Acts on 1 December 1770. The veto came at the direction of newly appointed prime minister Lord North who urged repeal because the acts taxed British manufactures. The tea tax, which brought an average yearly revenue of £12,000, was retained as a confirmation of Parliament's right to tax the colonies and to establish a source of revenue from which to pay the civil establishment.[13]

The predominantly landowning Livingstons wanted to continue nonimportation until the tea tax was also repealed. The DeLancey-led New York merchants, in dire straits, protested. British imports to New

York had declined in value by three-quarters in only one year. The merchants urged abandonment of nonimportation except for tea. The radical Sons of Liberty, supported by the Livingstons, immediately protested the merchants's decision and then "published an inflammatory anonymous advertisement," calling a meeting at City Hall. Leading the meeting were Sons of Liberty Isaac Sears, "Captn McDougald the American Wilks and some others of the same kidney." Sears swore to murder any merchant who did not support nonimportation.[14]

Undeterred by Sears's threat, New York's merchants conducted a door-to-door survey in which they asked New Yorkers if they objected to ending nonimportation except for tea. The overwhelming majority of New Yorkers—1180 in favor of ending nonimportation with 300 neutral, according to Colden—voted along with the merchants, much to the annoyance of the Sons. The ban was lifted, despite continued protests from a "restless Faction [the Livingstons], who from popular arguments, rumours and invectives are endeavouring to excite riots and opposition among the lower class of people."[15]

The Parliamentary tea tax alarmed New Yorkers because the £2,000 salary of the earl of Dunmore was to be taken "out of the Revenue arising in America by the duty upon Tea," leaving him, unlike most previous New York governors, thoroughly independent of the whims of the assembly. The paying of governors by the Crown significantly reduced the power of the provincial assembly. A financially independent governor made it much more difficult for a provincial legislative leader such as James DeLancey or William Livingston to exert undue influence on politics as they had in the past.[16]

With a steady source of income guaranteed by the tea tax and fees, Dunmore was in an enviable financial position. An indication of the monetary value of fees for New York's governors was the struggle that arose over Dunmore's suit against Lieutenant Governor Cadwallader Colden. Dunmore, as greedy as any governor, allied with the Livingston faction. Much to the delight of Livingston, Smith, and Scott, Dunmore demanded half of the money Colden received from fees for the time between Dunmore's appointment and his actual arrival in the colony. Heeding Smith's advice, Dunmore decided to hear the case in the juryless chancery court where the governor presided. Colden was outraged, both at the action and Dunmore's decision to file the "Bill in Chancery (where the Govr is the sole Judge and is to receive the benefit of the suit)." Colden believed that his enemies instigated the suit "to discover the Perquisites which I have received." Colden claimed the only money he "received was a voluntary donation for services done to individuals." Voluntary or not, the amount of money that came to Colden and other New York governors was considerable.[17]

William Livingston, an old enemy of Colden's, lost no time in adding to Colden's outrage by writing a "Soliloquy" in which Colden laments his late stand against jury verdicts during the *Forsey v. Cunningham* appeal. "What a Fool was I," Livingston has Colden say, "to kick up a Dust against Juries? 'Tis the best Tryal in the World; and the grand Bulwark of English Liberty." Colden, with good reason, objected strenuously to paying any money to Dunmore and cited as precedent the fact that Rip Van Dam, when faced with a similar demand from William Cosby in 1732, had refused to pay. Colden did not, however, mention his own defiance of Robert Monckton's similar 1761 demand. The Crown's attorney general agreed that Colden had no obligation to give Dunmore the money.[18]

Even without Colden's contribution, the profits from the New York post were so great that Dunmore protested bitterly when he found that he was reassigned to Virginia after only a few months in office. Until the moment his replacement, William Tryon, arrived on 9 July 1771, Dunmore hoped to change assignments with him so that he could retain his New York post. Tryon, who also knew the monetary worth of a New York governorship, refused. Dunmore was bitter. At a reception given shortly before he left for Virginia, he cried out in a drunken stupor, "Damn Virginia—did I ever seek it? Why is it forced upon me? I asked for New York—New York I took, and they have robbed me of it without my consent."[19]

The profits to be made from fees was one reason New York governors continued to grant land in defiance of the 1767 proclamation. In 1771, the Board of Trade, appalled by New Yorkers's wanton disregard for the interests of New Hampshire grantees, strongly recommended to the King-in-Council that past land-granting practices in New York be stopped: no more land should be granted "either upon the terms or in the manner in which they have hitherto exercised that power." Lands should be awarded solely according to the ability of the petitioner "to cultivate and improve the same." Even worse, as far as elite New Yorkers were concerned, was the board's recommendation that a limit be placed and enforced on the amount of acreage to be granted. They suggested "that no one of the said persons, so applying shall either in his or her own name or in the name or names of any other person or persons in trust for him or her receive more than five hundred Acres."[20]

American Secretary of State Hillsborough told Tryon in December 1771 that New York's method of granting land would "probably be the subject of serious consideration at a proper opportunity." He further warned, in this show of imperial authority, that, if people obtained patents under false pretenses or falsified patents as "a Colour for giving to any one person more than he is allowed by the King's Instructions," the ministry would take "some effectual measure" to halt "an abuse of so gross and fraudulent a nature."[21]

Despite the knowledge that an investigation was to be made into New York's land-granting practices and despite knowing that his instructions forbade the granting of land in New Hampshire, Tryon continued to ignore the best interests of the royal prerogative and to approve Green Mountain land grants. Tryon, who, like Dunmore, allied with the Livingstons on arrival, openly admitted to William Smith, Jr., that he was ready to break other of his instructions "whenever they [the Assembly] could shew equal Reasons of which he was to be the Judge, he would comply," ignoring the fact that his policies increased local privilege at the expense of imperial interests. Tryon excused his conduct to the home government by pointing out that large land grants controlled rising democratic tendencies. He considered it "good policy to lodge large Tracts of Land in the hands of Gentlemen of weight and consideration. They will naturally farm out their lands to Tenants; a method which will ever create subordination and counterpoise, in some measure, the general levelling spirit, that so much prevails in some of His Majty's Governts."[22]

The New York governor's grants heightened the fears of New Hampshire grantees about the security of their property and placed in jeopardy New York tenants who occupied the disputed Green Mountain land. Attacked by New Hampshire grantees, New Yorkers fought back, but were outnumbered. British troops had been used to quell the 1766 land riots in the Hudson Valley. Governor William Tryon appealed to generals Frederick Haldimand and Thomas Gage for military help in 1773 and again in 1774, but to no avail. The British, preoccupied with more pressing military problems in other colonies, did not consider the New York frontier situation serious enough to warrant the deployment of British troops there. In an attempt to cope with the chaos on the frontier, the New York assembly in 1774 passed harsh laws for the area, fixing penalties greater than those for similar offenses in other areas.[23]

Haldimand and Gage were convinced that Tryon had overestimated the strength of "a few lawless Vagabonds" on the frontier, but nothing alarmed New Yorkers more than a threat to their landholdings. Even more serious was a 1773 royal decree, issued in response to the Board of Trade's recommendations, which validated only those land grants in the Green Mountains that were improved. As Tryon observed, "scarce any measure can raise a more General discontent in this Colony, than a Law to vacate Patents for non-settlement." He further noted that "loud complaints will be made of the Crown's reseizing of unimproved lands . . . since the non improvements are to be imputed to the violence & power of the general opposition of the N. Hampshire Planters in the vicinity." The threat to seize undeveloped land was a serious concern for New York's manor lords, many of whom owned thousands of acres of unimproved land. In response to this threat, the elite sought to protect their manorial holdings with an assembly act passed in 1775 that prohibited the royal government from challenging any sixty-year old land grant.[24]

William Livingston's landholdings were among those threatened by the Crown's order since most of the 15,000 or more acres he owned in New York and Vermont were undeveloped. Livingston was able to sell about 700 acres of his Green Mountain land in 1775, but his remaining Vermont acreage was jeopardized by New Hampshire grantees who, in 1777, petitioned the Continental Congress for statehood. John Witherspoon in Congress tried to negotiate a settlement for Livingston with Vermont leaders. Livingston was unforgiving toward "the robbers of Vermont," who took "the best part of my Estate" and granted it to others. Offers by Vermont officials to substitute other land for the Vermont acres Livingston owned were scorned by him. As he told Witherspoon, "I want my own because I know them to be good but I do not know what kind of lands they will think proper to [substitute] . . . as an equivalent."[25]

Insecure land titles caused open contention in New York, as did friction between various interest groups and social classes. New York's lower classes grew increasingly alienated from the elite and resentful of the elite's power. Much of this resentment was directed at the DeLancey assembly, partially prompted by the assembly's persecution of Alexander McDougall. A series of letters published in 1772 stated categorically that it was the power of the assembly that the lower class feared, not "the power of the crown."[26]

Class contention in New York increased following the passage of the 1773 Parliamentary Tea Act, which gave a monopoly of the tea trade to the East India Company. The New York merchant consignees chosen to receive the tea were among the most socially prominent and politically active of the elite. The rank and file remained opposed to the importation of tea, circulating handbills and advocating nonconsumption. The merchants were equally determined to import and sell East India tea. A letter published in the 21 October 1773 issue of the *New York Journal* carried an overt threat of physical harm to the merchant elite. It warned the elite that "it will be impossible to shield or screen yourselves from the many darts that will incessantly be levelled against your persons." Well-aware of the importance of the services they performed, the lower-class writer further reminded the elite, "You cannot become your own cooks, butchers, butlers, nor bakers." The threat of violence was again made explicit when the writer pointed out that "A thousand avenues to death would be perpetually open to receive and swallow you, and ten thousand uplifted shafts, ready to strike the fatal stroke whenever a favourable opportunity offered for that purpose."[27]

The merchant consignees took the threats seriously as resistance continued through the fall of 1773, with demonstrations, broadsides, orations, and renewed threats. Despite the vocal opposition, Tryon told the ministry he still had "sanguine Hopes" that the tax would be peacefully accepted once the tea actually reached New York. The merchant consignees realized this was impossible and resigned on 1 December. All hope of peaceful acceptance vanished when news of the 16 December 1773, dumping of East India tea in Boston Harbor reached New York. New Yorkers renewed their determination not to pay the tax, causing Tryon to note that "the Commissioners appointed for vending those Teas finding it would be impossible to carry into Execution the Powers granted them, have this day presented a Memorial, requesting Government would take the Teas under its Protection . . . the General Voice is no Sales, no Consumption while the American Duty remains unrepealed by Parliament." New Yorkers remained determined in their opposition to "the Monopoly, and the Importation Duty in America." Tryon realized that the only way government officials could keep the tea safe was "under the protection of the Point of the Bayonet, and Muzle of the Canon, and even then I do not see how the consumption could be effected."[28]

Despite opposition to the Tea Act, New York had returned to a relative tranquility on 7 April 1774 when Tryon, in ill health, returned to England for a brief visit. He left Cadwallader Colden again in charge of government. Only a few weeks later, turmoil returned when New York staged its own tea party. Opposition to the tea tax was led by lower-class radicals who refused to permit the tea to be landed or stored in the fort. The crowd's insistence heightened fears among the elite of mob action and democracy.[29]

The ministry responded to Boston's destruction of property with the Intolerable Acts, which shut Boston's harbor and altered Massachusetts's government. Most Britons, including Lord Dartmouth, who replaced Hillsborough as American secretary in 1772, and prime minister Lord North, were convinced that Boston's defiant destruction of private property was an affront that called for severe punishment. The impossibility of finding the Boston culprits who dumped the tea led the ministry to the decision to punish the entire community.[30]

The ministry reacted strongly against Massachusetts because, as Lord North pointed out, the colonists "deny our legislative authority. . . . We must control them or submit to them." North believed the ministry must do "something immediate and effectual," since he realized "the degrees of Freedom or restraint in which they [the colonies] were to be held" was no longer the issue, but rather whether the colonies would "be totally seperated from" Great Britain.[31]

While most Britons, including members of Parliament, were as appalled as Lord North at Boston's destruction of the tea, a few members of Parliament spoke out against the Intolerable Acts, questioning the constitutional legality of making the entire city of Boston "dependant upon the Kings private pleasure." Such indiscriminate punishment, they believed, "was without Precedent, and of a most dangerous Example." Despite the misgivings of some representatives, Parliament passed and the king confirmed the Intolerable Acts in March 1774.[32]

Burke, who had opposed the Intolerable Acts in Commons, was pleased when New York Governor William Tryon arrived in London at the end of May 1774. The governor, Burke believed, would help him in his parliamentary resistance to the Quebec Bill. The act, soon passed by Parliament, granted religious toleration to Canadians and provided for a nonrepresentative government in that province. It also extended Canada's boundaries to include land claimed by American colonists in the Ohio Valley. Colonists saw parallels in the granting of toleration to Canada's Roman Catholics with James II's efforts to grant religious toleration as the first step to establishing Roman Catholicism as the state religion in England. Nonconformists feared the Quebec Act was a similar smokescreen for establishing the Church of England in all the colonies. Removal of western land put an end to the expansionist plans of provincials, which was exactly the ministry's intent. British officials believed their difficulties in America sprang from weak royal government and too rapid population growth, which put stresses on society. The rapid population growth in the colonies was also of concern to the English because there was a commensurate and unwelcome population drain from Great Britain and Ireland. Less land would mean a slower European exodus and a slower rate of colonial growth. The Quebec Act was thus seen by colonists as a double threat to religion and to expansion. The act was lumped by colonists with the Intolerable Acts because it was equally objectionable to them.[33]

In New York, the acts were "immediately publish'd in all our News Papers, and was the subject of all Conversation." A congress of all colonies was called to meet in Philadelphia in September 1774 to plan a common course of action against the British. The First Continental Congress banned imports from Great Britain after December 1774 and exports from Great Britain after 10 September 1775.[34]

Despite congressional action, popular fervor in New York City against the Intolerable Acts, particularly among the lower classes, remained so strong that the "principal Inhabitants" feared the "hot headed men" who comprised the Sons of Liberty "might run the City into dangerous measures." To forestall such extremism, the elite, acting on a prearranged plan, "appear'd in a considerable body, at the first Meeting of the People after the Boston Port Act was publish'd here." They dissolved "the former Committee" of Correspondence, created to keep in touch with other colonies. The Committee contained many lower-class radicals. In its place was "appointed a new one of 51 Persons, in which care was taken to have a number of the most prudent and considerate People of the Place." The Sons had proposed their own slate of candidates for this committee, but were outmanuevered by the elite who put up the familiar names of men from New York's traditional ruling class. The move of the elite to take control of the mob and reassert their authority was similar to that in November 1765 when the elite usurped control of a meeting called by the Sons to protest the Stamp Act. They were equally successful in this instance as the lower-class radicals fell back on customary forms of behavior. The result was the election of moderates and conservatives to outweigh the presence of such radicals as Alexander McDougall and Isaac Sears. The elite, conservative-dominated Committee of 51, included two Livingston brothers, and John Jay and James Duane (both of the latter two related to the Livingston family by marriage). This committee was itself soon replaced by an even more conservative Committee of 60 comprised of "several gentlemen of property and who are esteemed to favor moderate and conciliatory" measures.[35]

With the seizure of committee control by the moderate elite, the direction of New York's resistance passed from the radical lower classes to the elite, who used their considerable political acumen to outwit radical lower-class leaders. The elite were now forced by circumstance and by conviction to take a stand. The transition was noted at the time. The lower-class radicals, said Colden, who was well aware of the significance of the occurence, "have lost their influence, and are neglected." Orders for resistance to British measures were now being given, Colden continued, "by Men of different Principles, and who have much at stake." With the renewed influence of the elite, order returned briefly to New York, with "no more burning of Effigies, or puting cut-throat papers under Peoples Doors."[36]

This temporary lull in protests led Colden to assert "that a great Majority of this Province are very far from approving of the extravagant and dangerous Measures of the New England Governments," which was undoubtedly the case. Most provincials, like Britons, were appalled at the Bostonians' destruction of private property. The majority of colonists dreaded "a Civil War, and desire[d] nothing so much as to have an End put to this unhappy dispute with the Mother Country." There was little official support for civil war in New York, where the Tory DeLanceys remained in control of the assembly. With a substantial majority, the DeLanceys were able to block assembly approval of the resolutions for nonimportation and nonexportation passed by the First Continental Congress. Despite the assembly's unwillingness to give official sanction to Congress's recommendation, or even to appoint delegates for the Second Continental Congress, many New Yorkers chose to support Congress. As Colden reported, "the non importation association of the Congress is ever rigidly maintained in this Place."[37]

Part of the reason for this popular support among all social ranks was the awareness that, by 1774, power in the province had clearly shifted back to the King-in-Parliament. The elite were particularly aware that the Crown retained the appointive or confirmative power over such key officials as the governor, lieutenant governor, chief justices, attorney general, secretary, councillors, and clerk of the council. The assembly appointed and controlled the treasurer, agent, clerk and other personnel. The power of the purse had been largely lost by the assembly, since the governor, chief justice, auditor, and receiver and attorney generals, as well as the province's secretary, surveyor, customs officials, and vice-admiralty court officials, were all paid from the royal revenue. But this did not by any means ensure a prerogative triumph because the governed simply refused to be governed under a system they despised.[38]

To tighten its control even further, the Crown, in 1774, turned to its long-anticipated crackdown on New York landowners. On 7 April 1774, Colden laid before the council an additional instruction to Tryon dated 3 February 1774 for "establishing Regulations to be observed for the future, in the Disposal and granting of his Majesty's Lands within this Province." The instruction directed that surveys and maps be made of land not already granted, that available land be sold to the "best bidder," at a price of not less than 6d. per acre with a quit rent of 1/2 penny per acre. No bribes were to be permitted, with the only fees paid to be those allowed by law.[39]

Tryon did not take the order seriously. In fact, he assured Colden that he considered the instruction "a mere nullity" and that he had taken "the liberty to assure Ld. Dartmouth I did not beleive it could have any operation." The instructions may or may not have been capable of implementation, but New Yorkers feared they would be forced to accept the new regulations.[40]

This and other Parliamentary measures were seen by colonists as yet another threat to property, the foundation of all freedom and liberty. In an American Declaration of Rights, Americans reminded Britons that "we consider ourselves & do insist, that we are and out to be as free as our fellow Subjects in Britain, and that no power on Earth has a right to take our property from us without our Consent." What colonists wanted was for Britons to "place us in the same situation that we were at the close of the last War, & our former harmony will be restord."[41]

The declaration asserted that colonists, as British subjects, were "entitled to Life, liberty, and Property; and they have never ceded to any Sovereign Power whatever a right to dispose of either without Their Consent." Colonists would, however, "chearfully consent to the operation of such acts of the British Parliament, as are bona fide, restrained to the regulation of our external commerce, for the purpose of securing the Commercial advantages of the whole Empire to the Mother Country, & the commercial benefits of Its respective Members."[42]

The chief issue that alienated colonists from mother country remained Parliamentary-imposed taxation. The colonists wanted freedom from taxation "imposed on them without their Consent." As Colden noted, most Americans did not want separation, but rather "would rejoice in any prudent Plan for restoring Harmony and Security." What was necessary was for "Parliament to lay aside the right of raising money on the Subjects in America" on condition that "Assemblies, should grant and secure to the Crown, a sufficient and permanent" revenue for government expences. But in January 1775, when the ministry offered to give up its right to tax if the colonies would agree to pay for all government and military expenses, the offer was rejected by the Continental Congress, and protest within the colonies swelled.[43]

As the assemblies in other mainland colonies moved to independence, the DeLancey assembly in New York continued to proclaim its loyalty to the king, leaving New York at odds with most other colonies, which now favored open resistance. The loyalty of the New York assembly was noted by Lord North, who in the spring of 1775 planned to extend trade restrictions to include New Jersey, Pennsylvania, Maryland, Virginia, and South Carolina, as well as New England. North Carolina was excluded because of a lack of information about events in that colony. New York was also excluded "on account of your refusal to authenticate, by any Act of yours, the Non importation agreement" passed by the Continental Congress.[44]

Despite their loyalty to the crown, even the DeLancey assembly believed that Great Britain's actions toward the colonies were ill-conceived and threatened provincial liberties. The assembly was appalled at the measures taken by the ministry to discipline Boston, particularly the alteration of the Massachusetts charter. Pro-king or not, the DeLancey assembly continued in its long-standing objective of protecting and expanding provincial rights and privileges. In March 1775, the assembly voted affirmatively that the Intolerable Acts were "a Grievance that affects this Colony" because they might "form a Precedent for altering or taking away Charter Rights" in New York and other colonies. In petitions to king, Lords, and Commons, the DeLancey assembly made its position clear. Colonists believed their governmental charters guaranteed their freedoms and rights. If such rights were not immutable, then they could be altered or abolished at the whim of the ministry.[45]

Particularly distressing were "the late Acts for shutting up the Port of *Boston*, and altering the Charter of the *Massachusetts Bay* . . . which establish a dangerous Precedent, by inflicting Punishment without the Formality of a Trial." New Yorkers believed their constitution, even though not confirmed, had been in force since 1683 and could not be changed. The British believed that any colonial charter could be overturned simply because it was a colonial charter. To Britons the inferiority of colonial charters merely confirmed the supremacy of Parliament.[46]

Many New York representatives were convinced that other colonial constitutions, like that of Massachusetts, could, and probably would, be altered. Since the colonies were now mature, representatives advanced their claim for "an equal Participation of *Freedom* with their *Fellow Subjects in Britain*." The assembly stressed they did not want "to become independent of the *British* Parliament," but "only to enjoy the Rights of Englishmen." The New York assembly objected to such measures as paying governors from tax revenue, designed "to provide for the Support of civil Government," that took control of the executive from their hands.[47]

The assembly voiced its disapproval of the increasing use of admiralty courts and noted its irritation over the threat these courts presented to trial by jury. The advancement of such courts threatened provincial autonomy while significantly increasing metropolitan authority. The assembly also objected to the Quebec Act, which stripped Ohio Valley land from the seaboard colonies and gave it to Quebec. The tenure of judges controversy still rankled New Yorkers, who promised concessions on their own part if the king would "be graciously pleased to remove the distinction between your subjects in *England* and those in *America*, by commissioning your Judges *here* to hold their Offices on the same Tenure: In which case, we beg leave to assure your Majesty, that we stand ready to give them such adequate and permanent Salaries, as will render them *independent of the People*."[48]

The assembly reiterated its attachment to Great Britain. They said, "we desire no more than a Continuation of that ancient Government, to which we are intitled by the Principles of the *British* Constitution, and by which alone can be secured to us the Rights of Englishmen." New Yorkers remained "attached by every Tie of Interest and Regard to the *British* Nation . . . we harbour not an Idea of diminishing the Power and grandeur of the Mother Country. . . . To render this Union permanent and solid, we esteem it the undoubted Right of the Colonies, to participate of that Constitution, whose direct End and Aim is the Liberty of the Subject, fully trusting that this honorable House will listen with Attention to our Complaints, and Redress our Grievances, by adopting such Measures, as shall be found most conducive to the general Welfare of the whole Empire, and most likely to Restore Union and Harmony among all the different Branches."[49]

The constitutional platform, first loosely formed in the 1730s and then fully delineated in 1764 and 1765 by colonists opposing the Sugar and Stamp Acts, remained essentially unchanged ten years later. As the New York assembly pointed out, colonists wanted "only to obtain redress of Grievances & relief from fears & jelousies occasioned by the system of Statutes & regulations adopted since the close of the last War for raising a Revenue in America—extending the powers of Courts of Admiralty and Vice Admiralty—trying persons in Great Britain for Offences alledged to be committed in America—affecting the Province of Massachusetts Bay and altering the Government and extending the limits of Quebec, by the abolition of which System the harmony between Great Britain & those Colonies so necessary to the happiness of both" had been disturbed. New Yorkers wanted a return to conditions as they had been prior to 1763, or "a Restoration of those Rights which we enjoyed by General Consent, before the Close of the last War."[50]

The British Parliament refused to consider the New York assembly's petitions. The petitions were received by agent Edmund Burke on 5 April 1775. On 15 May Burke read the remonstrance in Commons and then moved for a discussion. The motion was rejected when Lord North expressed the "opinion that the house could not so much as receive any paper which tended to call in question, the Right of Parliament to make Laws to bind the subjects of this Empire in all cases whatsoever." The petition to Lords, presented to that body by the duke of Manchester, was also rejected. Following the rejection of the two petitions, Burke immediately "gave them to my Clerk to convey to the Newspapers," as the New York assembly had demanded. The petition to the king was also ignored, but not published.[51]

In rejecting the New York petitions, the ministry reaffirmed Parliamentary supremacy and colonial inferiority. While the ministry applauded "the moderation and good disposition" of the New York assembly, certain portions of its petitions to king, Lords, and Commons contained "claims which made it impossible for Parliament consistent with its justice and dignity to receive them." For a reconciliation to occur, the New York assembly should first realize, said Dartmouth, "how equally vain & improper it is to insist upon claims inconsistent with their dependance on the authority of Parliament."[52]

Britons agreed that "the most perfect Constitution for a dependent Province" was one "which approaches the nearest to that of the Sovereign Kingdom." Unfortunately, there was "no such Constitution in the American Colonies." That meant that the constitution of any colony "is capable of being improved." In other words, as New Yorkers and other colonists were quick to realize, what happened to Massachusetts, could happen to any colony.[53]

The ministry would not accept colonial claims of equality. The ministry agreed that colonials had the rights of Englishmen, or that "the Subjects of Great Britain residing in its external Dominions, are intitled to all the Rights and Privileges of British Subjects, which they are capable of enjoying." However, the ministry was quick to point out, "there are some Rights, and Privileges peculiar to the Inhabitants of Great Britain, which the British Subjects in the External Dominions are incapable of enjoying." One such right denied to colonists was enjoying "a Share in the Supreme Imperial Legislature."[54]

As for provincial assemblies, they "received the Power of Legislation" on condition that they would provide for "the Support of government." If they did not provide that support, "the Legislation must cease." Colonies, the ministry reiterated, "can have no more liberty than is consistent with their Dependance on Great Britain. . . . They can have no political power or share in their own Government, that is inconsistent with the Authority of the supreme Legislature, That is, of the King & parliament of Great Britain." There was no doubt in the minds of the king or his ministers that Great Britain was supreme. The ministry forthrightly declared that "the Kingdom of Great Britain is Imperial, that is, not subordinate to, or dependent upon any Earthly Power." The rejection of the three petitions meant New York would join the other mainland colonies in opposition to Great Britain. New York's elite called an election to send delegates to the Continental Congress.[55]

April 1775 witnessed continued rioting in New York City, sparked by worsening economic conditions. Nonimportation hurt the colonies far more than it did Great Britain, and the urban lower classes were particularly hard hit. On 4 April, Sons of Liberty seized 530 arms from City Hall and took the powder house. The Sons put fifty guards around the powder house and paraded through town with the weapons. They then called a meeting of the city's people to chose military officers. It was pointless for officials to call out the militia to restore order because it was the militiamen who were rioting. The assembly contacted militia officer "Colonel Lispenard [who on] being asked, whether He thought the Militia if duly summoned for that purpose would appear and Assist in restoring and Establishing good Order, replyed, that many of the Persons concerned in the present Disorders belonged to the Militia and that he did not believe the Militia or any considerable Part of it would meet to oppose the Perpetrators of those Disorders."[56]

Business came to a standstill in the city as riots continued, closing the port and customs house. The rioting was the worst the city had seen to date as "the Inhabitants of this City burst thro' all Restraints . . . emptied Vessels laden with Provisions." News of Lexington and Concord arrived in New York on 23 April to spark more riots, in which demonstrators "Seized the City Arms and in the Course of a few Days distributed them among the Multitude, formed themselves into Companies and Trained openly in the Streets, increased the Numbers and Power of the Committee . . . Convened themselves by Beat of drum for popular Resolution." Finally these separate incidents "combined to depress all legal Authority" in New York. Colden reported the actions of the crowd had "entirely prostrated the Powers of Government." The Sons took "a Number of small Cannon into the Country—Called all Parts of the Colony to a Provincial Convention—chosen twenty Delegates for this City—formed an Association." The radicals were determined "to resist the Acts of Parliament . . . and to repel every species of Force . . . for inforcing the Taxing Claims of Parliament at the risque of their Lives and Fortunes."[57]

Many formerly conservative members of the elite, spurred by the crowd's actions and the news of Lexington and Concord, joined the radicals and became patriot leaders. Even the formerly reluctant New York assembly was now forced by popular opinion to join "the General Association of the Colonies" to work "with the others in resisting the Acts of Parliament." Royal government effectively ended with "that scene of disorder and violence . . . which has entirely prostrated the Powers of Government" in New York. If royal government ended, revolutionary government began, as "congresses and Committees are now established . . . and are acting with all the confidence and authority of a legal Government." The New York provincial congress, with over one hundred members, represented the culmination of former committees of correspondence, inspection, and observation. The congress, with its colonial counterparts, provided government at the local level and executed "the determinations of the continental and Provincial Congresses." Part of the Continental Congress's task was to raise troops and money "to oppose the Kings Forces." The Second Continental Congress justified American resistance at Lexington, Concord, and Bunker's Hill by issuing a Declaration of Causes and Necessity of Taking Up Arms and by sending an Olive Branch Petition to the king in which they stressed Americans's desire for reconciliation.[58]

There was to be no reconciliation as royal authority collapsed in the colonies. The few British regulars in New York, in a "very disagreeable & critical situation," were moved to a ship in the harbor for their own safety and to prevent them from deserting. As the troops prepared to evacuate the city, "several People began to harangue them, exhorting them to desert and assuring them of sufficient Protection" if they did so. A few soldiers joined the crowd "and were immediately carried away by the People." Looking for weapons, the crowd then seized the soldiers' possessions so that "the Troops embarkd without their Baggage."[59]

Shortly after the troop evacuation, Governor William Tryon, full of foreboding for the future, returned to New York on 15 June 1775 "and received the next morning the Great Seal of the Province, and the diminished authority the Lieutenant Governor had to transfer to me." In the year Tryon had been in England, "the General Revolt that has taken place in the Colonies has put his Majestys civil Governors in the most degraded situation, left in the exercise of only such feeble executive powers as suit the present conveniences of the Country, and this dependant on the caprice of a moment."[60]

Aware that he could be seized by overly ardent patriots, Tryon, on 7 July 1775, complained to Dartmouth of the "delicate state of my health and public situation." It was "very probable," Tryon said, that he would "be either taken Prisoner, as a state Hostage, or obliged to retire on board one of His Majestys Ships of War to avoid the insolence of an inflamed Mob." He requested "discretionary leave to return to England" when the situation worsened. Such permission was granted on 6 September 1775.[61]

Tryon fully grasped the significance of events in America. On 7 August 1775 Tryon warned Dartmouth that Americans were determined "to pursue their dangerous Designs. Independency is shooting from the Root of the present Contest." Great Britain had to act quickly with "some new Plan of Accommodation" or "the Colonies will be severed from Her." Tryon's sympathies lay with Loyalists, who "will fall a Sacrifice . . . & their Estates be Confiscated to Defray in part the Expence of the Civil War." Tryon predicted that "the Ports of America will be declared Free: and the Powers of Europe Invited to guarantee the Independcy of the Colonies."[62]

Tryon's predictions proved true. His fears for his own safety were confirmed on 10 October 1775, when the Continental Congress ordered Tryon's arrest. On hearing this Tryon wrote to New York City Mayor Whitehead Hicks, telling Hicks that he put his security in the hands of the corporation and citizens of New York City. Should he be seized, Tryon continued, "The Commander of his Majestys ships of War in the Harbour will demand that the Inhabitants deliver me on Board the Fleet, and on refusal enforce the Demand with their whole Power." Tryon prudently decided not to place his trust in Hicks's protection and boarded *HMS Halifax* on 19 October.[63]

On 30 October 1775, Tryon transferred to *HMS Dutchess of Gordon*. Tryon was certain that New York's revolutionary government did not represent the majority of the people or even the majority of the voting population. He found this was not the case when he was forced by New York's septennial law to call assembly elections in December 1775. Loyalists won only four seats, and Tryon did not call the assembly. On 18 April 1776, Tryon informed Lord Germain that "the general Assembly of this Province is now dissolved," thus ending a stormy and contentious chapter in American history.[64]

Another even stormier chapter in American history began that summer when Tryon forwarded to Germain "a printed copy of their Declaration of Independency, which was published through the streets of New York the middle of last month." Royal government officially and symbolically ended in New York with the destruction of George III's statue. Loyalists in New York suffered, as Tryon predicted, caught "between Scylla and Charybdis, that is the dread of Parliamentary Taxation and the Tyranny of their present Masters." Those who could not support the new regime were "seized and secured, and even down to the meanest planters persecuted and tyrannized over." Among those who suffered from persecution were the DeLancey family. James DeLancey, Jr., and his wife were in England by August 1775 and remained there the rest of their lives. Others of their family who refused to take oaths of loyalty to the new country joined them in exile and had their estates confiscated by the new revolutionary regime.[65]

The old regime truly ended in New York on 21 September 1776, when Lieutenant Governor Cadwallader Colden died at Flushing. Colden's lifetime encompassed virtually the course of imperial politics in New York. Colden was a confidant of most New York governors after he settled in the province and witnessed the declining respect commanded by a series of inept placemen. In 1765, when Colden himself was governor, serious popular resistance to imperial policy became full-blown in New York. Colden was again in power in 1774 and 1775 when royal authority finally ended. Colden, 88 years old in

1776, heartsick at the rupture between colonies and mother country, died just before the British army retook New York on 24 September 1776 and Lord William Howe "made himself master of the City of New York." Howe and his men entered a city in flames, with fully one-quarter of the buildings destroyed. The British occupied New York City for the duration of the war. William Tryon remained governor until the 1780 arrival of Major General James Robertson, named royal governor on 1 April 1779.[65]

To Americans who supported the revolution, the fault for the break was clearly at Great Britain's door. The elite, including William Livingston, believed that Britain, while blessed with "the best Constitution in the world," had nevertheless, by 1776, deteriorated to "a pensioned Confederacy against Reason, & Virtue, and Honour, and Patriotism, & the Rights of Man." Parliament, "formerly the most august Assembly in the World," now consisted of nothing more than "venal Pensioners on the Crown." The effects of declining morals in Britain were reflected in its government, Livingston believed, which was characterized by the "Multiplication of Officers to strengthen the Court-Interest: Perpetually extending the Prerogatives of the King; & retrenching the Rights of the Subject: Advancing to the most eminent Stations, men without Education, & of dissolute Manners: Employing with the People's Money, a Band of Emissaries, to misrepresent & traduce the People: And (to crown the System of Miss-rule) sporting with our Persons & Estates, by filling the highest Seats of Justice with Bankrupts, Bullies and Blockheads." Royal governors sent to rule the colonies were nothing but "a set of political Craftsmen, flagiciously conspiring to erect the Babel DISPOTISM, on the Ruins of the antient and beautiful Fabric of LAW." What good was "the best Constitution," Livingston asked, when it was coupled "with the worst Administration."[67]

William Livingston had long since left New York City for New Jersey by the time the revolution began. Disgusted with New York politics, he admitted his alienation from that province to a friend when he commented that "From its [New York's] prolific production of public Scoundrels I could wish my Mother when pregnant with your humble Servant had better made choice of Siberia to usher me into this breathing World."[68]

Livingston's move out of New York City in 1772 spelled the effective end of the triumvirate. In fact, the trio had begun to move apart even before 1772. After Livingston's departure from New York, the relationship cooled quickly. Once the war started, there is no surviving correspondence between William Livingston and William Smith, Jr., and the only letters between William Livingston and John Morin Scott concern their Vermont landholdings. The disruption of their friendship was probably brought about by differing political outlooks. All three remained republicans, but reacted differently to the rising aspirations of the lower classes. Their diverging paths were typical for members of the elite.

William Smith, like many American colonists—a third according to John Adams—wanted no part of the Revolution. Smith could not reconcile himself to rising democratic tendencies in the provinces. To him, the rule of the lower class meant anarchy. Smith became more and more conservative as the Revolution approached. At the outbreak of hostilities he and his wife, Janet Livingston, fled to Livingston Manor. Smith repeatedly refused to take the oath of allegiance to the State of New York. He returned to British-occupied New York City in 1778 where he advised the British military command on American affairs. He later sailed to England and was then named chief justice of Canada.[69]

Scott was at the other end of the political spectrum from Smith. A radical who favored democracy, Scott worked for and welcomed the break with Great Britain. He was active in both civil and military capacities during the war and was a delegate to the Continental Congress, where he served to 1783.[70]

Livingston was every bit as much of an elitist as Smith. He was wary of the lower class whom he termed the "vulgar" or the "mobility" or the "degenerate." Livingston saw his elitist function as one of guiding the lower classes. In effect, his self-imposed role was to save the ignorant from their own ignorance. Livingston lacked the blind faith in mankind and democracy that characterized Scott, or, for that matter, Thomas Jefferson. Livingston was determined to lead the revolution to ensure that society emerged with the same social pecking order it had before.[71]

To Livingston, as to virtually all except a handful of American colonists, the separation from Great Britain was something to be approached with trepidation. Yet, in 1776, Livingston accepted the governorship of New Jersey and led its citizens in the struggle to achieve independence from Great Britain. Thoroughly committed to the revolutionary cause after 1776, Livingston worked untiringly to secure victory in the contest he had unwittingly helped to bring about. The propaganda campaign mounted by Livingston and other members of the elite to educate and politicize the lower classes during the colonial period had been all too effective. When the lower classes became politically active, the elite was faced with the choice of either going along with the rank and file or remaining loyal to Great Britain. The DeLanceys chose the latter alternative and lost their homes and their native land. The Livingstons became patriots. They joined the revolutionary movement with reservations and then only because they feared mob rule if the elite did not moderate the actions of the rabble by assuming its traditional leadership role. The Livingstons also believed that leading the movement would permit them and other members of the elite to retain their privileged and dominant places in American society. If that was a vain dream, they had no way of knowing. The Revolution brought the defeat of the prerogative but in the long run privilege was also defeated.

Conclusion

Distant from the seat of power, elite New Yorkers exploited their position to gain political sophistication and some measure of home rule. Attempts by the government to limit colonial autonomy led to heightened resistance. Ultimately, it was not only elite discontent with British imperial authority that caused the American Revolution. The independence movement also sprang from the determination of the lower classes to effect change in society. Increasingly knowledgeable and literate, the lower and middling sort responded to elite propaganda. When the elite, unwilling to alter the basic structure of society, was slow to initiate and effect change, the lower and middling sort took matters into their own hands through the formation of such radical groups as the Sons of Liberty. The Sons remained in control of New York's prerevolutionary movement until 1774, when the elite usurped from them the leadership of the independence movement. The elite still had the stature to ensure that the lower class would accept their leadership and the knowledge of the political system necessary to implement their design.

The lower classes in New York and other colonies shared the belief with the elite that New York and America were superior to and offered more opportunity for advancement than Great Britain, while the American people were more moral (virtuous) than Britons. In a sense, New York's lower classes bought into the American dream. They believed that they could also prosper in America, much as had the elite. They envied the upper class, but, far from wanting to destroy them, they believed it was possible to emulate and join them. This desire on the part of the lower class for upward mobility and the long-standing tradition of elite leadership permitted the oligarchs to assert their authority in 1774 and gain control of the colony and the revolutionary movement.

As the Revolution approached, New York's elite realized that they were caught in a bind. On the one hand was the imperial government threatening to reduce their liberties. On the other were the provincial lower classes, led by radicals and showing evidence of distinct levelling tendencies. The elite realized that they must take control of the movement to moderate the actions of lower-class radicals.

Some elite New Yorkers, like the DeLanceys, could not bring themselves to pander to the interests of the lower class. They, and thousands like them, were the Tories, who lost their homes, their fortunes, and, in many cases, their country, because they could not compromise their principles. Others of the elite, like the Livingstons, went along with lower-class leaders only after they realized they must do so to retain control of New York. They believed that their leadership would ensure that society emerged from the conflict with the same pecking order it had had before. They were successful to a degree, because moderate conservatives from New York and other states retained control of the revolutionary movement throughout the war, thus avoiding many of the excesses that accompanied and followed the radical-led French Revolution. But the elite also recognized that it would be impossible in the future to ignore the numerous and potentially volatile lower classes.

Even if the actions of the elite were largely self-serving, the constitutional arguments they used to justify their resistance to legitimate authority proved significant for the future nation and the world at large. New York's elite, and the elite of other colonies, based their resistance to perceived British tyranny on a broad platform of natural rights and the rights of Englishmen. This rhetoric produced and justified a colonial revolution against an imperial power. The defiance of the elite also established principles basic to American life— principles that were ultimately incorporated into state and national constitutions. Among these principles was the elite's insistance they could only be taxed by people they elected into office and that they were entitled to certain basic freedoms: of the press and religion, from arbitrary arrest, and from illegal search and seizure. Among the rights delineated by the elite was that of trial by a jury of one's peers. The elite also set a precedent for truth as a defense against libel in the John Peter Zenger trial, a case spurred by the elite in their struggle against an incompetent governor. William Livingston's *Independent Reflector* essays, written to prevent state support of religious education, demanded that there be a distinct separation between church and state. In the tenure of judges controversy, aimed at an ineffectual governor, the elite fought for the independence of the judiciary from executive control. Established in the *Forsey v. Cunningham* controversy was the assurance that jury decisions could not be overturned in a higher court.

Revolutionary rhetoric, with its emphasis on freedom and liberty, sparked an emancipation movement in the new nation and slave rebellions throughout the western hemisphere. The rhetoric of the American Revolution generated other major revolutions against colonial powers within western society. Whatever the varied motives of New York's elite in opposing British measures, the reasons they and the elite in other colonies set down on paper were true and valid and remained so.

In forming state and national governments, the intent of the elite was to emulate Great Britain, but to be selective in that emulation. Only the best of British law, politics, and society would be incorporated into America. But it perhaps was not possible to take only the best. Americans absorbed much that was not admirable from the British, including their pattern of exploitation of the white lower classes, black slaves and freemen, and Native Americans. Or perhaps the attitudes Americans inherited are those any imperial power adopts out of perceived necessity. Americans, like the British, insist that subordinate nations and peoples adopt our beliefs, customs, religion, and political philosophy. America continues to extend its sphere of influence in the interests of national aggrandisement and economic considerations, much as did the British. But, given the increased risk of destruction today, we apparently have yet to learn from the British that it is dangerous to overextend one's imperial interests.

Notes

Abbreviations

CSP	*Calendar of State Papers, Colonial Series, America and West Indies*
Colden, *Papers*	*The Letters and Papers of Cadwallader Colden, 1711–1775*
DHNY	*Documentary History of the State of New York*
DRNY	*Documents Relative to the Colonial History of the State of New York*
Livingston Papers	*The Papers of William Livingston*
Livingston, *Review of the Military Operations*	*Review of the Military Operations in North America, from the Commencement of the French Hostilities on the Fronties of Virginia in 1753, to the surrender of Oswego, on the 14th of August, 1756; in a Letter of to a Nobleman*
New York Assembly Journal	*Journal of the Votes and Proceedings of the Genercal Assembly of the Colony of New York, 1691–1765*

Preface

1. Robert C. Ritchie, *The Duke's Province: A Study of New York Politics and Society, 1664–1691* (Chapel Hill, 1977), 3–4.

2. Patricia U. Bonomi, *A Factious People: Politics and Society in Colonial New York* (New York and London, 1971), 5.

3. See Roger Champagne, "Family Politics versus Constitutional Principles: New York Assembly Elections of 1768 and 1769," *William and Mary Quarterly* 20 (1963): 57–79.

4. Jack P. Greene, *The Quest for Power: The Lower Houses of Assembly in the Southern Royal Colonies, 1689–1776* (New York, 1963), vii.

5. Petition to Lords Spiritual and Temporal, 25 Mar. 1775, Votes and Proceedings of the General Assembly of the Colony of New York, CO 5, 1220, Public Record Office.

6. Carl Lotus Becker, *The History of Political Parties in the Province of New York, 1760–1776* (Madison, Wisc., 1909, 1968), 22.

7. See, for instance, Gary B. Nash, *The Urban Crucible: Social Change, Political Consciousness, and the Origins of the American Revolution* (Cambridge, Mass. and London, 1979, 1986), 233.

8. Edward Countryman, *A People in Revolution: The American Revolution and Political Society in New York, 1760–1790* (Baltimore and London, 1981), xiii.

9. For a recent work on New York City mobs, see Paul A. Gilje, *The Road to Mobocracy, Popular Disorders in New York City, 1763–1834* (Chapel Hill and London, 1987). Gilje sees early mob violence as a movement whereby society reaffirmed its commitment to shared goals.

10. Sung Bok Kim, *Landlords and Tenants in Colonial New York: Manorial Society, 1664–1775* (Chapel Hill, 1978), especially chapter 6, "The Economics and Sociology of Tenancy," 235–80.

11. Jack P. Greene, *Pursuits of Happiness: The Social Development of Early Modern British Colonies and the Formation of American Culture* (Chapel Hill and London, 1988), 128, 139, 140–41.

12. Historians of eighteenth-century Britain are presently split between Lewis Namier and his adherents, who see family connections, not political loyalties, as governing politics, and historians such as Geoffrey Holmes, who believe the Whigs and Tories remained cohesive political parties throughout the eighteenth century. See Lewis B. Namier, *The Structure of Politics at the Accession of George III*, 2d ed. (London, 1957) and Geoffrey Holmes, *British Politics in the Age of Anne*, rev. ed (London and Ronceverte, W.V., 1967, 1987).

Chapter 1. Privilege and Perogative

1. Hints respecting the Civil Establishments in the American Colonys, 25 Feb. 1763, Liverpool Papers, Additional Mss. 38,335, British Library. Folios 14–33 have been printed with an introduction by Thomas C. Barrow in the *William and Mary Quarterly* 24 (1967): 108–26.

2. See, for instance, Robert Hunter to Board of Trade, 14 Mar. 1713, *Documents Relative to the Colonial History of the State of New York*, ed. Edmund B. O'Callaghan and Berthold Fernow, 15 vols. (Albany, 1853–87), 5:356 (hereafter cited as *DRNY*); Charles Worthen Spencer, *Royal Government in New York, 1694–1719* (Columbus, Ohio, 1905), 12; John M. Murrin, "English Rights as Ethnic Agression: The English Conquest, the Charter of Liberties of 1683, and Leisler's Rebellion in New York," in *Authority and Resistance in Early New York*, ed. William Pencak and Conrad Edick Wright (New York, 1988), 56–94.

3. David Beers Quinn, *Set Fair for Roanoke, Voyages and Colonies, 1584–1606* (Chapel Hill and London, 1985), 13, 413; Greene, *Pursuits of Happiness*, 7.

4. For Poynings's Law in Ireland and the crown's attempts to extend it to Jamaica and Virginia, see Sir George Clark, *The Later Stuarts, 1660–1714* (Oxford, 1934, 1976), 294, 305, 312, and 336; for English imperial administration in the seventeenth century, see Stephen Saunders Webb, *The Governors-General, The English Army and the Defin-*

ition of the Empire, 1569–1681 (Chapel Hill, 1979); Ian R. Christie, *Wars and Revolutions, Britain, 1760–1815* (Cambridge, Mass., 1981), 95–96; Jack P. Greene, *Peripheries and Center: Constitutional Development in the Extended Polities of the British Empire and the United States, 1607–1788* (New York and London, 1986), 61.

5. Bernard Bailyn, *The Peopling of British North America* (New York, 1986), 26; Greene, *Pursuits of Happiness*, 7; Quinn, *Set Fair for Roanoke*, 13; Christie, *Wars and Revolution*, 96; Robert Lacey, *Sir Walter Ralegh* (New York, 1979), 105–9. For religious controversy in Ireland, see Brendan Fitzpatrick, *Seventeenth Century Ireland, The War of Religions* (Totowa, N.J., 1989).

6. By the terms of the Alien Act, Scots would be considered foreigners and barred from exporting goods to England. For background on the act and the political union of England and Scotland, see Brian P. Levack, *The Formation of the British State, England, Scotland, and the Union, 1603–1707* (Oxford, England, 1987); see also William Ferguson, *Scotland, 1689 to the Present* (New York, 1968), 26–27, 44, 47–48; Christopher Harvie, *Scotland and Nationalism, Scottish Society and Politics, 1707–1977* (London, 1977), 27–28; P. W. J. Riley, *The Union of England and Scotland, a Study in Anglo-Scottish Politics of the Eighteenth Century* (Manchester, 1978), 209; James MacKinnon, *The Union of England and Scotland* (London, 1896), 9–10, 24–26, 38, 78.

7. Quinn, *Set Fair for Roanoke*, 6–7, 206, 257; Edmund S. Morgan, *American Slavery, American Freedom, The Ordeal of Colonial Virginia* (New York and London, 1975), 20; Lacey, *Sir Walter Ralegh*, 34, 39.

8. As Jack P. Greene points out, there were two important differences between English colonization in Ireland and America. The former had a large, Christian, and civilized population and colonizers were a minority of the population. See *Peripheries and Center*, 8.

9. Instructions for Coll. Thomas Dongan, Jan. 27, 1683, *DRNY*, 3:331; Ritchie, *The Duke's Province*, 164, 167, 170; Murrin, "English Rights as Ethnic Aggression," 56–94.

10. Petition of the Mayor and Common Council of New York for a new Charter, Nov. 9, 1683, *DRNY*, 3:357; Ritchie, *The Duke's Province*, 171–73. On the Dutch in America, see Donna Merwick, *Possessing Albany, 1630–1710: The Dutch and English Experience* (New York, 1990).

11. Ritchie, *The Duke's Province*, 178; Murrin, "English Rights as Ethnic Aggression," 56–94.

12. Veto of the Act entitled The Charter of Liberties and Privileges for the Province of New-York, 3 Mar. 1684, *DRNY*, 3:357–58.

13. For the nature of imperial administration, see Stephen Saunders Webb, "The Trials of Sir Edmund Andros," in *The Human Dimensions of Nation Making*, ed. James Kirby Martin (Madison, Wisc., 1976), 23–53.

14. Council of New York to Board of Trade, 29 July 1691, *Calendar of State Papers, Colonial Series, America and West Indies*, ed. W. N. Sainsbury, J. W. Fortescue, and Cecil Headlam, 42 vols. (London, 1860–1953), 513 (hereafter cited as *CSP*); *The Laws and Acts of the General Assembly for their Majesties province of New-York* (New York, 1893), cxi–cxii; *Charters of the Old English Colonies in America*, intro., Samuel Lucas (London, 1881), 109; Murrin, "English Rights as Ethnic Aggression", 56–94. Assembly Message to William Burnet, August 1728, quoted in Greene, *Peripheries and Center*, 39.

15. Robert Hunter to Board of Trade, 14 Nov. 1710, *DRNY*, 5:177; for factionalism in New York, see Bonomi's classic study, *A Factious People*.

16. Bernard Bailyn, *Origins of American Politics* (New York, 1968), 67–69; Holmes, *British Politics*, xx; Stanley Nider Katz, *Newcastle's New York, Anglo-American Politics in the Eighteenth Century, 1732–1753* (Cambridge, Mass., 1968), 40.

17. Hints respecting the Civil Establishments in the American Colonys, 25 Feb. 1763, Liverpool Papers, Additional Mss. 38,335, British Library.

18. Caroline Robbins, *The Eighteenth Century Commonwealthman* (Cambridge, Mass., 1959), 5, 8; Holmes, *British Politics in the Age of Anne*, 121, 129; Richard Pares, *King George III and the Politicians* (London, Oxford, New York, 1953, 1973), 44.

19. On the similarities between Whig and Tory country parties, see Isaac Kramnick, *Bolingbroke and His Circle: The Politics of Nostalgia in the Age of Walpole* (Cambridge, Mass., 1968), 236–37. For Tory alienation from the Whig government, see Eveline Cruickshanks, *Political Untouchables, The Tories and the '45* (New York, 1979).

20. Philip Livingston to Jacob Wendell, 23 July 1737, Museum of the City of New York, New York City.

21. For a revisionist study of the religious and political motives behind Leisler's Rebellion, see David William Voorhees, "In Behalf of the true Protestants religion: The Glorious Revolution in New York," (Ph.D. diss., New York University, 1988) particularly 62–67, 365–71.

22. Mary Lou Lustig, *Robert Hunter (1666–1734), New York's Augustan Statesman* (Syracuse, N.Y., 1983), 118–19. On the ideological basis of Whigs and Tories and their endurance as cohesive political parties in England during the eighteenth century, see Holmes, *British Politics in the Age of Anne*, particularly xii, 2–20; for the development of Whig philosophy and its affect on eighteenth century Americans, see J. G. A. Pocock, "Machiavelli, Harrington and English Political Ideologies in the Eighteenth Century," *William and Mary Quarterly* 22, (1965):549–83. See also Pares, *King George III and the Politicians,* 71.

23. Alison Gilbert Olson, *Anglo-American Politics, 1660–1775: The Relationship Between Parties in England and Colonial America* (New York & Oxford, 1973), vii; Katz, *Newcastle's New York*, 9.

24. Lustig, *Robert Hunter*, 217–30.

25. Cadwallader Colden to Board of Trade, 20 Sept. 1764, *DRNY*, 7:655; Spotswood, *Official Letters*, 2:124, quoted in Morgan, *American Slavery, American Freedom*, 360.

26. Gary Nash, *The Urban Crucible*, 235; for New York political history, see Becker, *The History of Political Parties,*particularly 5–22.

27. Duke of Newcastle to Horace Walpole, 25 Oct. 1755, Newcastle Papers, Additional Mss. 32,860, British Library.

28. Charles Hardy to duke of Newcastle, 8 Nov. 1756, Newcastle Papers, Additional Mss. 32,868, British Library; Holmes, *British Politics in the Age of Anne*, 224.

29. Alured Popple to Cadwallader Colden, 1 Nov. 1734, Cadwallader Colden, *The Letters and Papers of Cadwallader Colden, 1711–1775*, 9 vols., *New-York Historical Society, Collections, 1917–1923, 1934–1935* (New York, 1918–1937), 1:110, 2:114–15 (hereafter cited as Colden, *Papers*).

30. Lustig, *Robert Hunter*, 158; William Smith, Jr., *The History of the Province of New York*, ed., Michael Kammen, 2 vols. (Cambridge, Mass., 1972), 1:187.

31. Smith, *History of New York*, 1:98–99.

32. On the development of the New York court system, see Herbert L. Osgood, *The American Colonies in the Seventeenth Century*, 3 vols. (Gloucester, Mass., 1957), 2:279, 283; see also Peter Charles Hoffer, *Law and People in Colonial America* (Baltimore and London, 1992); Rex Maurice Naylor, "The Royal Prerogative in New York, 1691–1775," *Quarterly Journal*, New York State Historical Association 5 (1924): 221–55; Douglas Greenberg, *Crime and Law Enforcement in the Colony of New York, 1691–1776* (Ithaca, 1974), 34–35; Milton M. Klein, "The Rise of the New York Bar: The Legal Career of William Livingston," *William and Mary Quarterly* 15 (1958): 334–58; *The Colonial Laws of New York from the Year 1664 to the Revolution*, 5 vols. (Albany, 1894), 1:226–31.

33. Hints respecting the Civil Establishments in the American Colonys, 25 Feb. 1764, Liverpool Papers, Additional Mss. 38,335, British Library. Slaughter was authorized by his instructions to name twelve councillors, Fletcher fifteen, Bellomont thirteen, and Cornbury twelve. The number remained at twelve after Cornbury's administration. See Spencer, *Royal Government in New York*, 47.

34. Hints respecting the Civil Establishments in the American Colonys, 25 Feb. 1763, Liverpool Papers, Additional Mss. 38,335, British Library; Assembly Minutes, 30 Apr. 1712, CO 5,1185, 196, Public Record Office.

35. Hints respecting the Civil Establishments, Liverpool Papers, Additional Mss. 38,335, British Library.

36. Ibid.

37. Earl of Hillsborough to Cadwallader Colden, 17 Feb. 1770 *DRNY*, 8:207.

38. Thucydides, *The Peloponnesian War*, trans. Rex Warner (Penguin Books, 1954, 1975), 213.

39. Robert Hunter quoted in Osgood, *The American Colonies in the Eighteenth Century*, 2:106.

Chapter 2. This Unsettled and Ungovernable Province, 1710–1719

1. Robert Hunter to Board of Trade, 25 July 1715, *DRNY*, 5:416–18.

2. Cadwallader Colden to James Alexander, n.d., quoted in William A. Whitehead, *Contributions to the Early History of Perth Amboy, N. J.* (New York, 1856), 149.

3. Duke of Marlborough to Sidney Godolphin, 23 June 1707, Sidney Godolphin to duke of Marlborough, 17 Aug. 1709, 18 Aug. 1709, duke of Marlborough to Sidney Godolphin, 22 Aug. 1709, 7 Sept. 1709, Blenheim Papers, British Library.

4. For Hunter's career see Lustig, *Robert Hunter*, particularly 217–30.

5. Cadwallader Colden to Alexander Colden, 25 Sept. 1759 in Smith, *History of New York*, 1:300; Robert Hunter to James Alexander, 4 Nov. 1727, *Documents Relating to the Colonial History of the State of New Jersey*, ed. William Adee Whitehead, 10 vols. (Newark, 1880), 5:179; Robert Hunter to James Alexander, 10 Aug. 1728, Rutherfurd Collection, New-York Historical Society.

6. Robert Hunter to Board of Trade, 3 Nov. 1718, *DRNY*, 5:520.

7. Robert Hunter to Bishop of London, 1 Jan. 1712, Robert Hunter to Henry St. John,1 Jan. 1712, *DRNY*, 5:311, 296–97; Lustig, *Robert Hunter*, 42, 59, 218–19.

8. Robert Hunter to John Chamberlayne, 27 Feb. 1712, *DRNY*, 5:316; Lustig, *Robert Hunter*, 109–10.

9. Robert Hunter to Henry St. John,1 Jan. 1712, *DRNY*, 5:296–97.

10. Robert Hunter to Henry St. John, 11 Sept. 1711, *DRNY*, 5:255–56.

11. Robert Hunter to Board of Trade, 25 July 1715, *DRNY*, 5:417; Robert Hunter to William Popple, 14 Nov. 1715, *CSP*, #674, 341.

12. Robert Hunter to Board of Trade, 3 Oct. 1710, *DRNY*, 5:170; Cadwallader Colden to Alexander Colden, 15 Oct. 1759, Smith, *History of New York*, 1:308.

13. Robert Hunter to Board of Trade, 14 Nov. 1710, *DRNY*, 5:180.

14. Ibid.

15. Order in Council, 1 March 1711, Robert Hunter to earl of Stair,18 Oct. 1714, postscript, 8 Nov. 1714, *DRNY*, 5:103, 454.

16. Cadwallader Colden to Alexander Colden, 15 Oct. 1759, Smith, *History of New York*, 1:308; Robert Hunter to Board of Trade, 7 May 1711, *DRNY*, 5:209.

17. Board of Trade to Robert Hunter, 29 June 1711, Robert Hunter to Board of Trade, 1 Jan. 1712; *DRNY*, 5:252, 298.

18. Lustig, *Robert Hunter*, 76, 98.

19. Robert Hunter to Board of Trade, 18 May 1712, *DRNY*, 5:341–42.

20. Robert Hunter to Board of Trade, 14 March 1713, *DRNY*, 5:356.

21. Robert Hunter to Board of Trade, 12 Sept. 1711, *CSP*, #95, 97.

22. Robert Hunter to Board of Trade, 14 March 1713, *DRNY*, 5:356.

23. Vesey also hated the Whig governor Bellomont (1698–1701), who complained in 1699 that the minister did not include him in his prayers. Bellomont vowed that he would "never go to Church while he's [Vesey's] minister." Earl of Bellomont to Board of Trade, *DRNY*, 5:534; John Talbot to Bishop of London, 21 Oct. 1714, Robert Hunter, A Proclamation, 3 March 1714, Remarks on the Preceding Addressed to General Nicholson, *Documentary History of the State of New York*, ed., Edmund B. O'Callaghan, 4 vols. (Albany, 1849–51), 3:451, 452, 455–57, 458 (hereafter cited as *DHNY*).

24. Robert Hunter to Board of Trade, 27 Aug. 1714, *DRNY*, 5:379–80; Lustig, *Robert Hunter*, 121–22.

25. Robert Hunter to Board of Trade, 25 July 1715, *DRNY*, 5:416.

26. Assembly Journal, 1702–1713, 12 May 1713, 214, C O 5,1185, Public Record Office.

27. George Clinton to Board of Trade, 25 Nov. 1749, *DRNY*, 6:535–36.

28. Robert Hunter to Board of Trade, 3 May 1715, *DRNY*, 5:406.

29. Robert Hunter, *Androboros, A Biographical Farce in Three Acts*, ed. Lawrence H. Leder, *Bulletin of the New York Public Library* 68 (1964):173; Cadwallader Colden to Alexander Colden, 15 Oct. 1759, in Smith, *History of New York*, 1:306; John Anderson, *The American Theatre* (New York, 1938), 8–10; Lustig, *Robert Hunter*, 126.

30. Eugene R. Sheridan, *Lewis Morris, 1671–1746, A Study in Early American Politics* (Syracuse, 1981), 1, 5–6, 8, 15, 52, 108.

31. Robert Hunter to Board of Trade, 8 Feb. 1715, *DRNY*, 5:400; *Calendar of New York Colonial Commissions, 1680–1770*, abstracted by Edmund B. O'Callaghan (New York, 1929), 17; Lustig, *Robert Hunter*, 50, 118–20.

32. Lawrence H. Leder, *Robert Livingston (1654–1728) and the Politics of Colonial New York* (Chapel Hill, 1961), 3, 7, 9, 21, 33, 35.

33. Order to the Attorney General to Prepare Draft of Letters Patent for the Manor of Livingston, 1 Oct. 1715, Governor Hunter's Patent, *DHNY*, 3:689–90, 690–702.

34. Petition Samuel Mulford, n.d., *DRNY*, 5:474; Address of General Assembly to Robert Hunter, 4 Oct. 1717, *CSP*, #126, 52–53.

35. Robert Hunter to Board of Trade, 2 Oct. 1716, see also undated letter, Hunter to Board of Trade, probably written in 1718, *DRNY*, 5:480, 498–99; Samuel Mulford's Speech to the Assembly of New York, 2 Apr. 1714, CO 5,1051, ff. 185–87, Public Record Office; David Jamison, Writ of Attachment, 2 Apr. 1714, Address from General Assembly to Robert Hunter, 4 Oct. 1717, *CSP*, #49, 16, #125, 53.

36. Samuel Mulford to Board of Trade, 24 Aug. 1716, *CSP*, # 49, 16; Charles Warren, *A History of the American Bar* (Boston, 1911), 91; Board of Trade to earl of Stanhope, 3 Aug. 1715, CO 5,1051, Public Record Office; *Journal of the Legislative Council of the Colony of New York*, 9 Apr. 1691–17 Sept, 1743, 2 vols. (Albany, 1861), 1:401.

37. Frederick Seaton Siebert, *Freedom of the Press in England, 1476–1776* (Urbana, Ill., 1952), 2, 5, 119, 120; Leonard W. Levy, *Legacy of Suppression* (Cambridge, Mass., 1960), 13–14.

38. Ibid., 170, 381–82; Holt quoted in Siebert, *Freedom of the Press*, 271.

39. Siebert, *Freedom of the Press*, 306–12, 313; Sir William Blackstone, *Commentaries on the Laws of England* (Oxford, 1765–69), 4:151–52; Levy, *Legacy of Suppression*, 9–10.

40. Draft of Instructions for Robert Hunter, Governor of New-York, 27 Dec. 1709, *DRNY*, 5:142.

41. Siebert, *Freedom of the Press*, 306, 312, 313.

42. Lustig, *Robert Hunter*, 120; A. Aspinall, *Politics and the Press, 1780–1850* (London, 1949), 34.

43. Robert Hunter to Board of Trade, 2 Oct. 1716, Robert Hunter to Alured Popple, 3 June 1718, *DRNY*, 5:480–81, 504–5; Samuel Mulford to Board of Trade, 28 Aug. 1717, *CSP*, #49, 16; Privy Council Register, 10 Mar. 1717, 20 Mar. 1717, 15 July 1717, 29 Jan. 1718, 6 Jan. 1719, PC 2/86, ff. 11, 58, 65, 84, 213, Public Record Office.

44. Warren, *History of the American Bar*, 4; Robert Hunter to Board of Trade, 7 Aug. 1718, *CSP*, #650, 329.

45. Lustig, *Robert Hunter*, 129–30.

46. Robert Hunter to Board of Trade, 7 July 1718, 7 Aug. 1718, *DRNY*, 5:510, 515.

47. *Messages from the Governors, 1683–1776*, ed. Charles Z. Lincoln (Albany, 1909), 24 June 1719, 189.

Chapter 3. To Prepare the Way and Alarm the People, 1720–1735

1. *New York Weekly Journal*, 19 Nov. 1733.

2. For a statement of the American position toward Great Britain prior to the Revolution see American Declaration of Rights, 14 Oct. 1774, Liverpool Papers, Additional Mss. 38,342, British Library.

3. Smith, *History of New York*, 1:167.

4. Ibid., 1:167–70; Sheridan, *Lewis Morris*, 124, 127; William Burnet to Board of Trade, DRNY, 5:579.

5. For imperial politics during this era see James A. Henretta, *Salutary Neglect: Colonial Administration under the Duke of Newcastle* (Princeton, 1972), particularly Chapter I, "The Structure and Politics of Colonial Administration, 1721–1730."

6. Lord Hervey's *Memoirs*, ed. Romney Sedgwick (Middlesex, England and New York, 1963, 1984), 31.

7. Katz, *Newcastle's New York*, 23.

8. J. H. Plumb, *Robert Walpole, The Making of a Statesman*, 2 vols. (London, 1956), 1:293–95, 300, 301; Kramnick, *Bolingbroke*, 43, 56–57, 72; James Harrington quoted in ibid., 247; on the importance of property to freedom see Paschal Larkin, *Property in the Eighteenth Century, A Special Reference to England and Locke* (London and New York, 1930).

9. E. P. Thompson, *Whigs and Hunters: The Origins of the Black Act* (New York, 1975), 22–23.

10. Robert Hunter to James Alexander, 10 Feb. 1728, Rutherfurd Collection, New-York Historical Society; Lustig, *Robert Hunter*, 175.

11. William Burnet to Board of Trade, 26 Nov. 1720, 9 Mar. 1721, *DRNY*, 5:579, 584; Robert Hunter to Cadwallader Colden, 18 Feb. 1720, Lewis Morris to Marquess of Lothian, 26 Mar. 1735, Cadwallader Colden to Peter Collinson, May 1742, Cadwallader Colden to duke of Newcastle, 21 Mar. 1748, Colden, *Papers*, 1:100–1, 2:125–27, 2:261–62, 3:24. There is not as yet an adequate biography of Cadwallader Colden, but see Alice M. Keys, *Cadwallader Colden: A Representative Eighteenth Century Official* (New York, 1906) and Stephen Charles Steacy, "Cadwallader Colden: Statesman and Savant of Colonial New York," 2 vols. (Ph.D. diss., University of Kansas, 1987).

12. William Burnet to Board of Trade, 26 Nov. 1720, 9 Mar. 1721, *DRNY*, 5:579, 584; Smith, *History of New York*, 1:166–67.

13. George Clarke to Horace Walpole, 24 Nov. 1725, *DRNY*, 5:768; Smith, *History of New York*, 1:182.

14. For 1715 Naturalization Act, see Robert Hunter to Board of Trade, 25 July 1715, *DRNY*, 5:416; Smith, *History of New York*, 1:181–82; George Clarke to Horace Walpole, 24 Nov. 1725, *DRNY*, 5:769; W. Hay to duke of Newcastle, 9 Aug. 1733, Newcastle Papers, Additional Mss. 32,688, British Library.

15. George Clarke to Horatio Walpole, 24 Nov. 1729, *DRNY*, 5:769; Sheridan, *Lewis Morris*, 147.

16. Smith, *History of New York*, 1:185–86; William Burnet to Board of Trade, 21 Dec. 1727, *DRNY*, 5:848.

17. William Burnet to Board of Trade, 21 Dec. 1727, *DRNY*, 5:847–48; James Alexander to Cadwallader Colden, 5 May 1728, Colden, *Papers*, 1:259–60.

18. Holmes, *British Politics in the Age of Anne*, xviii–xix; Siebert, *Freedom of the Press*, 270, 271; David Harrison Stevens, *Party Politics and English Journalism, 1702–1742* (New York, 1916, 1967), 126–28; Kramnick, *Bolingbroke*, 63, 73–74. See also Malcolm G. Largmann, "The Political Image of Sir Robert Walpole Created by Literary Satire in the Opposition Press, 1721–1742" (Ph.D. diss., New York University, 1965).

19. On the influence of English opposition writers on Americans, see, for instance, Richard Buel, Jr., "Freedom of the Press in Revolutionary America: The Evolution of Libertarianism, 1760–1820," in *The Press and the American Revolution*, ed. Bernard Bailyn and John B. Hench (Boston, 1981), 66, 69–70; *New York Weekly Journal*, 17 Dec. 1733. On the exposure of provincials to English publications in general, see Norman S. Fiering, "The Transatlantic Republic of Letters: A Note on the Circulation of Learned Periodicals to Early Eighteenth-Century America," *William and Mary Quarterly* 33 (1976):642–60. On the influence of Enlightenment thought on Americans' concept of a free press, see Jeffery A. Smith, *Printers and Press Freedom: The Ideology of Early American Journalism* (New York and Oxford, 1988), particularly Ch. 3, "Ideals of Enlightenment."

20. *New York Weekly Journal*, 19 Nov. 1733.

21. A. Aspinall, *Politics and the Press*, 67; Kramnick, *Bolingbroke*, 52.

22. Siebert, *Freedom of the Press*, 382; Stevens, *Party Politics and English Journalism*, 126–28.

23. Smith, *History of New York*, 1:188; James Alexander to Cadwallader Colden, 5 May 1728, Colden, *Papers*, 1:260; Earl of Townshend to Board of Trade, 12 Aug. 1727, John Montgomery to Board of Trade, 30 Nov. 1728, Board of Trade to John Montgomery, 28 May 1729, *DRNY*, 5:823, 874–75, 876–77; Lustig, *Robert Hunter*, 175.

24. Bonomi, *A Factious People*, 99.

25. Edward F. DeLancey, "Memoir of the Honorable James DeLancey, lieutenant governor of the Province of New York," *DHNY*, 4:627.

26. George Clinton to Board of Trade, 22 June 1747, George Clinton to John Russell, duke of Bedford, 30 Oct. 1748, *DRNY*, 6:352, 465.

27. DeLancey, "Memoir of James DeLancey," *DHNY*, 4:628, 629; William Livingston, *Review of the Military Operations in North America, from the Commencement of the French Hostilities on the Frontiers of Virginia in 1753, to the surrender of Oswego, on the 14th of August, 1756; in a Letter to a Nobleman (1757)*, Massachusetts Historical Society, *Collections*, 1800, 1st series, 7 (Boston, 1801, 1846), 83 (hereafter cited as Livingston, *Review of the Military Operations*). While there is not as yet a biography of James DeLancey, two books deal in part with his life and career: see Katz, *Newcastle's New York*, particularly chapter 7, "Governor Clinton: New York, 1743–1753," 164–93 and Bonomi, *A Factious People*, particularly chapter 5, "James DeLancey, Anglo-American: The Politics of New York at Mid-Century," 143–78.

28. John Montgomery to Board of Trade, 30 June 1729, John Montgomery to

Charles Delafaye, 2 Aug. 1729, *DRNY*, 5:880–81, 888; James Alexander to Cadwallader Colden, 18 June 1729, Colden, *Papers*, 2:283–85; Sheridan, *Lewis Morris*, 144–45.

29. Duke of Newcastle to Board of Trade, 12 Jan. 1732, *DRNY*, 5:930; James Alexander to Cadwallader Colden, 3 July 1731, 21 Feb. 1732, Colden, *Papers*, 2:23, 50; Smith, *History of New York*, 1:187; Cadwallader Colden, *History of Governor William Cosby's Administration*, New-York Historical Society, *Collections*, 68 (1935), 283–85; Katz, *Newcastle's New York*, 61–62.

30. Colden, *History of Cosby's Administration*, 288.

31. Rip Van Dam to Board of Trade, 1 July 1731, William Cosby to Board of Trade, 18 Sept. 1732, William Cosby to duke of Newcastle, 3 May 1733, Lewis Morris to Board of Trade, 27 Aug. 1733, *DRNY*, 5:921, 936, 944–49, 951; Smith, *History of New York*, 1:195; Colden, *History of Cosby's Administration*, 289–92; Bonomi, *A Factious People*, 106–7.

32. William Cosby to Board of Trade, 18 Dec. 1732; William Cosby to duke of Newcastle, 18 Dec. 1732, *DRNY*, 5:939, 940; Katz, *Newcastle's New York*, 63–64.

33. Colden, *History of Cosby's Administration*, 289–90.

34. William Cosby to duke of Newcastle, 18 Dec. 1733, *DRNY*, 5:945, 948; Katz, *Newcastle's New York*, 82.

35. Cadwallader Colden to James Alexander, 27 Mar. 1735, Alured Popple to Cadwallader Colden, 16 Sept. 1735, Colden, *Papers*, 2:131, 140–41; on governors' use of courts to punish political enemies, see, for instance, Robert Hunter to Board of Trade, n.d. [1718], *DRNY*, 5:499.

36. Katz, *Newcastle's New York*, 82.

37. Lewis Morris to Board of Trade, 27 Aug. 1733, *DRNY*, 5:953; Katz, *Newcastle's New York*, 33, 80–81.

38. Ibid., 90.

39. Reed Browning, *The Duke of Newcastle* (New Haven, London, 1975), 64; Thomas Hurdes to duke of Newcastle, 16 Aug. 1733, 4 Sept. 1733, Newcastle Papers, Additional Mss. 32,688, British Library.

40. Kramnick, *Bolingbroke*, 54–55; Browning, *Newcastle*, 65–66.

41. Colden, *History of Cosby's Administration*, 286; James Alexander to Robert Hunter, 8 Nov. 1733, *Documents Relative to the Colonial History of the State of New Jersey*, 5:359.

42. Lincoln, ed. Messages from the Governors, 1683–1776, 25 Apr. 1734, 1:245–46.

43. James Alexander, *A Brief Narrative of the Case and Trial of John Peter Zenger . . . by James Alexander*, ed. Stanley Nider Katz (Cambridge, Mass., 1963); Bonomi, *A Factious People*, 304.

44. *Dictionary of American Biography*, ed. Dumas Malone, 20 vols. (New York, 1936), s.v. "Zenger, John Peter."

45. Colden, History of Cosby's Administration, 322; James Alexander to Robert Hunter, 8 Nov. 1733, Documents Relating to the Colonial History of the State of New Jersey, 5:360; New York Weekly Journal, 12 Nov. 1733, 19 Nov. 1733, 7 Oct. 1734, 8 June 1733; see also Alexander, Zenger, 8–9, 115, 129, 133.

46. "A Song Made Upon the Foregoing Occasion," Alexander, *Zenger*, 111; *Journal of the Votes and Proceedings of the General Assembly of the Colony of New York, 1691–1765*, 2 vols. (New York, 1764–1766), 1:687 (hereafter cited as *New York Assembly Journal*), also quoted in Katz, *Newcastle's New York*, 81.

47. *New York Weekly Journal*, 5 Nov. 1733; Bonomi, *A Factious People*, 114–15.

48. *New York Weekly Journal*, 5 Nov. 1733; Lewis Morris, Jr., was also elected to the assembly in 1733, Alexander, *Zenger*, 5; Katz, *Newcastle's New York*, 84; Bonomi, *A Factious People*, 304–5.

49. "A Song Made Upon the Election of New Magistrates for This City," *New York Weekly Journal*, quoted in Alexander, *Zenger*, 109.

50. William Cosby to Board of Trade, 19 June 1734, *DRNY*, 6:7; Katz, *Newcastle's New York*, 86–87; Cosby quoted in Alexander, *Zenger*, 10.

51. Lewis Morris to the marquis of Lothian, 26 Mar. 1735, Colden, *Papers*, 2:125; Alexander, *Zenger*, 7.

52. Daniel Horsmanden to Cadwallader Colden, 23 July 1735, Colden, *Papers*, 2:153; Sheridan, *Lewis Morris*, 160–77, 181.

53. William Cosby to Board of Trade, 10 June 1735 and 19 June 1735, 31, 32.

54. *New York Weekly Journal*, 8 Apr. 1734, 12 Sept. 1734. See also Alexander, *Zenger*, 135–37.

55. Alexander, *Zenger*, 59; *Journal of the Legislative Council of the City of New York*, 1:637, 641; Sheridan, *Lewis Morris*, 160–77, 181.

56. Katz, ed., Alexander, *Zenger*, 18–19, 49.

57. Siebert, *Freedom of the Press*, 270, 271.

58. Ibid, 381–82.

59. *New York Weekly Journal*, 18 Aug. 1735; Alexander, *Zenger*, 54, 62, 68–69, 101.

60. Colden, *History of Cosby's Administration*, 339; Alexander, *Zenger*, 3, 30; Levy, *Legacy of Suppression*, 6; Smith, *Printers and Press Freedom*, 83.

61. Buel, "Freedom of the Press in Revolutionary America," 74.

62. "A Song Made Upon the Foregoing Occasion," *New York Weekly Journal,* Oct. 1734, quoted in Alexander, *Zenger*, 110–11.

Chapter 4. Obstruct all Parts of Government
1735–1753

1. Board of Trade's Report to the Privy Council upon the State of New York, 2 Apr. 1751, *DRNY*, 6:614.

2. Bonomi, *A Factious People*, 143, 147–48.

3. George Clarke to Board of Trade, 16 Mar. 1735, and Clarke to duke of Newcastle and Board of Trade, 7 Oct. 1736, *DRNY*, 6:42, 76–77, 80; Daniel Horsmanden to Cadwallader Colden, 19 Dec. 1735, Colden, *Papers*, 2:142.

4. Colden, *History of Cosby's Administration*, 346; Katz, *Newcastle's New York*, 134–38; Sheridan, *Lewis Morris*, 178.

5. George Clarke to duke of Newcastle, 7 Oct. 1736, Clarke to Board of Trade, 9 May 1737, *DRNY*, 6:76, 94–95; Katz, *Newcastle's New York*, 150–51.

6. Cadwallader Colden to Mrs. Colden, 11 Sept. 1737, Colden, *Papers*, 2:179; on the similar intensity of emotion stirred by elections in England, see Holmes, *British Politics in the Age of Anne*, 25.

7. On voting practices in New York, see Becker, *History of Political Parties in the Province of New York*, 5–22; Countryman, *A People in Revolution*, 76–77; Nicholas Varga, "Election Procedures and Practices in Colonial New York," *New York History* 61 (1960):149–77; Gary Nash estimates two-thirds of free white adult males qualified to vote in New York City as opposed to less than one-half in Boston and Philadelphia, *The Urban Crucible*, 233.

8. George Clarke to Board of Trade, 17 June 1737, *DRNY*, 6:96; Katz, *Newcastle's New York*, 151–53.

9. Daniel Horsmanden to Cadwallader Colden, 23 July 1735, Colden, *Papers*, 2:153; Sheridan, *Lewis Morris*, 160–77, 181.

10. According to William Smith, Jr., Clarke returned to Englan in 1745 with an estate worth £100,000, *History of New York*, 2:60; Katz, *Newcastle's New York*, 151, 153.

11. George Clarke to Board of Trade, 13 June 1740, *DRNY*, 6:160–61; Katz, *Newcastle's New York*, 154–55.

12. George Clarke to Board of Trade, 30 Nov. 1739, George Clarke's Answers of Enquiries of Board of Trade, 2 June 1738, *DRNY*, 6:151, 120; the Triennial Act was disallowed by the crown, but a subsequent Septennial Act, passed in 1743, was finally approved. See Bonomi, *A Factious People*, 135.

13. George Clarke to Board of Trade, 28 Jan. 1740, *DRNY*, 6:158–59; Cadwallader Colden to Mrs. Colden, 11 Sept. 1737, Colden, *Papers*, 2:179.

14. Katz, *Newcastle's New York*, 157; Livingston, *Review of the Military Operations*, 79, 85.

15. George Clarke to Board of Trade, 22 Apr. 1741, George Clarke to duke of Newcastle, 20 June 1741, *DRNY*, 6:186, 196; Daniel Horsmanden to Cadwallader Colden, 7 Aug. 1741, Colden, *Papers*, 2:225–26; Smith, *History of New York*, 2:60; for a full and lucid account of the slave rebellion see T. J. Davis, *A Rumor of Revolt, The "Great Negro Plot" in Colonial New York* (New York and London, 1985). Davis convincingly argues that slaves were indeed engaged in a plot, but it was one to gain their freedom. The "great plot" feared by Clarke and other members of the elite was largely a product of their collective imaginations.

16. Browning, *Duke of Newcastle*, 112; W. A. Speck, *Stability and Strife, England, 1714–1760* (Cambridge, Mass., 1979), 125, 203, 210, 238.

17. Browning, *Duke of Newcastle*, 113–16, 117–18, 120.

18. Duke of Newcastle to Board of Trade, 30 Apr. 1741, *DRNY*, 6:187.

19. George Clinton to Board of Trade, 27 Jan. 1744 and 22 June 1747, *DRNY*, 6:254, 353.

20. George Clinton to Board of Trade, 22 June 1747, *DRNY*, 6:353.

21. Katz, *Newcastle's New York*, 167; Dudley Ryder and William Murray on the Appointment of Chief Justice DeLancey, 25 July 1753, *DRNY*, 6:792.

22. Governor Hunter's Patent, 1715, *DHNY*, 3:690–702.

23. Michael Kammen, *Colonial New York* (Millwood, N. Y., 1975), 311.

24. Robert Hunter also had a negative opinion of Albany Indian traders, whom he referred to as "that vile race." Hunter believed traders were "more intent on their private profit than the publick good." Robert Hunter to Board of Trade, 29 Sept. 1715, *DRNY*, 5:436; Philip Livingston to Cadwallader Colden, 17 Apr. 1739, Cadwallader Colden to Peter Collinson, May 1742, John Ayscough to Cadwallader Colden, 2 Dec. 1749, Colden, *Papers*, 2:195, 259–60, 3:167.

25. Conference between Commissioners of Colonies and Indians, 9 Oct. 1745, *DRNY*, 6:294–95;

26. Robert Hunter to the Board of Trade, 7 July 1718, *DRNY*, 5:511.

27. George Clarke to Cadwallader Colden, 10 May 1736, Colden, *Papers*, 2:149–50.

28. George Clinton to duke of Newcastle, 18 Nov. 1745, 9 Dec. 1746, *DRNY*, 6:286, 313–14.

29. The earl of Clarendon, who as Lord Cornbury governed New York, thought Robert Livingston to be "a very ill man." Clarendon claimed that Livingston, who had the victualling contract for the Albany garrison, "was guilty of most notorious frauds by which he greatly improv'd his Estate." Robert Hunter believed Robert Livingston to be "ye most selfish man alive." See earl of Clarendon to Lord Dartmouth, 8 Mar. 1711, *DRNY*, 5:196 and Robert Hunter to Francis Nicholson, 22 Oct. 1711, *DHNY*, 3:676. George Clinton to Board of Trade, 30 Nov. 1747, George Clinton to duke of Newcastle, 30 Nov. 1747, *DRNY*, 6:413, 414.

30. Verner W. Crane, *The Southern Frontier, 1670–1732* (Ann Arbor, 1929, 1956), 160–61; Lewis Henry Morgan, *The League of the Iroquois* (Secaucus, N. J., 1851, 1975), 24; on Iroquois wars of conquest, see George T. Hunt, *The Wars of the Iroquois* (Madison, 1960).

31. George Clinton to Board of Trade, 5 June 1744, Conference between Governor Clinton and the Indians, 18 June 1744, George Clinton to duke of Newcastle, 9 Oct. 1744, George Clinton to Board of Trade, 25 July 1745, *DRNY*, 6:255, 262, 265, 282; Douglas Edward Leach, *The Northern Colonial Frontier, 1607–1763* (New York, 1966), 192.

32. Francis Jennings, *The Ambiguous Iroquois Empire* (New York and London, 1984), 356, 360–62.

33. George Clinton to duke of Newcastle, 10 June 1746, *DRNY*, 6:309–10; see also George Clinton to Cadwallader Colden, 29 Mar. 1748, Colden, *Papers*, 3:27.

34. George Clinton to duke of Newcastle, 30 Nov. 1745, *DRNY*, 6:305–6; on Clinton's attempts to launch a military campaign against Canada see Bonomi, *A Factious People*, 156–57.

35. George Clinton to Board of Trade, 22 June 1747, *DRNY*, 6:353; Katz, *Newcastle's New York*, 172–73.

36. *DHNY*, 4:632; George Clinton to Board of Trade, 22 June 1747, *DRNY*, 6:352, 356–57; Smith, *History of New York*, 2:73; two modern historians of New York differ in offering causes for the split. Stanley Katz believes the duo broke over animosity raised when DeLancey killed an assembly bill favored by the governor. Patricia Bonomi believes DeLancey broke with Clinton because he thought the latter's military policies against Canada were disastrous. See Katz, *Newcastle's New York*, 169–70, and Bonomi, *A Factious People*, 156–57.

37. See, for instance, George Clinton to Board of Trade, 22 June 1747, *DRNY*, 6:353.

38. Livingston, *Review of the Military Operations*, 85; George Clinton to Board of Trade, 22 June 1747, George Clinton to John Russell, duke of Bedford, 30 Oct. 1748, *DRNY*, 6:357, 464–65; Cadwallader Colden to William Shirley, 25 July 1749, Colden, *Papers*, 4:124–25, 163.

39. George Clinton to Board of Trade, 30 Nov. 1747, George Clinton to duke of Newcastle, 30 Nov. 1747, *DRNY*, 6:413, 414.

40. Cadwallader Colden to George Clinton, 9 Feb. 1749, Colden, *Papers*, 3:94.

41. Smith, *History of New York*, 2:124–25,

42. George Clinton to duke of Newcastle, 30 May 1747, *DRNY*, 6:351; Bonomi, *A Factious People*, 306–8.

43. George Clinton to duke of Newcastle, 13 Feb. 1747 and 9 Nov. 1747, *DRNY*, 6:409, 416; George Clinton to Cadwallader Colden, 31 Jan. 1748, Cadwallader Colden to George Clarke, 14 Feb. 1748, Colden, *Papers*, 3:10–11, 13; Smith, *History of New York*, 2:142–43; Katz, *Newcastle's New York*, 174.

44. George Clinton to duke of Bedford, 30 Oct. 1748, George Clinton to the duke of Newcastle, 13 Feb. 1747, *DRNY*, 6:465, 417.

45. George Clinton to duke of Bedford, 30 Oct. 1748, *DRNY*, 6:464.

46. George Clinton to Board of Trade, 22 Apr. 1748, 22 June 1747, George Clinton to duke of Bedford, 15 Aug. 1748, *DRNY*, 6:425, 353, 430.

47. George Clinton to Board of Trade, 22 June 1747, *DRNY*, 6:353.

48. George Clinton to Board of Trade, 22 Apr. 1748, Board of Trade to George Clinton, 29 June 1748, George Clinton to duke of Bedford, 15 Aug. 1748, *DRNY*, 6:420, 427, 430.

49. George Clinton to Board of Trade, 26 Nov. 1749, *DRNY*, 6:535–36.

50. Lustig, *Robert Hunter*, 77–78, 87, 100–3, 118, 124–25; George Clinton to Board of Trade, 24 Oct. 1752, *DRNY*, 6:766.

51. Cadwallader Colden to John Catherwood, 21 Nov. 1749, Colden, *Papers*, 3:162.

52. George Clinton to duke of Newcastle, 9 Nov. 1747, *DRNY*, 6:410; Speck, *Stability and Strife*, 248–51.

53. William Shirley to George Clinton, 13 Aug. 1748, Clinton and Shirley to Board of Trade, 18 Aug. 1748, *DRNY*, 6:432–37, 437–40.

54. George Clinton to duke of Newcastle, 30 Nov. 1745, 9 Dec. 1746; George Clinton to Board of Trade, 27 Sept. 1747 and 29 Sept. 1747; Governor Clinton's Reasons for Suspending Mr. Horsmanden, 27 Sept. 1747; George Clinton to duke of Bedford, 15 Aug. 1748, 30 Oct. 1748, 24 Feb. 1749, Board of Trade to George Clinton, 29 June 1748, *DRNY*, 6:306, 312–13, 379, 380–82, 404, 428, 429, 465, 476; John Ayscough to Cadwallader Colden, 30 Apr. 1750, Colden, *Papers*, 3:208; Katz, *Newcastle's New York*, 173–74.

55. George Clinton to duke of Bedford, 15 Aug. 1748, *DRNY*, 6:430.

56. Peter Collinson, May 1742, Colden, *Papers*, 2:262.

57. George Clinton to Mr. Catherwood, 17 Feb. 1749, George Clinton to duke of Bedford, 28 June 1749, *DRNY*, 6:471, 514; Copy of Complaint, *King v. Oliver DeLancey*, July 1749, Colden, *Papers*, 3:117–18.

58. Speck, *Stability and Strife*, 251; Browning, *Duke of Newcastle*, 181–82.

59. Jack P. Greene, "An Uneasy Connection, An Analysis of the Preconditions of the American Revolution," in *Essays on the American Revolution*, ed. Stephen G. Kurtz and James H. Hutson (Chapel Hill and New York, 1973), 32–80.

60. Browning, *Duke of Newcastle,* 167–69.

61. An example of the cavalier attitude of the Royal Navy to impressment occurred in 1757. New York governor Sir Charles Hardy, returning to duty with the Royal Navy, was prevented from sailing because many of his seamen had deserted to join privateers. With the military assistance of commander Lord Loudoun, Hardy rounded up the deserters "and I believe, some additional Strength to the Ships of War." Fully staffed with reluctant New York seamen, Hardy set sail. Lord Loudoun to William Pitt, 30 May 1757, *Correspondence of William Pitt with Colonial Governors and Military and Naval Commissioners in America*, ed. Gertrude Selwyn Kimball, 2 vols. (London and New York, 1906, 1969), 1:69; John Ayscough to Cadwallader Colden, 18 June 1750, Cadwallader Colden to George Clinton, 19 June 1750, Colden, *Papers*, 3:216–18; Douglas Edward Leach, *Roots of Conflict, British Armed Forces and Colonial Americans, 1677–1763* (Chapel Hill and London, 1986), 142–43. Leach gives the maid's name as Abigail Stibbins.

62. Suggestions for Letter drafted by Cadwallader Colden, n.d., Draft prepared by Cadwallader Colden to send to the Board of Trade, n.d., Colden, *Papers*, 3:224.

63. George Clinton to Board of Trade, 15 Nov. 1748, 2 Dec. 1750, *DRNY*, 6:468, 598.

64. George Clinton to duke of Bedford, 13 Dec. 1750, *DRNY*, 6:602–3; George Clinton to Cadwallader Colden, 27 Nov. 1750, James Alexander to Cadwallader Colden, 2 Jan. 1751, Colden, *Papers*, 3:237, 245; Katz, *Newcastle's New York*, 185–87.

65. For election results see *New York Gazette*, 3 Sept. 1750; Petition to Governor Clinton, 16 Apr. 1752, *DHNY*, 3:727–30.

66. William Livingston to Robert Livingston, 25 Nov. 1751, Livingston Redmond Collection, Franklin Delano Roosevelt Library, Hyde Park.

67. Report of Surveyor General on Robert Livingston's Petition, 4 May 1752, Report of Council, 28 Feb. 1753, *DHNY*, 3:733, 734–48.

68. Another Petition of the Proprietor of Livingston Manor to Governor Clinton, 31 May 1753, George Clinton to Lt. Gov. Spencer Phips, 30 July 1753, Proclamation to Arrest Rioters in Manor of Livingston, 28 July 1753, Henry Van Renseallear to Robert

Livingston, 11 Aug. 1753, Robert Livingston to Lt. Gov. James DeLancey, 12 Feb. 1754, Abraham Yates, Jr., to James DeLancey, 29 Mar. 1755, Affidavit of Robert Livingston, 8 May 1755, *DHNY*, 3:739–49, 749–50, 751–52, 754–56, 768, 784–85, 792–93; for an overly optimistic view of landlord-tenant relations, see Kim, *Landlord and Tenant in Colonial New York*, particularly "The Economics of Land and Landlords," and "The Economics and Sociology of Tenancy," 129–61, 235–80.

69. Captain de Celaron's Certificate, 10 Aug. 1749, Hendrick's Speech to Colonel Johnson, 2 Feb. 1750, *DRNY*, 6:532, 548–49; Browning, *Duke of Newcastle*, 181.

70. Ibid. 172–73, 182.

71. Francis Jennings, *Empire of Fortune, Crown, Colonies and Tribes in the Seven Years War in America* (New York and London, 1988), 185.

72. Greene, "An Uneasy Connection," 32–80; Olson, *Anglo-American Politics*, 147.

73. George Clinton to John Russell, duke of Bedford, 28 Feb. 1751, Report of the Privy Council upon the State of New-York, 2 April 1751, George Clinton to Board of Trade, 2 Aug. 1752, James DeLancey to Board of Trade, 15 Oct. 1753, *DRNY*, 6:612, 614–39, 762, 803–4; Livingston, *Review of the Military Operations*, 128.

74. Ibid., 129.

75. Board of Trade to King, 5 July 1753, *DRNY*, 6:788–91; *DHNY*, 4:633; Livingston, *Review of the Military Operations*, 128–89.

76. Thomas Pownall to Board of Trade, 14 Oct. 1753, James DeLancey to Board of Trde, 15 Oct. 1753, *DRNY*, 6:802–3, 803–4; Livingston, *Review of the Military Operations*, 82; Cadwallader Colden to Mrs. Colden, 14 Oct. 1753, Colden, *Papers*, 3:407; Irving Mark, *Agrarian Conflicts in Colonial New York, 1711–1775* (New York, 1940), 31; Clinton's wealth came in only a small part from his yearly salary of £950. Most of the money came from rake-offs on appropriations and from charging exorbitantly high fees for land patents. Clinton also used fictitious names and bought large tracts of land for himself in New York and in 1752 demanded one-quarter of all land patented in the province. Smith, *History of New York*, 2:61, 138; George Clinton to Cadwallader Colden, 28 July 1752, Colden, *Papers*, 3:342; Enclosure in George Clinton's letter to duke of Newcastle, 20 Nov. 1755, George Clinton to duke of Newcastle, 30 Jan. 1756, Newcastle Papers, Additional Mss. 32,861, 32,862, British Library. For additional information on the income of New York's royal governors, see Beverly McAnear, *The Income of the Colonial Governors of British North America* (New York, 1967), 14–27, 37–38; for the imperial structure within which Clinton and all other royal governors functioned, see Rex Maurice Naylor, "The Royal Prerogative in New York, 1691–1775," *New York History* 5(1924):221–53.

77. John Watts to Moses Franks, 9 Nov. 1765, quoted in Katz, *Newcastle's New York*, 39.

78. For offices at the disposal of New York's governor, see Naylor, "The Royal Prerogative in New York, 1691–1775," 221–55.

Chapter 5. Republicans in Principle, 1753–1757

1. Thomas Jones, *History of New York during the Revolutionary War*, ed. Edward Floyd DeLancey, 2 vols. (New York, 1879), 1:6.

2. Cadwallader Colden to earl of Hillsborough, 7 July 1770, *DRNY*, 8:217.

3. As Patricia Bonomi warns, "It may be unwise to view these groupings *too* narrowly, as though they were mere family factions, like Capulets and Montagues, or provincial Guelphs and Ghibellines." Even though quarrels were often sparked by "petty"

motives, "more seems to have been at stake here than mere personal prestige or family reputation." See *A Factious People*, 13–14.

4. Ibid., 159–61.

5. Livingston, *Review of the Military Operations*, 82.

6. Ibid.; *DHNY*, 4:634; Bonomi, *A Factious People*, 173.

7. James DeLancey to Board of Trade, 3 Jan. 1754, James DeLancey to Sir Thomas Robinson, 15 Dec. 1754, Board of Trade to Lords Justices, 22 Apr. 1755, *DRNY*, 6:820, 924, 948.

8. Smith, *History of New York*, 2:178; *Ecclesiastical Records of the State of New York*, ed. Hugh Hastings, 6 vols. (Albany, 1901–1905), 5:3456–57.

9. See, for instance, Buel, "Freedom of the Press in Revolutionary America," 69–70; Bailyn, *Origin of American Politics*, 52–57.

10. Bailyn, *The Ideological Origins of the American Revolution*, 26–30; John Redwood, *Reason, Ridicule and Religion, the Age of Enlightenment in England, 1660–1750* (Cambridge, Mass., 1976), 198.

11. Countryman, *A People in Revolution*, 3–4; William Livingston to Noah Welles, 18 Feb. 1749, Johnson Family Papers, Yale University.

12. Jones, *History of New York*, 1:6; Smith, *History of New York*, 1:98–99, 2:168–69.

13. George F. Sensabaugh in *Milton in Early America* (New York, 1964, 1979) says Livingston's poetry "scarcely rose to mediocrity." He notes Milton's influence on Livingston, whom he terms "a sometime Milton disciple," 58.

14. Redwood, *Reason, Ridicule and Religion*, 198, 214; for an example of Livingston's anti-Catholicism, see *Independent Reflector*, ed. Milton M. Klein (Cambridge, Mass., 1963), 81; William Livingston to James Sprout, 22 Sept. 1744, in Theodore Sedgwick, Jr., *A Memoir of the Life of William Livingston* (New York, 1833), 55. For an excellent and complete review of William Livingston's New York career, see Milton M. Klein, "The American Whig: William Livingston of New York," (Ph.D. diss. Columbia University, 1954).

15. Jones, *History of New York*, 1:3–4.

16. See, for instance, "Remarks on the Excise," or "The Abuses of the Road, and City-Watch," in *The Independent Reflector*, 61–68, 69–75.

17. *Independent Reflector*, 172; on the link between religion and politics, see Patricia U. Bonomi, *Under the Cope of Heaven, Religion , Society and Politics in Colonial America* (New York and Oxford, 1986), particularly "The Religious Prospect," 3–10.

18. *Ecclesiastical Records*, 5:3515–17, 3517–18; Bailyn, *Origin of American Politics*, 94–95.

19. *Colonial Laws of New York from the Year 1664 to the Revolution*, 3:607, 679, 899, 908, 930, 1027; *Ecclesiastical Records*, 5:3297–98, 3389–95; Donald Gerardi, "The King's College Controversy 1753–1756 and the Ideological Roots of Toryism in New York," in *Perspectives in American History* 11 (1977–1978), 145–98; David Humphrey, *From King's College to Columbia* (New York, 1976), especially chapter 4.

20. *Ecclesiastical Records*, 5:3220; *Independent Reflector,* 171–214, 367–75; the population of New York County in 1749 was 10,926 whites and 2,368 blacks, with a total province-wide population of 73,448 black and white, *DRNY*, 6:550; Smith, in his *History of New York*, said there were only thirteen college graduates in New York in the 1740s, 2:82–83; *Independent Reflector*, 192–95. On the need for a college in New York, see also "The Advantage of Education," *Independent Reflector*, 419–21.

21. *Independent Reflector*, 393.

22. Samuel Johnson to archbishop of Canterbury, 29 June 1753, *DRNY*, 6:777.

23. *Independent Reflector*, 76–81, 287–89, 319–26, 328–34; see also Bailyn, *Origin of American Politics*, 114, 128–30.

24. *Independent Reflector,* 306–18

25. Levy, *Legacy of Suppression*, 6–7.

26. William Livingston, "Of the Use, Abuse and Liberty of the Press," *Independent Reflector*, 336–44; Blackstone, *Commentaries on the Laws of England*, 4:151–52; Siebert, *Freedom of the Press*, 262–63; Levy, *Legacy of Suppression*, 9, 14–15.

27. *Independent Reflector*, 12–13; *Freedom of the Press from Zenger to Jefferson*, ed. Leonard W. Levy (Indianapolis, New York, Kansas City, 1966), xxxi, xxxiii.

28. Smith, *History of New York*, 2:168–69.

29. *Ecclesiastical Records*, 5:3456–57, 3457–59.

30. *Ecclesiastical Records*, 5:3515–17, 3517–18.

31. Livingston, *Review of the Military Operations*, 63.

32. Smith, *History of New York*, 2:150; Proceedings of the Colonial Congress held at Albany, June 19, 1754, *DRNY*, 6:853; Klein, "American Whig," 451–54.

33. James DeLancey to Board of Trade, 22 Apr. 1754, *DRNY*, 6:833; *DHNY*, 4:635; Livingston, *Review of the Military Operations*, 75; on French incursion, see "Inscription," *DRNY*, 6:610.

34. Livingston, *Review of the Military Operations*, 74–75; James DeLancey to Board of Trade, 22 July 1754, *DRNY*, 6:850–52.

35. On the significance of Iroquois neutrality, see Anthony F. C. Wallace, "Origins of Iroquois Neutrality, The Grand Settlement of 1701," *Pennsylvania History* 24(July 1957): 223–35; for Iroquois involvement in the French and Indian War, see Francis Jennings, *Empire of Fortune* (New York and London, 1988).

36. James DeLancey to Board of Trade, 22 July 1754, Proceedings of the Colonial Congress, July 8, 1754, *DRNY*, 6:850, 879–80; Jennings, *Empire of Fortune*, 95–97.

37. Proceedings of the Colonial Congress, *DRNY*, 6:879–80; Jennings, *Empire of Fortune*, 100.

38. Livingston, *Review of the Military Operations*, 162.

39. Ibid., 77; Proceedings of the Colonial Congress, 10 July 1754, *DRNY*, 6:882, 889, 891.

40. Speck, *Stability and Strife*, 257–58; Browning, *Duke of Newcastle*, 209.

41. William Livingston to Chauncey Whittelsey, 22 Aug. 1754, Sedgwick, *Livingston*, 91–92.

42. *DHNY*, 4:635; William Livington to Noah Welles, 8 Oct. 1754, Sedgwick, *Livingston*, 94.

43. William Livingston to Noah Welles, 7 Dec. 1754, Sedgwick, *Livingston*, 104; *Ecclesiastical Records*, 5:3523–25, 3525–26; *New York Assembly Journal*, 2:413–19.

44. Order in Council, 29 Jan. 1755, *DRNY*, 6:934–35.

45. *DHNY*, 4:634; Board of Trade to King George, 4 Feb. 1756, Board of Trade to Charles Hardy, 4 Mar. 1756, *DRNY*, 7:32–33, 40; Charles Hardy Message, 24 Sept. 1756, Votes and Proceedings of the General Assembly of the Colony of New York, CO 5,1216, Public Record Office; see also Greene, "An Uneasy Connection," 32–80.

46. Hints respecting the Civil Establishments in the American Colonys, 25 Feb. 1763, Liverpool Papers, Additional Mss. 38,335, British Library; Greene, "An Uneasy Connection," 32–80.

47. Livingston, *Review of the Military Operations*, 85, 139–40, 142; Thomas Elliot Norton, *The Fur Trade in Colonial New York, 1686–1776* (Madison, Wisc., 1974), 171, 197, 198, 202; Milton M. Klein, "William Livingston's A Review of the Military Operations," in *The Colonial Legacy*, ed. Lawrence H. Leder, 2 vols. (New York, 1971), 2:107, 121, 122, 128.

48. John A. Schutz, *William Shirley, King's Governor of Massachusetts* (Chapel Hill, 1961), 224.

49. For the Cartagena expedition and the antagonism of Americans to British offi-

cers, see Douglas Edward Leach, *Roots of Conflict,* especially "Florida, the Caribbean, and Georgia," 42–63 and "The Great War for the Empire, Joint Operations," 107–33; see also Fred Anderson, *A People's Army, Massachusetts Soldiers and Society in the Seven Years' War* (New York and London, 1984), 111–41; Browning, *Duke of Newcastle,* 210; Speck, *Stability and Strife,* 259, 261, 262; Sir George Lyttelton to duke of Newcastle, 7 Oct. 1756, Newcastle Papers, Additional Mss. 32,868, British Library.

50. Browning, *Duke of Newcastle,* 210. For an example of British indignation at money spent in defense of Hanover see the cartoon reproduced in Vincent Carretta, *George III and the Satirists from Hogarth to Byron* (Athens, Georgia and London, 1990), 19–20. The cartoon shows Newcastle and Pelham disemboweling a corpse representing Britannia while a white horse, the emblem of Hanover, drinks the blood spilled from the corpse.

51. Jennings, *Empire of Fortune,* 124; Browning, *Duke of Newcastle,* 211.

52. Livingston, *Review of the Military Operations,* 92–93; Jennings, *Empire of Fortune,* 157–59.

53. Board of Trade to Charles Hardy, 17 Feb. 1756, *DRNY,* 7:36–37; Speck, *Stability and Strfie,* 263–65; duke of Newcastle to Lord Halifax,1 Jan. 1756, Intelligence from Versailles, 12 Jan. 1756, duke of Newcastle to Lord Chancellor, 8 May 1756, Lord Barrington to duke of Newcastle, 11 Dec. 1756, Newcastle Papers, Additional Mss. 32,861, 32,864, 32,869, British Library.

54. Samuel Fellows, John Burton, and H. Butler to duke of Newcastle, 25 Aug. 1756, duke of Newcastle to J. Willes, 27 Aug. 1756, Duke of Newcastle to Lord Chancellor, Newcastle Papers, 28 Aug. 1756, Additional Mss. 32,867, British Library.

55. *London Evening Post,* 24–26 Aug. 1756, British Library.

56. Duke of Newcastle to Lord Chancellor, 8 May 1756, J. Willes to duke of Newcastle, 21 Aug. 1756, Additional Mss. 32,864, 32,867, British Library.

57. Message from Charles Hardy to Assembly, 24 June 1756, Votes and Proceedings of the General Assembly of the Colony of New York, CO 5,1216, Public Record Office; Jennings, *Empire of Fortune,* 185–86; Browning, *Duke of Newcastle,* 230, 231; Schutz, *Shirley,* 209, 225–26, 234–35; *The Papers of William Livingston,* 5 vols., vol. 1, ed., Carl E. Prince, vol. 2, ed., Carl E. Prince and Dennis P. Ryan, vol. 3, ed., Carl E. Prince, Mary Lou Lustig, and Dennis P. Ryan, vol. 4, ed., Carl E. Prince and Mary Lou Lustig, vol. 5, ed., Carl E. Prince, Mary Lou Lustig, and David William Voorhees (vols. 1 and 2, Trenton, 1979, 1980, vols. 3, 4, and 5, New Brunswick, 1986, 1987, 1988), 5:476 (hereafter cited as *Livingston Papers*).

58. William Livingston to Noah Welles, 8 Aug. 1757, Johnson Family Papers, Yale University.

59. Livingston, *Review of the Military Operations,* 159.

60. Speck, *Stability and Strife,* 264–65; Browning, *Duke of Newcastle,* 255; duke of Newcastle to Lord Barrington, 13 Oct. 1756, duke of Newcastle to Lord Chancellor, 14 Oct. 1756, duke of Newcastle to duke of Grafton, 15 Oct. 1756, duke of Newcastle to Mr. O'Brien, 21 Oct. 1756, duke of Newcastle to duke of Devonshire, 26 Oct. 1756, duke of Newcastle to Mr. Arundel, 30 Oct. 1756, Newcastle Papers, Additional Mss. 32,868, British Library.

61. Jennings, *Empire of Fortune,* 355; Speck, *Stability and Strife,* 265–67; Browning, *Duke of Newcastle,* 257–58.

62. Browning, *Duke of Newcastle,* 260–61; Mr. Sutton to duke of Newcastle, 10 July 1757, Newcastle Papers, Additional Mss. 32,872, British Library; duke of Newcastle to Mr Obrien, 21 Oct. 1756, Newcastle Papers, Additional Mss. 32,868, British Library.

63. Jennings, *Empire of Fortune,* 360–61; for Newcastle's efforts to finance the European war, see Reed Browning, "The Duke of Newcastle and the Financial Manage-

ment of the Seven Years War in Germany, *Society for Army Historical Research Journal* 49 (1972):20–35.

64. Board of Trade to Charles Hardy, 10 Mar. 1757, Charles Hardy to Board of Trade, 24 May 1757, James DeLancey to Board of Trade, 3 June 1759, *DRNY*, 7:220, 222, 225; Schutz, *William Shirley*, 234.

65. Livingston, *Review of the Military Operations*, 85.

66. Ibid.

67. Schutz, *William Shirley*, 243–46.

68. For background on the publication of the *Review* see Klein, "William Livingston's A Review of the Military Operations," 1:109–39; William Livingston to Noah Welles, 8 Aug. 1757, 3 Jan. 1758, Johnson Family Papers, Yale University; C. V. Wedgwood, *The King's Peace, 1637–1741* (Middlesex, Eng., 1955, 1983), 107.

69. Jennings, *Empire of Fortune*, 361–62; William Livingston to Noah Welles, 21 Mar. 1950, Johnson Family Papers, Yale University.

Chapter 6. Property Reputation and Extensive Connections, 1758–1765

1. William Smith, *Historical Memoirs, March 16, 1763–July 9, 1776*, ed. William H. W. Sabine (New York, 1956), 95.

2. Ibid.

3. Cadwallader Colden to Board of Trade, 20 Sept. 1764, *DRNY*, 7:655; Nash, *The Urban Crucible*, 233.

4. See Greene, *The Quest for Power*, particularly Part V, "Control Over Executive Affairs," 223–354.

5. For the most complete accounts of the war see Jennings, *Empire of Fortune,* and Ian K. Steele, *Betrayals, Fort William Henry and the 'Massacre'"* (New York and Oxford, 1990), 1993.

6. William Livingston to Noah Welles, 24 Aug. 1757, Johnson Family Papers, Yale University; James DeLancey to Board of Trade, 17 Dec. 1758, *DRNY*, 7:353; *New York Assembly Journal*, 2:584.

7. Cadwallader Colden to Board of Trade, 7 Aug. 1740 [1760]; same to same, 26 Sept. 1760; Board of Trade Proposal, 17 March 1761; Cadwallader Colden to Board of Trade, 12 Aug. 1761, *DRNY*, 7:444, 460, 468.

8. Cadwallader Colden to James Alexander, n.d., quoted in Whitehead, *Contributions to the Early History of Perth Amboy*, 149.

9. Cadwallader Colden to Charles Windham, 1st earl of Egremont, 13 Sept. 1763, Cadwallader Colden to earl of Halifax, 22 Feb. 1765, *DRNY*, 7:549, 705.

10. Cadwallader Colden to Board of Trade, 10 Jan. 1761, *DRNY*, 7:453; see also Milton M. Klein, "Prelude to Revolution in New York: Jury Trials and Judicial Tenure," in *Willliam and Mary Quarterly* 17 (1960): 439–62.

11. Smith, *History of New York*, 2:251; for a similar provincial struggle over crown control of the judiciary in New Jersey, see Jerome J. Nadelhaft, "Politics and the Judicial Tenure Fight in Colonial New Jersey," *William and Mary Quarterly* 28 (1971):46–63.

12. Browning, *Duke of Newcastle*, 275, 276, 280, 281, 282, 288; John Derry, *English Politics and the American Revolution* (London, 1976), 41.

13. Cadwallader Colden to Board of Trade, 2 June 1761, *DRNY*, 7:466–67; *New York Assembly Journal*, 2:646.

14. Cadwallader Colden to Board of Trade, 12 Aug. 1761, *DRNY*, 7:468.

15. Cadwallader Colden to Board of Trade, 25 Sept. 1761, *DRNY*, 7:469–70.

16. Board of Trade Proposal, 17 March 1761, *DRNY*, 7:460; Benjamin Prat to Cadwallader Colden, 22 Aug. 1761, 3 Oct. 1761, Colden, *Papers*, 6:68, 81.

17. Cadwallader Colden to Board of Trade, 11 Jan. 1762; Benjamin Prat to Board of Trade, 24 May 1762, Board of Trade Representation to King, 11 June 1762, *DRNY*, 7:500, 505–6.

18. Benjamin Prat to Thomas Pownall, 7 Jan. 1762, Colden, *Papers*, 6:115; on Pownall's continuing influence on colonial affairs, see Franklin B. Wickwire, "John Pownall and British Colonial Policy," *William and Mary Quarterly* 20 (1963):543–54, and idem. *British Subministers and Colonial America, 1763–1783* (Princeton, 1966), 87.

19. The "Lion's Mouth" appeared from 3 April to 24 May 1762; *American Chronicle*, 20 Mar. 1762.

20. Cadwallader Colden to Board of Trade, 4 Apr. 1762, Colden, *Papers*, 9:186–92.

21. For Colden's use of satire to attack his enemies, see James Alexander to Cadwallader Colden, 5 May 1728, Colden, *Papers*, 1:259–61; for Colden's career as a member of the country opposition, see Cadwallader Colden to Mrs. Elizabeth Hill, 19 Jan. 1734; Daniel Horsmanden to Cadwallader Colden, 19 Nov. 1734; Lewis Morris to Marquis of Lothian, 26 Mar. 1735; Cadwallader Colden to James Alexander, 27 Mar. 1735, Colden, *Papers*, 2:102, 121, 124–28, 128–31.

22. Robert Monckton to Cadwallader Colden, 11 Nov. 1761, Colden, *Papers*, 6:88–89.

23. Board of Trade Proposal, 17 Mar. 1761; Benjamin Prat to Board of Trade, 24 May 1762, Cadwallader Colden to Board of Trade, 8 July 1763, *DRNY*, 7:460, 500, 528.

24. Cadwallader Colden to Board of Trade, 8 July 1763, *DRNY*, 7:527.

25. Anthony F. C. Wallace, *The Death and Rebirth of the Seneca* (New York, 1969, 1972), 114–22.

26. Derry, *English Politics and the American Revolution*, 51.

27. "Hints respecting the Settlement of our American Provinces," 25 Feb. 1763, Liverpool Papers, Additional Mss. 38,335, British Library. In the *William and Mary Quarterly* 24 (1967):108–26, Thomas C. Barrow tentatively identifies the author as William Knox, a former royal official in Georgia who returned to England in 1761. Knox served both Bute and Grenville and was then undersecretary to the southern secretary of state.

28. Ibid.; P. D. G. Thomas, *British Politics and the Stamp Act Crisis: The First Phase of the American Revolution, 1763–1767* (Oxford, 1975), 35–36.

29. Hints respecting the Settlement of our American Provinces," 25 Feb. 1763, Liverpool Papers, Additional Mss. 38,335, British Library.

30. Ibid; Thomas, *British Politics and the Stamp Act Crisis*, 37–38.

31. *British Royal Proclamations Relating to America, 1603–1783*, ed. Clarence S. Brigham (New York, 1911), 216.

32. Smith, *Historical Memoirs*, 24–25, 26; Cadwallader Colden to Board of Trade, 7 Nov. 1764, *DRNY*, 7:677.

33. George Hansen to Cadwallader Colden, 24 Nov. 1765, John Tabor Kempe to Cadwallader Colden, 31 Oct. 1764, Reasons offered by Daniel Horsmanden, Esq., Chief Justice of the Province of New York, 19 Nov. 1764, Colden, *Papers*, 6:388, 368–71, 379–86; Smith, *Historical Memoirs*, 25, 28; on *Forsey v. Cunningham,* see Herbert Johnson, *Essays on New York Colonial Legal History* (Wesport, Conn., 1981), 171–92; Joseph H. Smith, *Appeals to the Privy Council from the American Plantations* (New York, 1950), 390–416.

34. Reasons offered by Daniel Horsmanden, Esq., 19 Nov. 1764, Colden, *Papers*, 6:379–81; Cadwallader Colden to Board of Trade, 13 Dec. 1764, *DRNY*, 7:679–80.

35. William Smith, Jr., to Robert Monckton, 3 Dec. 1764, Smith, *Historical Memoirs*, 27.

36. Cadwallader Colden to Board of Trade, 14 Apr. 1765, *DRNY*, 7:710; *New York Gazette*, 28 Feb. 1765.

37. Mr. Colden's Account of the State of the Province of New York, 6 Dec. 1765, *DRNY*, 7:778.

38. Mr. Colden's Account of the State of the Province of New York, 6 Dec. 1765, *DRNY*, 7:795; Irving Mark notes that of thirty three attorneys who passed the bar in New York from 1730 to 1776, thirty were related to the manorial families. Mark, *Agrarian Conflicts*, 91) Renssaerwyck had 1,000,000 acres, Highland Patent (Philipse Manor) 205,000 acres, Livingston Manor 160,000 acres, Philipsborough with 156,000 acres, and Cortlandt Manor with 86,000 acres (Mark, *Agrarian Conflicts*, 21).

39. Cadwallader Colden to earl of Halifax, 22 Feb. 1765; Cadwallader Colden to Board of Trade, 20 Sept. 1764, *DRNY*, 7:654, 705.

40. Cadwallader Colden to earl of Halifax, 22 Feb. 1765; Colden to Board of Trade, 20 Sept. 1764, *DRNY*, 7:654, 705; on the New York slave rebellion of 1712, see Lustig, *Robert Hunter*, 105–6.

41. *Independent Reflector*, 133.

42. Cadwallader Colden to Board of Trade, 7 Nov. 1764, Cadwallader Colden, *Letter Books, 1760–1775*, 2 vols., New-York Historical Society, *Collections, 1876, 1877* (New York, 1877, 1878), 1:397, 2:73.

43. Colden, *Papers*, 6:329–39.

44. On the difficulty in collecting quit rents see Milton M. Klein, "Archibald Kennedy, Imperial Pamphleteer," in *The Colonial Legacy*, 2:82–83; Cadwallader Colden to Board of Trade, 8 Feb. 1764; Sir Henry Moore to William, earl of Shelburne, 20 Feb. 1767, *DRNY*, 7:608, 900–5; Henry Brockholst Livingston to William Livingston, 18 Aug. 1785, 20 Feb. 1788, 12 Mar. 1788, *Livingston Papers*, 5:202, 330–31, 332. Klock was notorious for cheating Indians of both land and money. He consistently refused to release the Canajohary tract to the Indians, despite the fact that a release had been signed by all other proprietors. The result was that Klock complained he was "several Times Assaulted and Robbed by the Conojohary Indians." In 1774, Lt. Gov. Colden advised Klock that "unless he does execute the same [release], the Matter will be laid before the General Assembly, and such Measures entered into as will compel him to do them [the Mohawks] Justice." See Minutes of the Council, 1 Sept.1774, 7 Dec. 1774, CO 5,1201, Public Record Office.

45. William Johnson to Cadwallader Colden, 20 Feb. 1761, 19 Mar. 1761, Colden, *Papers*, 6:12, 18; William Livingston to Charles Stewart, 15 Mar. 1785, William Livingston to William Livingston, Jr., 6 Mar. 1787, *Livingston Papers*, 5:175–77, 282.

46. Cadwallader Colden to Board of Trade, 1 Mar. 1762, *DRNY*, 7:491; Cadwallader Colden to Board of Trade, June 8, 1765, Colden, *Letter Books*, 1:406; Mark, *Agrarian Conflicts*, 41, 43.

47. Cadwallader Colden to Board of Trade, 20 Sept. 1764, *DRNY*, 7:655.

48. Lustig, *Robert Hunter*, 125–26, 222.

49. Nash, *The Urban Crucible*, 235; for New York political history see Becker, *History of Political Parties in the Province of New York*, particularly 5–22; Countryman, *A People in Revolution*, 36, 45, 58. For the political behavior of a lower class group see Graham Russell Hodges, *New York City Cartmen, 1667–1850* (New York, 1986). For mob behavior, see George Rude, *Paris and London in the Eighteenth Century* (New York, 1952, 1970), and George Rude, *Ideology and Popular Protest* (New York, 1980); E. J. Hobsbawm, *Primitive Rebels* (New York 1959); Pauline Maier, *From Resistance to Revolution, Colonial Radicals and the Development of American Opposition to Britain* (New York, 1974).

50. For the theory of relative deprivation, see Ted Robert Gurr, *Why Men Rebel* (Princeton, 1970). Gurr contends that unrest and revolution usually occur in times of rising prosperity. He argues that expectations rise when one social group achieves success. This produces heightened expectations among other groups. See particularly 105–6, 114.

51. Klein, "The American Whig," 537–39; Colden, *Letters*, 6:137, 138.

52. General Assembly of New York to Cadwallader Colden, 11 Sept. 1764, Liverpool Papers, Additional Mss. 38,338, British Library.

53. Cadwallader Colden to Board of Trade, 20 Sept. 1764, *DRNY*, 7:653–55; Dorothy Rita Dillon, *The New York Triumvirate* (New York, 1949), 87.

54. Board of Trade quoted in Thomas, *British Politics and the Stamp Act Crisis*, 87.

55. George Clinton to duke of Newcastle, *DRNY*, 6:268.

56. Thomas, *British Politics and the Stamp Act Crisis*, 107; see also Charles R. Ritcheson, "The Preparation of the Stamp Act," *William and Mary Quarterly* 10 (1953):543–59.

57. Smith, *Historical Memoirs*, 31; Paul Gilje, in *The Road to Mobocracy*, argues that mobs in this period acted to defend shared communal interests and that rioting was not indicative of a splintered society, 5–6; Henry Moore to Board of Trade, 22 Feb. 1765, *DRNY*, 7:814.

58. Edmund S. Morgan and Helen M. Morgan, *The Stamp Act Crisis, Prologue to Revolution*, rev. ed. (New York, 1963), 39–40, 47–48, 96–98.

59. Dillon, *New York Triumvirate*, 87; the suggestion to establish committees of correspondence in America came initially from a New York Sons meeting held either 31 Oct. or 6 Nov. 1765. See Maier, *From Resistance to Revolution*, 78.

60. Morgan and Morgan, *The Stamp Act Crisis*, 239–40; Countryman, *A People in Revolution*, 83.

61. Thomas Gage to Cadwallader Colden, 31 Aug. 1765, Colden, *Papers*, 7:57–58.

62. Klein, American Whig, 550; *The Constitutional Courant*, 21 Sept. 1765; *Independent Reflector*, 61.

63. Cadwallader Colden to Henry Seymour Conway, 12 Oct. 1765, *DRNY*, 7:767–68.

64. Bernard Bailyn, *The Ordeal of Thomas Hutchinson* (Cambridge, Mass., 1974), 68–69; Maier, *From Resistance to Revolution*, 56–60; Cadwallader Colden to Sir Henry Conway, 2 Sept. 1765, James McEwers to Cadwallader Colden, n.d., *DRNY*, 7:760, 761; Thomas Gage to Sir Henry Conway, 23 Sept. 1765, *Correspondence of General Thomas Gage with the Secretaries of State, 1763–1775*, ed. Clarence Edwin Carter (New Haven, 1931), 67–68; *New York Gazette* comment quoted in Maier, *From Resistance to Revolution*, 54.

65. Cadwallader Colden to Sir Henry Conway, 23 Sept. 1765, *DRNY*, 7:760; *Independent Reflector*, 145; *New York Gazette*, 26 Dec. 1768; Sedgwick, *Livingston*, 126.

66. Mr. Colden's Account . . . , *DRNY*, 7:798.

67. Robert W. Tucker and David C. Hendrickson, *The Fall of the First British Empire* (Baltimore and London, 1982), 218–19.

68. Cadwallader Colden to earl of Halifax, 22 Feb. 1765, *DRNY*, 7:705.

Chapter 7. The Spirit of Mobbing, 1765–1770

1. *Independent Reflector*, 145.

2. Cadwallader Colden to earl of Hillsborough, 25 Apr. 1768, *DRNY*, 8:61.

3. Ibid.

4. On Livingston's limited interpretation of "the people," see Charles H. Levermore, "The Whigs of Colonial New York," *American Historical Review* 1(1896):238–50.

5. Newcastle Papers, Additional Mss. 33,030, vol. 1, British Library; Thomas Gage to Henry S. Conway, *Correspondence of Thomas Gage*, 1:71; Becker, *History of Political Parties in the Province of New York*, 27; *New York Mercury*, 14 Oct. 1765.

6. Enclosure, Cadwallader Colden to Henry S. Conway, 26 Oct. 1765, *DRNY*, 7:770.

7. Cadwallader Colden to duke of Newcastle, 23 Sept. 1765, Newcastle Papers, Additional Mss. 33,030, vol. 1, British Library; Cadwallader Colden to Board of Trade, 6 Dec. 1765, *DRNY*, 7:792.

8. Montresor, *Journals*, ed. G. D. Scull, New-York Historical Society, *Collections*, 14:335; Anonymous Letter, n.d., delivered 1 Nov. 1765, *DRNY*, 7:775.

9. Richard Maxwell Brown, "Violence in the American Revolution," in *Essays on the American Revolution*, 92; Maj. James Thomas [sic], Account of the Riot at New York, n.d., Newcastle Papers, Additional Mss. 33,030, Vol. 1, British Library.

10. Maier, *From Resistance to Revolution*, 67–68.

11. To replace his lost chariot, Colden quickly ordered another from England. The carriage was to be "made of the Best Seasond timber lin'd with a light Coloured Cloth . . . with 2 rows of fringe 2 fore Glasses Door Glasses and a sett of mahogany shutters with rose lights . . . Painted a fine Glaizd Crimson with light Crimson flowers on silver all over the Pannels" at a cost of £88 9s. plus £25 for shipping. The coach was shipped 12 May 1766. Peter Collinson to Cadwallader Colden, 20 March 1766, Jacob and Elliott's Bill, Colden, Papers, 7:108–9, 110; Montresor, *Journals*, 14:337; Smith, *Historical Memoirs*, 31; F. L. Engelman, "Cadwallader Colden and the New York Stamp Act Riots," *William and Mary Quarterly* 10 (1953):560–78; Cadwallader Colden to Henry S. Conway, 5 Nov. 1765, 9 Nov. 1765, *DRNY*, 7:771, 773; Thomas Gage to Henry S. Conway, 4 Nov. 1765, *Correspondence of Thomas Gage*, 1:71; Cadwallader Colden to Board of Trade, 6 Dec. 1765, *DRNY*, 7:792; James claimed that his losses were in excess of £2000 sterling. He accepted £1765 15s. 2d. offered as settlement by the New York Assembly on 29 Nov. 1766 and said "he was well satisfied" with the sum. On 9 Dec. 1766 the assembly declined to compensate Colden for losses sustained in the 1 Nov. 1765 riot, claiming the disturbance "was occasioned by his own Misconduct." Major James Account of the Riot at New York, n.d., Newcastle Papers, Additional Mss. 33,030, vol. 1, British Library; Votes and Proceedings of the General Assembly of New York, CO 5,1217, Public Record Office.

12. Thomas Gage to Henry S. Conway, 21 Dec. 1765, *Correspondence of Thomas Gage*, 1:79; *DRNY*, 7:773; Montresor, *Journals*, 14:339; Becker, *History of Political Parties in the Province of New York*, 32, 40, 49;

13. Ibid., 32, 40, 49; Dunlap quoted in Bernard Friedman, "The Shaping of the Radical Consciousness in the Province of New York," *Journal of American History* 4(March 1970), 56:781–801; on the symbolism and ritual that motivated New York mobs, see Peter Shaw, *American Patriots and the Rituals of Revolution* (Cambridge, Mass., 1981), 5–25, 179, 227–31; Sean Wilentz, *Chants Democratic, New York City and the Rise of the American Working Class, 1788–1850* (New York, 1984), 65; see also Paul A. Gilje, "Republican Rioting," in *Authority and Resistance in Colonial New York*, 202–25; and idem., *The Road to Mobocracy*, particularly Part 1, "Traditions," 3–92.

14. Cadwallader Colden to earl of Shelburne, 26 Dec. 1766, *DRNY*, 7:886–87; on the reaction of the elite to lower class initiative, see Carl Becker, "Growth of Revolutionary Parties and Methods in New York Province, 1765–1774," *American Historical Review* 7(1901):56–76.

15. Colden, *Letters*, 7:66–71; Montresor, *Journals*, 14:339.

16. Smith, *Historical Memoirs*, 31; Cadwallader Colden to Henry Conway, 5 Nov. 1765, 9 Nov. 1765, 13 Dec. 1765, 15 Dec. 1765, *DRNY*, 7:771, 773, 800, 801; Montre-

sor, *Journals*, 14:339. Moore was appointed governor 20 June 1765. See Board of Trade to the King, 20 June 1765, Cadwallader Colden to Henry Conway, 21 Feb. 1766, Henry Moore to earl of Hillsborough, 9 May 1768, *DRNY*, 7:745, 812, 8:67.

17. Henry Moore to earl of Hillsborough, 9 May 1768, *DRNY*, 8:67.

18. Henry Moore to earl of Dartmouth, 21 Nov. 1765, *DRNY*, 7:789.

19. Henry Moore to Henry Conway, 21 Dec. 1765, Cadwallader Colden to Henry Conway, 13 Dec. 1765, *DRNY*, 7:802, 794.

20. Henry Moore to Henry S. Conway, 21 Dec. 1765, *DRNY*, 7:802.

21. Henry Moore to earl of Shelburne, 9 June 1767, *DHNY*, 4:366; Thomas Gage to Henry S. Conway, 21 Dec. 1765, *Correspondence of Thomas Gage*, 1:79; Smith, *Historical Memoirs*, 95.

22. Address of the Sons of Liberty to the Assembly, 29 Nov. 1765, *DHNY*, 3:495–96.

23. Thomas Gage to Henry S. Conway, 21 Dec. 1765, *Correspondence of Thomas Gage*, 1:79.

24. Montresor, *Journals*, 14:342, 349, 350; *DHNY*, 3:496; Henry Moore to Henry S. Conway, 16 Jan., 26 Mar. 1766, Henry S. Conway to Governors, 31 Mar. 1766, *DRNY*, 7:805, 818, 823.

25. Votes and Proceedings of the General Assembly of the Colony of New York, CO 5,1217, Public Record Office.

26. Montresor, *Journals*, 353–54, 357; Votes and Proceedings of the General Assembly of the Colony of New York, CO 5,1221, Public Record Office; Cadwallader Colden to Henry S. Conway, 21 Feb. 1766, Henry Moore to Henry S. Conway, 20 Feb. 1766, *DRNY*, 7:812, 810.

27. Montresor, *Journals*, 353–54, 357; Thomas, *British Politics and the Stamp Act Crisis*, 151–52.

28. Montresor, *Journals*, 353–54, 357; Testimony of Merchants Trading with the American Colonies, n.d., Newcastle Papers, Additional Mss. 33,030, vol. 1, British Library; Tucker and Hendrickson, *The Fall of the First British Empire*, 224, 226.

29. On the Irish Declaratory Act, see Christie, *Wars and Revolutions*, 96; Declaratory Act, Newcastle Papers, Additional Mss. 33,030, Vol. 1, British Library.

30. Votes and Proceedings of the General Assembly of the Colony of New York, CO 5,1217, Public Record Office.

31. Representation of Board of Trade on Appeals, 24 Sept. 1765; Henry Moore to Board of Trade, 22 Feb. 1766, *DRNY*, 7:762–63, 803, 814.

32. Cadwallader Colden to Thomas Gage, 2 Sept. 1765, Henry Moore to Henry Conway, 20 Feb. 1766, *DRNY*, 7:758, 800; Montresor, *Journals*, 346.

33. Tucker and Hendrickson, *The Fall of the First British Empire*, 220–22n.

34. Henry Moore to Board of Trade, 28 March 1766, Henry Moore to earl of Shelburne, 23 Feb. 1767, *DRNY*, 7:820–21, 909; Klein, "American Whig," 575.

35. Henry Moore to Henry S. Conway, 30 Apr. 1766, *DRNY*, 7:825.

36. Cadwallader Colden to Henry S. Conway, 24 June 1766, *DRNY*, 7:833; Montresor, *Journals*, 383.

37. Ibid., 366, 374–75; Smith, *Historical Memoirs*, 34; Oscar Handlin, "The Eastern Frontier of New York," *New York History* 18(1937):50–75.

38. Thomas Gage to Henry S. Conway, 24 June 1766, *Correspondence of Thomas Gage*, 1:95.

39. Montresor, *Journals*, 376; Henry Moore to Henry S. Conway, 14 July 1766, *DRNY*, 7:846.

40. Klein, "The Rise of the New York Bar," 334–58; L. F. S. Upton, *The Loyal Whig, William Smith of New York and Quebec* (Toronto, 1969), 55–56; Henry Moore to Board of Trade, 12 Aug. 1766, *DRNY*, 7:849; Countryman, *A People in Revolution*, 67.

41. Earl of Shelburne to Henry Moore, 11 Dec. 1766, Cadwallader Colden to Henry S. Conway, 24 June 1766, *DRNY*, 7:879, 833; Montresor, *Journals*, 384.

42. Ibid., 382.

43. Smith, *Historical Memoirs*, 95; Henry Moore to Henry S. Conway, 20 June 1766, *DRNY*, 7:831–32.

44. Thomas, *British Politics and the Stamp Act Crisis*, 284–85.

45. Thucydides, *Peloponnesian War*, 58.

46. Derry, *English Politics and the American Revolution*, 17, 20; see also Greene, *Peripheries and Center*, particularly "Parliament and the Colonies," 55–76.

47. Shelburne quoted in Thomas, *British Politics and the Stamp Act Crisis*, 300–2.

48. Ibid., 305–6; Charles R. Ritcheson, *British Politics and the American Revolution* (Norman, Okla., 1954), 90–91; Lustig, *Robert Hunter*, 7.

49. Smith, *Historical Memoirs*, 95; Henry Moore to Henry S. Conway, 20 June 1766, earl of Shelburne to Henry Moore, 18 July 1767, *DRNY*, 7:831, 945.

50. Earl of Shelburne to Governors, 11 Dec. 1766, Henry Moore to earl of Shelburne, 20 Feb. 1767 and 21 Feb. 1767, *DRNY*, 7:880, 900–1, 906; Tucker and Hendrickson, *The Fall of the First British Empire*, 247.

51. Earl of Shelburne to Henry Moore, 18 July 1767, *DRNY*, 7:945; An Estimate of Tea, Sugar and Molasses, Nov. 1763, British Library, Liverpool Papers, Additional Mss. 38,335; Maier, *From Resistance to Revolution*, 113n; Thomas C. Barrow, "The Old Colonial System from an English Point of View," *Anglo-American Political Relations, 1675–1775*, ed. Alison G. Olson and Richard M. Brown (New Brunswick, 1970), 136; for the continued extensive smuggling of tea by Americans, see Benjamin Woods Labaree, *The Boston Tea Party* (London, Oxford, New York, 1966), 8–13.

52. Thomas, *British Politics and the Stamp Act Crisis*, 337, 346–47, 361–62.

53. Tucker and Hendrickson, *The Fall of the First British Empire*, 252, 255.

54. Cadwallader Colden to earl of Hillsborough, 25 Apr. 1768, *DRNY*, 8:61; the animosity of New Yorkers to attorneys was of long standing and was shared by aspiring lawyers. In 1745, William Livingston, then serving an apprenticeship with James Alexander, wrote an anonymous essay dealing with "the Gentlemen of the Long Robe" who were deservedly distrusted by the lower class, or the "Vulgar," as Livingston termed them. Lawyers, he said, lacked integrity and "deserve[d] the Imputation of Injustice and dishonesty." Livingston observed that attorneys's injustices were particularly evident in their exploitation of apprentices. See *New-York Weekly Post Boy*, 19 Aug. 1745; Sedgwick, *Livingston*, 58. The popular Lewis Morris, running in Westchester was also defeated. Champagne, in "Family Politics versus Constitutional Principles: The New York Assembly Elections of 1768 and 1769," says Morris was defeated because DeLancey representatives prevented many lawful voters and some propertyless people from voting, as they were accustomed to do in the past (see 57–79).

55. Cadwallader Colden to earl of Hillsborough, 25 Apr. 1768, *DRNY*, 8:61.

56. Broadside to the Worthy Freeholders and Freeman, 8 Mar. 1768, New York Public Library.

57. Sedgwick, *Livingston*, 142; William Livingston to Noah Welles, 2 Feb. 1768, Johnson Family Papers, Yale University; Christie, *Wars and Revolutions*, 96.

58. Lustig, *Robert Hunter*, 109–10, 118–19.

59. Thomas Bradbury Chandler, "An Appeal to the Public in Behalf of the Church of England in America" (1767); Upton, *Loyal Whig*, 63; *Independent Reflector*, 9 Aug. 1973, 312.

60. John, bishop of Landaff, *A Sermon, Feb. 20, 1767* (London, 1767); William Livingston, *A Letter to the Right Reverend Father in God, John, Lord Bishop of Landaff* (New York, 1768); *Livingston Papers*, Appendix II, Biographical Essays, 5:547–49; Sedgwick, *Livingston*, 132, 133–34, 137.

61. On the DeLanceys's tactics, see Champagne, "Family Politics versus Constitutional Principles: The New York Assembly Elections of 1768 and 1769," 57–79; on the Massachusetts circular letter, see Pauline Maier, *From Resistance to Revolution*, 169–70.

62. Henry Moore to earl of Hillsborough, 7 July 1768, 4 Jan. 1769, *DRNY*, 8:80, 143; Champagne, "Family Politics versus Constitutional Principles: The New York Assembly Elections of 1768 and 1769," 57–79.

63. Smith, *Historical Memoirs*, 48, 49; *New York Assembly Journal*, 7 Apr. 1769.

64. Assembly Petition to king, Assembly Petition to the Right Honorable the Lords Spiritual and Temporal of Great-Britain, Assembly Petition to the Knights, Citizens and Burgesses of Great-Britain in Parliament assembled, Dec. 31, 1768, Votes and Proceedings of the General Assembly, CO 5, 1218, Public Record Office.

65. Henry Moore to earl of Hillsborough, 4 Jan. 1769, *DRNY*, 8:143; Moore tried to play down the defiant assembly petitions but they did not escape the notice of the ministry. Hillsborough complained that Moore neglected to "point them out in your correspondence." 15 July 1769, *DRNY*, 8:177; Champagne, "Family Politics versus Constitutional Principles: The New York Assembly Elections of 1768 and 1769," 57–79; Becker, *The History of Political Parties in the Province of New York*, 60–61, 69.

66. Henry Moore to earl of Hillsborough, 4 Jan. 1769, Cadwallader Colden to earl of Hillsborough, 7 Jan. 1769, *DRNY*, 8:144, 146; Petition from the Freeholders of Livingston Manor, 12 May 1769, Votes and Proceedings of the General Assembly, CO 5,1218, Public Record Office. In 1772, John DeLancey was elected from the borough of Westchester. Although he had previously lived in Westchester, he moved to New York City prior to the election. On asking the House for a ruling, he was informed that the move disqualified him since "no person is capable of being elected a Representative . . . unless he be an actual Resident." The assembly at the same time ruled on Robert R. Livingston's continuing insistence that he serve in the house and decided that permitting him to serve would "subvert the principles of the Constitution of the Colony." See Votes and Proceedings of the General Assembly of the Colony of New York, CO 5,1131, Public Record Office; Sedgwick, *Livingston*, 46, 47; Lawrence H. Leder, "The New York Elections of 1769: An Assault on Privilege," *The Mississippi Valley Historical Review*, 49 (Mar. 1963) 675–82.

67. Ibid.

68. Henry Moore to earl of Hillsborough, 3 June 1768, *DRNY*, 8:170.

69. Philip Livingston, Jr., to earl of Hillsborough, 11 Sept. 1769, Cadwallader Colden to earl of Hillsborough, 13 Sept. 1769, *DRNY*, 8:187–88.

70. Smith, *Historical Memoirs*, 53, 95.

71. John Cruger to Henry Moore, 20 May 1769, Votes and Proceedings of the General Assembly, CO 5, 1218, Public Record Office; Becker, *The History of Political Parties in the Province of New York*, 79.

72. Cadwallader Colden to earl of Hillsborough, 4 Oct. 1769, 16 Dec. 1769, 6 Jan. 1770, 21 Feb. 1770, Cadwallader Colden to Board of Trade, 6 Jan. 1770, earl of Hillsborough to Cadwallader Colden, 17 Feb. 1770, *DRNY*, 8:189, 193, 199, 205, 207.

73. *DHNY*, 3:528–32.

74. Cadwallader Colden to Hillsborough, 2 Feb. 1770, *DRNY*, 8:208; Countryman, *A People in Revolution*, 63–64.

75. Cadwallader Colden to earl of Hillsborough, 21 Feb. 1770, *DRNY*, 8:208; *Correspondence of Thomas Gage*, 1:250.

76. Votes and Proceedings of the General Assembly, 18 Dec. 1769, 19 Dec. 1769, CO 5,1219, Public Record Office; *DHNY*, 3:521–25.

77. George Francis Markham, "An Analysis of the Treatment of George III in New York City Newspapers, 1761–1776" (Ph.D. diss., New York University, 1963), 119–20, 173.

78. Cadwallader Colden to earl of Hillsborough, 21 Feb. 1770, *DRNY*, 8:208; Kammen, *Colonial New York*, 362.

79. Cadwallader Colden to earl of Hillsborough, 25 Apr. 1770, *DRNY*, 8:213; Jones, *History of New York*, 1:28–30.

80. *New York Journal*, 5 Apr. 1770.

81. Votes and Proceedings of the General Assembly of the Colony of New York, 13 Dec. 1770, CO 5,1219, Public Record Office; Dillon, *The New York Triumvirate*, 121.

82. Cadwallader Colden to earl of Hillsborough, 16 May 1770, *DRNY*, 8:214.

83. *New York Journal*, 12 Apr. 1770.

84. Burke quoted in Ian R. Christie, *Stress and Stability in Late Eighteenth Century Britain* (Oxford, 1984), 11.

Chapter 8. To Restore Union and Harmony, 1770–1776

1. Votes and Proceedings of the General Assembly of the Colony of New York, Petition to the Lords Spiritual and Temporal, 25 Mar. 1775, CO 5, 1220, Public Record Office.

2. Cadwallader Colden to earl of Hillsborough, 18 Aug. 1770, *DRNY*, 8:245.

3. William Tryon to George Germain, 14 Aug. 1776, *DRNY*, 8:684.

4. Christie, *Stress and Stability*, 12.

5. On migration to the Green Mountains see Handlin, "The Eastern Frontier of New York," 50–75.

6. Benning Wentworth to George Clinton, 17 Nov. 1749, same to same, 25 Apr. 1750, George Clinton to Benning Wentworth, 6 June 1750, Benning Wenthworth to George Clinton, 22 June 1750, Proclamation, 28 Dec. 1764, Order in Council, 20 July 1764, *DHNY*, 4:331, 333, 346–47, 355; Cadwallader Colden to Board of Trade, 20 Jan. 1764, same to same, 8 Feb. 1764, *DRNY*, 7:595–96, 608.

7. Henry Moore to earl of Shelburne, 9 June 1767, *DHNY*, 4:366.

8. Sheriff Har. Schuyler to Cadwallader Colden, 17 Aug. 1764, *DHNY*, 4:356; Cadwallader Colden to Board of Trade, 20 Jan. 1764, *DRNY*: 7:598; Countryman, *A People in Revolution*, 48.

9. Earl of Shelburne to Henry Moore, 11 Apr. 1767, *DRNY*, 7:917–18; Order of King-in-Council, 24 July 1767, *DHNY*, 4:375–76.

10. Mark, *Agrarian Conflicts*, 22, 42–43.

11. Earl of Dunmore to earl of Hillsborough, 24 Oct. 1770, earl of Hillsborough to earl of Dunmore, 11 Dec. 1770, William Tryon to earl of Hillsborough, 9 July 1771, earl of Dunmore to earl of Hillsborough, 9 July 1771, *DRNY*, 8:249, 260, 278; Smith, *Historical Memoirs*, 1:106–7.

12. Edmund Burke to John Cruger, 9 June 1771, Edmund Burke to Committee of Correspondence of the General Assembly, 4 Dec. 1771, 30 June 1772, *Correspondence of Edmund Burke*, ed. Lucy S. Sutherland, 10 vols. (Cambridge and Chicago, 1960), 2:213, 193, 313.

13. Becker, *History of Political Parties in the Province of New York*, 87–90.

14. Alexander Colden to Anthony Todd, 11 July 1770, *DRNY*, 8:218–20; Derry, *English Politics*, 97.

15. Nash, *Urban Crucible*, 233–34; Carl Lotus Becker, "Revolutionary Parties and Methods in New York Province," *American Historical Review* 7(1901): 56–76; Cadwallader Colden to earl of Hillsborough, 16 May 1770, 7 July 1770, 5 Oct. 1770, *DRNY*, 8:214, 216–17, 248–49.

16. Earl of Hillsborough to earl of Dunmore, 16 July 1770, *DRNY*, 8:223.

17. Cadwallader Colden to earl of Hillsborough, 10 Nov. 1770, earl of Dunmore to earl of Hillsborough, 5 Dec. 1770, Cadwallader Colden to earl of Hillsborough, 6 Dec. 1770, *DRNY*, 8:250–51, 257, 257–58.

18. William Livingston, "A Soliloquy" (New York, 1771); Cadwallader Colden to earl of Hillsborough, Nov. 10, 1770, *DRNY*, 8:250.

19. Earl of Dunmore to earl of Hillsborough, 24 Oct. 1770, earl of Hillsborough to earl of Dunmore, 11 Dec. 1770, William Tryon to earl of Hillsborough, 9 July 1771, earl of Dunmore to earl of Hillsborough, 9 July 1771, *DRNY*, 8:249, 260, 278; Smith, *Historical Memoirs*, 1:106–7.

20. Earl of Dunmore to earl of Hillsborough, 12 Nov. 1770, *DRNY*, 8:252.

21. Earl of Hillsborough to William Tryon, 4 Dec. 1771, *DRNY*, 8:285–86.

22. William Tryon to earl of Hillsborough, 11 Apr. 1772, earl of Dartmouth to William Tryon, 4 Nov. 1771, *DRNY*, 8:293, 318.

23. William Tryon to Frederick Haldiman, 1 Sept. 1773, Frederick Haldimand to William Tryon, 1 Sept. 1773, earl of Dartmouth to William Tryon, 14 Oct. 1773, Cadwallader Colden to earl of Dartmouth, 4 Oct. 1774, *DRNY*, 8:394, 395, 399, 491; *Colonial Laws*, 5:647–55.

24. Frederick Haldiman to William Tryon, 1 Sept. 1773, William Tryon to earl of Dartmouth, 1 July 1773, *DRNY*, 8:395, 382–83; *Colonial Laws*, 5:850–56.

25. William Livingston to John Morin Scott, 6 Mar. 1780, William Livingston to Catharine Lawrence, 21 Apr. 1781, William Livingston to John Witherspoon, *Livingston Papers*, 3:315–16, 4:182–83, 192.

26. Becker, *History of Political Parties in the Province of New York*, 87–90; letters quoted in part in Countryman, *A People in Revolution*, 92–93. Countryman points out that the letters "vilified the assembly as had never been done before."

27. 21 October 21, 1773, *New York Journal*, quoted in Labaree, *Boston Tea Party*, 90–92.

28. William Tryon to earl of Dartmouth, 1 Dec. 1773, same to same, 3 Jan. 1774, *DRNY*, 8:403, 407–8; Labaree, *Boston Tea Party*, 154.

29. Cadwallader Colden to Dartmouth, 4 May 1774, *DRNY*, 8:431; Minutes of the Council, 7 Apr. 1774–13 Apr. 1775, CO 5,1201, Public Record Office; Becker, *History of Political Parties in the Province of New York*, 106–11.

30. P. D. G. Thomas, *Lord North* (New York, 1976), 75; Derry, *English Politics*, 102–3.

31. Lord North quoted in Thomas, *Lord North*, 76; Edmund Burke to New York Committee of Correspondence, 6 April 1774, *Correspondence of Edmund Burke*, 2:527.

32. Edmund Burke to New York Committee of Correspondence, *Correspondence of Edmund Burke*, 6 April 1774, 2:528, 533.

33. Edmund Burke to New York Committee of Correspondence, 30 May, 2 Aug. 1774, *Correspondence of Edmund Burke*, 2:539, 3:15–18; Thomas, *Lord North*, 78; Bailyn, *The Peopling of British North America*, 9; Bernard Bailyn, *Voyagers to the West* New York, 1986), 31, 36–37.

34. Derry, *English Politics*, 110.

35. Cadwallader Colden to earl of Dartmouth, 1 June 1774, same to same, 7 Dec. 1774, same to same, 4 Jan. 1775, *DRNY*, 8:433, 512–13, 528; Labaree, *Boston Tea Party*, 27–28; Countryman, *A People in Revolution*, 137–40.

36. Cadwallader Colden to earl of Dartmouth, 7 Sept. 1774, *DRNY*, 8:488.

37. Cadwallader Colden to earl of Dartmouth, 1 Feb. 1775, same to same, 1 Mar. 775, *DRNY*, 8:532, 543.

38. William Tryon to earl of Dartmouth, *DRNY*, 11 June 1774, 8:454–56.

39. Minutes of the Council, 7 Apr. 1774–13 Apr. 1775, CO 5,1201, Public Record Office.

40. William Tryon to Cadwallader Colden, 30 June 1774, Colden, *Papers*, 7:227.

41. American Declaration of Rights, 14 Oct. 1774, Liverpool Papers, Additional Mss. 38,342, British Library; Greene argues that conditions between mother country and colonies had started to deteriorate well before 1763. See "An Uneasy Connection," 32–80.

42. American Declaration of Rights, 14 Oct. 1774, Liverpool Papers, Additional Mss. 38,342, British Library.

43. Cadwallader Colden to earl of Dartmouth, 2 Aug. 1774, William Tryon to earl of Dartmouth, 5 Sept. 1775, *DRNY*, 8:486, 633; American Declaration of Rights, 14 Oct. 1774, Liverpool Papers, Additional Mss. 38,342, British Library.

44. Edmund Burke to New York Committee of Correspondence, *Correspondence of Edmund Burke*, 14 Mar. 1775, 3:135; Derry, *English Politics*, 117.

45. Cadwallader Colden to earl of Dartmouth, 2 Nov. 1774, *DRNY*, 8:510; Votes and Proceedings of the General Assembly of the Colony of New York, Petition to King, 25 Mar. 1775, CO 5,1220, Public Record Office.

46. Votes and Proceedings of the General Assembly of New York, Petition to King, 31 Dec. 1768, CO 5,1218, Public Record Office.

47. Votes and Proceedings of the General Assembly of the Colony of New York, Petition to King, 25 Mar. 1775, CO 5,1220, Public Record Office.

48. Ibid.

49. Ibid.

50. Ibid.

51. Edmund Burke to New York Committee of Correspondence, *Correspondence of Edmund Burke*, 7 June 1775, 3:165–66.

52. Earl of Dartmouth to William Tryon, 23 May 1775, *DRNY*, 8:574–75.

53. Proposed Plan for Colonies, 1775, Principles of Law and Policy Applied to the British Colonies in America, 1775[?], Liverpool Papers, Additional Mss. 38,342, British Library.

54. Address to the People of Great Britain, Petition to the King, 1774, Additional Mss. 38,342, Liverpool Papers, British Library.

55. Proposed Plan for Colonies, 1775, Principles of Law and Policy Applied to the British Colonies in America, Liverpool Papers, Additional Mss. 38,342, British Library; Ritcheson, *British Politics and the American Revolution*, 191.

56. Minutes of the Council, 7 Apr. 1774–13 Apr. 1775, CO 5,1201, Public Record Office.

57. Ibid.; Cadwallader Colden to earl of Dartmouth, 3 May 1775, 7 June 1775, *DRNY*, 8:571, 579–80; Derry, *English Politics*, 110–17.

58. Cadwallader Colden to earl of Dartmouth, 7 June 1775, *DRNY*, 8:579–80; Derry, *English Politics*, 122–23.

59. Cadwallader Colden to earl of Dartmouth, 7 June 1775, *DRNY*, 8:583.

60. William Tryon to earl of Dartmouth, 4 July 1775, *DRNY*, 8:589.

61. William Tryon to earl of Dartmouth, 7 July 1775, J. Pownall to William Tryon, 6 Sept. 1775, *DRNY*, 8:592, 635.

62. William Tryon to earl of Dartmouth, 7 Aug. 1775, Copies of Letters of Thomas Jefferson and others relating to North America, 1775–1780, Additional Mss. 38,650A, British Library.

63. William Tryon to Whitehead Hicks, 10 Oct. 1775, same to same, 19 Oct. 1775 *DRNY*, 8:638, 641.

64. William Tryon to Lord George Germain, 18 Apr. 1776, *DRNY*, 8:676–77; Countryman, *A People in Revolution*, 95–96.

65. William Tryon to earl of Dartmouth, 7 Aug. 1775, William Tryon to George Germain, 14 Aug. 1776, *DRNY*, 8:604, 684; Edmund Burke to Marquess of Rockingham, 23 Aug. 1775, *Correspondence of Edmund Burke*, 3:195, 195n.

66. William Tryon to George Germain, 24 Sept. 1776, Germain to Tryon, 1 April 1779, *DRNY*, 8:686–87, 761.

67. William Livingston to the New Jersey Legislature, 25 Feb. 1777, *Livingston, Papers*, 1:254–59.

68. William Livingston to An Unknown Person, 7 March 1774, Livingston Papers, Vol. A, Massachusetts Historical Society.

69. *Livingston, Papers*, Appendix II, Biographical Essays, 5:589–90.

70. Ibid., 5:590–91.

71. William Livingston to William Hooper, 29 Aug. 1776, William Livingston to Henry Laurens, 8 Jan. 1778, *Livingston Papers*, 1:128–29, 2:170–71.

Bibliography

Primary Sources

Manuscripts

British Library
    Blenheim Papers
    Liverpool Papers, Additional Mss.
    Newcastle Paper; Additional Mss.

Public Records: England

Public Record Office, London
    Admiralty
    Chancery, 7
    Colonial Office, 5
    High Court of Admiralty
    Privy Council Register, 2

Public Records: U.S.A.

Franklin D. Roosevelt Library, Hyde Park, N.Y.
    Livingston–Redmond Manuscripts

Historical Society of Pennsylvania
    Gratz Collection

New York Historical Society
    James Alexander Papers
    Cadwallader Colden Papers
    Daniel Horsmanden Papers
    Jay Papers
    Rutherfurd Collection

New York State Library
    New York Colonial Manuscripts

Yale University
    Johnson Family Papers

Published Primary Sources

Alexander, James. *A Brief Narrative of the Case and Trial of John Peter Zenger. . . James Alexander.* Edited by Stanley Nider Katz. Cambridge Mass., 1963.

Blackstone, Sir William, *Commentaries on the Laws of England.* Oxford, 1765–69.

Burke, Edmund. *Correspondence of Edmund Burke.* 10 vols. Edited by Lucy S. Sutherland. Cambridge and Chicago, 1960.

Charters of the Old English Colonies in America. Introduction by Samuel Lucas. London, 1881.

Colden, Cadwallader, *The Letters and Papers of Cadwallader Colden, 1711–1775,* 9 vols. New–York Historical Society, *Collections,* 1917–23, 1934–35. New York, 1918–37.

————. *History of Governor William Cosby's Administration.* New–York Historical Society, *Collections,* 68. New York, 1935.

Great Britain. *Appeals to the Privy Council from the American Plantations.* New York, 1950.

————. *British Royal Proclamations Relating to America, 1603–1783.* Edited by Clarence S. Brigham. New York, 1911.

————. *Calendar of Treasury Books Preserved in the Public Record Office, 1660–1718,* 32 vols. Edited by William Shaw. London, 1904–57.

————. *Calendar of Treasury Papers.* 6 vols. Edited by Joseph Redington and William A. Shaw. London, 1868–97.

————. Public Record Office. *Calendar of State Papers, Colonial Series, America and West Indies, 1574–1736.* 42 vols. Edited by W. Noel Sainsbury, et al. London, 1860–1953.

Gage, Thomas. *Correspondence of General Thomas Gage with the Secretaries of State, 1763–1775.* Edited by Clarence Edwin Carter. New Haven, 1931.

Hunter, Robert. *Androboros, A Biographical Farce in Three Acts.* Edited by Lawrence H. Leder. *Bulletin of the New York Public Library* 68 (1964):173.

Jones, Thomas. *History of New York during the Revolutionary War.* Edited by Edward Floyd DeLancey. 2 vols. New York, 1879.

Livingston, William. *Review of the Military Operations in North America . . .,* 1757. Massachusetts Historical Society, *Collections,* 1800, 1st series, 7. Boston, 1801, 1846.

————. *Independent Reflector.* Edited by Milton M. Klein. Cambridge, Mass., 1963.

———— *A Letter to the Right Reverend Father in God, John, Lord Bishop of Landaff.* New York, 1768.

————. *A Soliloquy.* New York, 1771.

————. *The Papers of William Livingston.* 5 vols. Vol. 1, edited by Carl E. Prince; Vol. 2, edited by Carl E. Prince and Dennis P. Ryan; Vol. 3, edited by Carl E. Prince, Mary Lou Lustig, and Dennis P. Ryan; Vol. 4, edited by Carl E. Prince and Mary Lou Lustig; Vol. 5, edited by Carl E. Prince, Mary Lou Lustig, and David William Voorhees. Vols. 1 and 2, Trenton, 1979, 1980; Vols. 3, 4, 5. New Brunswick, N.J., 1986, 1987, 1988.

Lord Hervey's Memoirs. Edited by Romney Sedgwick. Middlesex, England and New York, 1963, 1984.

Montresor, *Journals.* Edited by G. D. Schull. New–York Historical Society, *Collections,* 14:33S.

New Jersey. *Documents Relating to the Colonial History of the State of New Jersey,* 10 vols. Edited by William Adee Whitehead. Newark, N.J., 1880.

New York City. *Calendar of Council Minutes, 1668–1783.* Edited by Berthold Fernow and A. J. F. Van Laer. New York State Library Bulletin No. 58, History 6. Albany, N.Y., 1902.

————. *Minutes of the Common Council of the City of New York, 1675–1776,* 8 vols. Edited by Herbert L. Osgood, et al. New York, 1905.

New York, Colony. *Calendar of New York Colonial Commissions, 1680–1770.* New York, 1929.

————. *Colonial Laws of New York from the Year 1664 to the Revolution,* 5 vols. Albany, N.Y., 1894–96.

————. *Ecclesiastical Records of the State of New York.* Edited by Hugh Hastings. 6 vols. Albany, 1901–5.

———— *Journal of the Legislative Council of the Colony of New York,* 9 April 1691–17 September 1743. 2 vols. Albany, N.Y., 1861.

————. *Journal of the Votes and Proceedings of the General Assembly of the Colony of New York, 1691–1765.* 2 vols. New York, 1764–66.

————. *The Laws and Acts of the General Assembly for their Majesties Province of New–York.* New York, 1893.

————. *Messages from the Governors, 1683–1776,* Edited by Charles Z. Lincoln. Albany, N.Y., 1909.

————. O'Callaghan, Edmund B., ed. *The Documentary History of the State of New York,* 4 vols. Albany, N.Y., 1850–51.

————, O'Callaghan, Edmund B. and Berthold Fernow, eds., and John R. Brodhead, comp. *Documents Relative to the Colonial History of the State of New York.* 15 vols. Albany, N.Y., 1856–87.

Pitt, William. *Correspondence of William Pitt with Colonial Governors and Military and Naval Commissioners in America.* Edited by Gertrude Selwyn Kimball. 2 vols. London and New York. 1906, 1969.

Sedgwick, Theodore, Jr. *A Memoir of the Life of William Livingston.* New York, 1833.

Smith, William. *The History of the Province of New–York.* 2 vols. Edited by Michael Kammen. Cambridge, Mass., 1972.

————. *Historical Memoirs, March 16, 1763–July 9, 1776.* Edited by William H. W. Sabine. New York, 1956.

Stock, Leo. F., ed. *Proceedings and Debates of the British Parliaments Respecting North America.* 5 vols. Washington, D.C., 1924–41.

Wraxall, Peter. *Peter Wraxall's An Abridgment of the Indian Affairs In the Colony of New York. . . , 1678–1751.* Edited by Charles H. McIlwain. Cambridge, Mass., 1915.

Newspapers

American Chronicle
Constitutional Courant
London Evening Post
New York Gazette
New York Weekly Journal
New York Weekly Post Boy

Secondary Sources

Books

Anderson, Fred. *A People's Army, Massachusetts Soldiers and Society in the Seven Years' War.* New York and London, 1984.

Anderson, John. *The American Theatre.* New York 1938.

Aspinall, A. *Politics and the Press, 1780–1850.* London, 1949.

Bailyn, Bernard. *Origins of American Politics.* New York, 1968.
——. *Ideological Origins of the American Revolution.* Cambridge, Mass., 1967.
—— *The Peopling of British North America.* New York, 1986.
Becker, Carl Lotus. *The History of Political Parties in the Province of New York, 1760–1776.* Madison, Wisc., 1909, 1968.
Bonomi, Patricia U. *A Factious People, Politics and Society in Colonial New York.* New York and London, 1971.
——. *Under the Cope of Heaven: Religion, Society and Politics in Colonial America.* New York and Oxford, 1986.
Carretta, Vincent. *George III and the Satirists from Hogarth to Byron.* Athens, Ga. and London, 1990.
Christie, Ian R. *Stress and Stability in Late Eighteenth Century Britain.* Oxford, 1984.
——. *Wars and Revolutions, Britain, 1760–1815.* Cambridge, Mass., 1981.
Countryman, Edward. *A People in Revolution, The American Revolution and Political Society in New York, 1760–1790.* Baltimore and London, 1981.
Crane, Verner W. *The Southern Frontier, 1670–1732.* Ann Arbor, Mich., 1929, 1956.
Cruickshanks, Eveline. *Political Untouchables, The Tories and the '45.* New York, 1979.
Davis, T. J. *A Rumor of Revolt, The "Great Negro Plot" in Colonial New York.* New York and London, 1985.
Derry, John. *English Politics and the American Revolution.* London, 1976.
Dillon, Dorothy Rita. *The New York Triumvirate.* New York, 1949.
Ferguson, William. *Scotland, 1689 to the Present.* New York 1968.
Fitzpatrick, Brendan. *Seventeenth Century Ireland, The Wars of Religions.* Totowa, N.J., 1989.
Gilje, Paul A. *The Road to Mobocracy, Popular Disorders in New York City, 1763–1834.* Chapel Hill, N.C. and London, 1987.
Greenberg, Douglas. *Crime and Law Enforcement in the Colony of New York, 1691–1776.* Ithaca, N.Y., 1974.
Greene, Jack P. *Peripheries and Center, Constitutional Development in the Extended Polities of the British Empire and the United States, 1607–1788.* New York and London, 1986.
——. *Pursuits of Happiness: The Social Development of Early Modern British Colonies and the Formation of American Culture.* Chapel Hill, N.C. and London, 1988.
——. *The Quest for Power: The Lower Houses of Assembly in the Southern Royal Colonies, 1689–1776.* New York, 1963.
Gurr, Ted Robert. *Why Men Rebel.* Princeton, 1970.
Harvie, Christopher. *Scotland and Nationalism, Scottish Society and Politics, 1707–1977.* London, 1977.
Henretta, James A. *Salutary Neglect, Colonial Administration under the Duke of Newcastle.* Princeton, 1972.
Hobsbawm, E. J. *Primitive Rebels.* New York, 1958.
Hodges, Graham Russell. *New York City Cartmen, 1667–1850.* New York, 1986.
Hoffer, Charles. *Law and People in Colonial America.* Baltimore and London, 1992.
Holmes, Geoffrey. *British Politics in the Age of Anne,* rev. ed. London and Ronceverte, W.Va., 1967, 1987.
Humphrey, David. *From King's College to Columbia.* New York, 1976.
Hunt, George T. *The Wars of the Iroquois.* Madison, Wisc., 1960.
Jennings, Francis. *The Ambiguous Iroquois Empire.* New York and London, 1984.
——. *Empire of Fortune: Crown, Colonies and Tribes in the Seven Years War in America.* New York and London, 1988.
Kammen, Michael. *Colonial New York.* Millwood, N.Y., 1975.

Katz, Stanley Nider. *Newcastle's New York, Anglo–American Politics in the Eighteenth Century, 1732–1753.* Cambridge, Mass., 1968.

Keys, Alice M. *Cadwallader Colden: A Representative Eighteenth Century Official.* New York, 1906.

Kim, Sung Bok, *Landlords and Tenants in Colonial New York Manorial Society, 1664–1775.* Chapel Hill, N.C., 1978.

Kramnick, Isacc. *Bolingbroke and his Circle, The Politics of Nostalgia in the Age of Walpole.* Cambridge, Mass., 1968.

Labaree, Benjamin Wood. *The Boston Tea Party.* London, Oxford, and New York, 1966.

Lacey, Robert. *Sir Walter Ralegh.* New York, 1979.

Larkin, Paschal. *Property in the Eighteenth Century, A Special Reference to England and Locke.* London and New York, 1930.

Leach, Douglas Edward. *The Northern Colonial Frontier, 1607–1763.* New York, 1966.

———. *Roots of Conflict, British Armed Forces and Colonial Americans, 1677–1763.* Chapel Hill, N.C. and London, 1986.

Leder, Lawrence H. *Robert Livingston (1654–1728) and the Politics of Colonial New York.* Chapel Hill, N.C., 1961.

Levack, Brian P. *The Formation of the British State, England, Scotland, and the Union, 1603–1707.* Oxford, 1987.

Levy, Leonard W. *Legacy of Suppression.* Cambridge, Mass., 1960.

———. Editor. *Freedom of the Press from Zenger to Jefferson.* Kansas City, Mo., 1966.

Lustig, Mary Lou. *Robert Hunter (1666–1734): New York's Augustan Statesman.* Syracuse, N.Y., 1983.

McAnear, Beverly. *The Income of the Colonial Governors of British North America.* New York, 1967.

MacKinnon, James. *The Union of England and Scotland.* London, 1896.

Maier, Pauline. *From Resistance to Revolution, Colonial Radicals and the Development of American Opposition to Britain.* New York, 1974.

Mark, Irving. *Agrarian Conflicts in Colonial New York, 1711–1775.* New York, 1940.

Merwick, Donna. *Possessing Albany, 1630–1710: The Dutch and English Experience.* New York, 1990.

Morgan, Edmund S. *American Slavery, American Freedom, The Ordeal of Colonial Virginia.* New York and London, 1975.

———. and Helen M. Morgan. *The Stamp Act Crisis, Prologue to Revolution.* Rev. ed. New York, 1953, 1963.

Morgan, Lewis Henry. *The League of the Iroquois.* Secaucus, N.J., 1851, 1975.

Namier, Lewis B. *The Structure of Politics at the Accession of George III.* 2nd ed. London, 1957.

Nash, Gary B. *The Urban Crucible: Social Change, Political Consciousness, and the Origins of the American Revolution.* Cambridge, Mass. and London, 1979, 1986.

Norton, Thomas Elliot. *The Fur Trade in Colonial New York, 1686–1776.* Madison, Wisc., 1974.

Olson, Alison Gilbert. *Anglo–American Politics, 1660–1775: The Relationship Between Parties in England and Colonial America.* New York and Oxford, 1973.

Osgood, Herbert L. *The American Colonies in the Seventeenth Century.* 3 vols. Gloucester, Mass., 1957.

———. *The American Colonies in the Eighteenth Century,* 4 vols. Gloucester, Mass., 1958.

Pares, Richard. *King George III and the Politicians.* London, Oxford, New York, 1953, 1973.

Plumb, J. H. *Robert Walpole, The Making of a Statesman.* 2 vols. London, 1956.

Quinn, David Beers. *Set Fair for Roanoke, Voyages and Colonies, 1584–1606.* Chapel Hill, N.C. and London, 1985.

Redwood, John. *Reason, Ridicule, and Religion, the Age of Enlightenment in England, 1660–1750.* Cambridge, Mass., 1976.

Riley, P. W. J. *The Union of England and Scotland, A Study in Anglo–Scottish Politics of the Eighteenth Century.* Manchester, 1978.

Ritchie, Robert C. *The Duke's Province, A Study of New York Politics and Society, 1664–1691.* Chapel Hill, N.C., 1977.

Robbins, Caroline. *The Eighteenth Century Commonwealthman.* Cambridge, Mass., 1959.

Rude, George. *Paris and London in the Eighteenth Century.* New York, 1952, 1970.
———. *Ideology and Popular Protest.* New York, 1980.

Schutz, John A. *William Shirley, King's Governor of Massachusetts.* Chapel Hill, N.C., 1961.

Sensabaugh, George F. *Milton in Early America.* New York, 1964, 1979.

Shaw, Peter. *American Patriots and the Rituals of Revolution.* Cambridge, Mass., 1981.

Sheridan, Eugene R. *Lewis Morris, 1671–1746, A Study in Early American Politics.* Syracuse, N.Y., 1981.

Siebert, Frederick Seaton. *Freedom of the Press in England, 1476–1776.* Urbana, Ill., 1952.

Smith, Jeffery A. *Printers and Press Freedom: The Ideology of Early American Journalism.* New York and Oxford, 1988.

Speck, W. A. *Stability and Strife, England, 1714–1760.* Cambridge, Mass., 1979.

Spencer, Worthen. *Royal Government in New York, 1694–1719.* Columbus, Ohio, 1905.

Steele, Ian K. *Betrayals, Fort William Henry and the 'Massacre.'* New York and Oxford, 1990, 1993.

Stevens, David Harrison. *Party Politics and English Journalism, 1702–1742.* New York, 1916, 1967.

Thomas, P. D. G. *British Politics and the Stamp Act Crisis, The First Phase of the American Revolution, 1763–1767.* Oxford, 1975.

Thompson, E. P. *Whigs and Hunters, The Origins of the Black Act.* New York, 1975.

Thucydides. *The Peloponnesian War.* Translated by Rex Warner. New York, 1954, 1975.

Tucker, Robert W. and David C. Hendrickson. *The Fall of the First British Empire.* Baltimore and London, 1982.

Upton, L. F. S. *The Loyal Whig, William Smith of New York and Quebec.* Toronto, 1969.

Wallace, Anthony F. C. *The Death and Rebirth of the Seneca.* New York, 1969, 1972.

Warren, Charles. *A History of the American Bar.* Boston, 1911.

Webb, Stephen Saunders. *The Governors–General, The English Army and the Definition of the Empire, 1569–1681.* Chapel Hill, N.C., 1979.

Wedgwood, C. V. *The King's Peace, 1637–1741.* Middlesex, England, 1955, 1983.

Whitehead, William A. *Contributions to the Early History of Perth Amboy, N.J.* New York, 1856.

Wickwire, Franklin B. *British Subministers and Colonial America, 1763–1783.* Princeton, 1966.

Wilentz, Sean. *Chants Democratic, New York City and the Rise of the American Working Class, 1788–1850.* New York, 1984.

Articles

Barron, Thomas C. "The Old Colonial System from an English Point of View." In *Anglo–American Political Relations, 1675–1775,* edited by Alison G. Olson and Richard M. Brown. New Brunswick, N.J., 1970.

Becker, Carl Lotus. "Growth of Revolutionary Parties and Methods in New York Province, 1765–1774." *American Historical Review* 7 (1901): 56–76.

Brown, Richard Maxwell. "Violence in the American Revolution." In *Essays on the American Revolution,* edited by Stephen G. Kurtz and James H. Hutson. Chapel Hill, N.C., 1973.

Browning, Reed. "The Duke of Newcastle and the Financial Management of the Seven Years War in Germany." *Society for Army Historical Research Journal* 49 (1972): 20–35.

Buel, Richard, Jr. "Freedom of the Press in Revolutionary America, The Evolution of Libertarianism, 1760–1820." In *The Press and the American Revolution,* edited by Bernard Bailyn and John B. Hench. Boston, 1981.

Champagne, Roger. "Family Politics versus Constitutional Principles: New York Assembly Elections of 1768 and 1769." *William and Mary Quarterly* 20 (1963): 57–79.

Fiering, Norman S. "The Transatlantic Republic of Letters: A Note on the Circulation of Learned Periodicals to Early Eighteenth–Century America." *William and Mary Quarterly* 33 (1976): 642–60.

Friedman, Bernard. "The Shaping of the Radical Consciousness in the Province of New York." *Journal of American History* 4 (March 1970), 56:781–801.

Gerardi, Donald. "The King's College Controversy, 1753–1756 and the Ideological Roots of Toryism in New York." In *Perspectives in American History* 11 (1977–1978): 145–98.

Gilje, Paul A. "Republican Rioting." In *Authority and Resistance in Colonial New York,* edited by William C. Pencak and Conrad Edick Wright. New York, 1988.

Greene, Jack P. "An Uneasy Connection, An Analysis of the Preconditions of the American Revolution." In *Essays on the American Revolution,* edited by Stephen G. Kurtz and James H. Hutson. Chapel Hill, N.C. and New York, 1973.

Handlin, Oscar. "The Eastern Frontier of New York." *New York History* 18 (1937): 50–75.

Klein, Milton M. "Archibald Kennedy, Imperial Pamphleteer." In *The Colonial Legacy.* 2 vols. Edited by Lawrence H. Leder. New York, 1971.

———. "Prelude to Revolution in New York: Jury Trials and Judicial Tenure." In *William and Mary Quarterly* 17 (1960): 4394–62.

———. "The Rise of the New York Bar: The Legal Career of William Livingston." *William and Mary Quarterly* 15 (1958): 334–58.

———. "William Livingston's A Review of the Military Operations." In *The Colonial Legacy.* 2 vols. Edited by Lawrence H. Leder. New York, 1971.

Leder, Lawrence H. "New York Elections of 1769: An Assault on Privilege." *Mississippi Valley Historical Review* 49 (March 1963): 675–82.

Levermore, Charles H. "The Whigs of Colonial New York." *American Historical Review* 1 (1896): 238–50.

Murrin, John M. "English Rights as Ethnic Aggression: The English Conquest, the Charter of Liberties of 1683, and Leisler's Rebellion in New York." In *Authority and Resistance in Early New York,* edited by William Pencak and Conrad Edick Wright. New York, 1988.

Nadelhaft, Jerome J. "Politics and the Judicial Tenure Fight in Colonial New Jersey." *William and Mary Quarterly* 28 (1971): 46–63.

Naylor, Rex Maurice. "The Royal Prerogative in New York, 1691–1775." *Quarterly Journal,* New York State Historical Association, 5 (1924): 221–55.

Pocock, J. G. A. "Machiavelli, Harrington and English Political Ideologies in the Eighteenth Century." *William and Mary Quarterly* 22 (1965): 549–83.

Ritcheson, Charles R. "The Preparation of the Stamp Act." *William and Mary Quarterly* 10 (1953): 543–59.

Varga, Nicholas. "Election Procedures and Practices in Colonial New York." *New York History* 61 (1960): 149–77.

Wallace, Anthony F. C. "Origins of Iroquois Neutrality, The Grand Settlement of 1701." *Pennsylvania History* 24 (July 1957): 223–35.

Webb, Stephen Saunders. "The Trials of Sir Edmund Andros." In *The Human Dimensions of Nation Making,* edited by James Kirby Martin. Madison, Wisc., 1976.

Wickwire, Franklin B. "John Pownall and British Colonial Policy." *William and Mary Quarterly* 20 (1963): 543–54.

Unpublished Ph.D. Dissertations

Klein, Milton M. "The American Whig: William Livingston of New York." Columbia University, 1954.

Largmann, Malcolm G. "The Political Image of Sir Robert Walpole Created by Literary Satire in the Opposition Press, 1721–1742." New York University, 1965.

Markham, George Francis. "An Analysis of the Treatment of George III in New York City Newspapers, 1761–1776." New York University, 1963.

Steacy, Stephen Charles. "Cadwallader Colden: Statesman and Savant of Colonial New York." 2 vols. University of Kansas, 1987.

Voorhees, David William. "In Behalf of the true Protestant religion: The Glorious Revolution in New York." New York University, 1988.

Index